Anonymous

Sermons Preached in Boston on the Death of Abraham Lincoln

Anonymous

Sermons Preached in Boston on the Death of Abraham Lincoln

ISBN/EAN: 9783744753999

Printed in Europe, USA, Canada, Australia, Japan

Cover: Foto ©ninafisch / pixelio.de

More available books at **www.hansebooks.com**

SERMONS

PREACHED IN BOSTON

ON THE DEATH OF

ABRAHAM LINCOLN.

TOGETHER WITH THE FUNERAL SERVICES IN
THE EAST ROOM OF THE EXECUTIVE
MANSION AT WASHINGTON.

BOSTON:
J. E. TILTON AND COMPANY.
1865.

Entered according to Act of Congress, in the year 1865,
BY J. E. TILTON AND CO.,
In the Clerk's Office of the District Court for the District of Massachusetts.

STEREOTYPED BY C. J. PETERS & SON,
No. 13 Washington Street.

PRESS OF GEO. C. RAND & AVERY.

CONTENTS.

FUNERAL SERVICE AT WASHINGTON.

		Page.
I.	BURIAL SERVICE READ BY REV. MR. HALL.	7
II.	OPENING PRAYER BY BISHOP SIMPSON.	9
III.	SERMON BY REV. D. P. GURLEY.	16
IV.	CLOSING PRAYER BY REV. E. H. GRAY.	28

SERMONS IN BOSTON.

V. REV. E. N. KIRK. 33
    Psalms xlvi. : 10.

VI. REV. CYRUS A. BARTOL. 51

VII. REV. J. M. MANNING. 59
    Deuteronomy xxxiv. : 4, 5.

VIII. REV. JOHN E. TODD. 75
    Psalms xciii. : 1.

IX. REV. JAMES FREEMAN CLARKE. . . . 91
    2 Tim. i : 10.

X. REV. GEORGE H. HEPWORTH. 109
    Matthew ix. : 15.

XI. REV. W. R. NICHOLSON. 125

XII. REV. WILLIAM HAGUE. 129
    Samuel iii. : 38.

XIII.	REV. E. B. WEBB.	145
	ISAIAH xxi. : 11, 12.	
XIV.	REV. R. H. NEALE.	163
	MATTHEW ix. : 15.	
XV.	REV. HENRY W. FOOTE.	179
XVI.	REV. F. D. HUNTINGTON.	193
XVII.	REV. WARREN H. CUDWORTH.	199
	DANIEL iv. 35.	
XVIII.	REV. CHANDLER ROBBINS.	215
	PSALMS lxxvii. : 19.	
XIX.	REV. W. S. STUDLEY.	227
	LAMENTATIONS v. : 15, 16, 17, 19.	
XX.	REV. RUFUS ELLIS.	235
	LUKE xxiv. : 5, 6.	
XXI.	REV. SAMUEL K. LOTHROP.	245
	2 SAMUEL xix : 2.	
XXII.	REV. EDWARD E. HALE.	267
	1 CORINTHIANS xv. : 57.	
XXIII.	REV. A. A. MINER.	279
	PSALMS lxxxix. : 18.	
XXIV.	REV. JAMES REED.	295
XXV.	REV. GEORGE PUTNAM.	309
XXVI.	REV. GEORGE L. CHANEY.	325
	JOHN xiv. : 18.	
XXVII.	REV. A. L. STONE.	337
	LAMENTATIONS v. : 15, 16.	
XXVIII.	REV. J. D. FULTON.	359
	DEUTERONOMY xxxiv. : 7.	

REV. P. D. GURLEY, D. D.

Entered according to Act of Congress, in the year 1865,
BY J. E. TILTON AND CO.,
In the Clerk's Office of the District Court for the District of Massachusetts.

STEREOTYPED BY C. J. PETERS & SON,
No. 13 Washington Street.

PRESS OF GEO. C. RAND & AVERY.

CONTENTS.

FUNERAL SERVICE AT WASHINGTON.

		Page.
I.	BURIAL SERVICE READ BY REV. MR. HALL.	7
II.	OPENING PRAYER BY BISHOP SIMPSON.	9
III.	SERMON BY REV. D. P. GURLEY.	16
IV.	CLOSING PRAYER BY REV. E. H. GRAY.	28

SERMONS IN BOSTON.

V.	REV. E. N. KIRK.	33
	PSALMS xlvi.: 10.	
VI.	REV. CYRUS A. BARTOL.	51
VII.	REV. J. M. MANNING.	59
	DEUTERONOMY xxxiv.: 4, 5.	
VIII.	REV. JOHN E. TODD.	75
	PSALMS xciii.: 1.	
IX.	REV. JAMES FREEMAN CLARKE.	91
	2 TIM. i: 10.	
X.	REV. GEORGE H. HEPWORTH.	109
	MATTHEW ix.: 15.	
XI.	REV. W. R. NICHOLSON.	125
XII.	REV. WILLIAM HAGUE.	129
	SAMUEL iii.: 38.	

BURIAL SERVICE.

At ten minutes past 12, Rev. Mr. HALL opened the services by reading from the Episcopal burial service for the dead as follows:

"I am the resurrection and the life saith the Lord; he that believeth in me, though he were dead, yet shall he live, and whosoever liveth and believeth in me shall never die.—*John* xi: 25, 26.

"I know that my Redeemer liveth, and that He shall stand at the latter day upon the earth and though after my skin worms destroy this body, yet in my flesh shall I see God, whom I shall see for myself, and mine eyes shall behold and not another.—*Job* xix: 25, 26, 27.

"We brought nothing into this world, and it is certain we can carry nothing out. The Lord gave and the Lord hath taken away. Blessed be the name of the Lord."—1 *Timothy* vi: 7, and *Job* i: 21.

"Lord, let me know my end and the number of my days, that I may be certified how long I have to live. Behold, Thou hast made my days as it were but a span long, and mine age is even as nothing in respect of Thee. And verily every man living is altogether vanity; for man walketh in a vain shadow, and disquieteth himself in vain. He heapeth up riches, and cannot tell who shall gather them. And now, Lord, what is my hope? Truly my hope is ever in Thee; deliver me from all my offences, and make me not a rebuke unto the foolish. When Thou, with rebukes dost chasten man for sin, Thou makest his beauty to consume away, like as it were a moth fretting a garment. Every man is, therefore, but vanity. Hear my prayer, O Lord, and with Thine ears consider my calling. Hold not Thy peace at my tears, for I am a stranger with thee and a sojourner, as all my fathers were. O, spare me a little, that I may recover my strength before I go hence and be no more seen. Lord, Thou hast been our refuge from one generation to another. Before the mountains were brought forth, or even the earth and the world were made, Thou art God from everlasting, and world without end. Thou turnest man to destruction; again thou sayest, come again, ye children of men, for a thousand years in thy sight are but as yesterday, seeing that it is past as a watch in the night. As soon as Thou scatterest them, they are even as sheep, and fade away suddenly like the grass. In the morning it is green and groweth up, but in the evening it is cut down, dried up, and withered. For we consume away in Thy displeasure, and are afraid at thy wrathful indignation. Thou hast set our misdeeds before Thee, and our secret sins in the light of Thy countenance; for when thou art angry all our days are gone. We bring our years to an end, as it were a tale that is told. The days of our age are threescore years and ten, and though men be so strong that they come to fourscore years, yet is their strength then but labor and sorrow, so soon passeth it away, and we are gone. So teach us to number our days that we may apply our hearts unto wisdom. Glory be to the Father, and to the Son, and to the holy Ghost; as it was in the beginning, is now, and ever shall be, world without end. Amen."

Then was read the lesson from the 15th chapter of St. Paul to the Corinthians, beginning with the 20th verse:

But now is Christ risen from the dead, and become the first-fruits of them that slept.

For since by man came death, by man came also the resurrection of the dead.

For as in Adam all die, even so in Christ shall all be made alive.

But every man in his own order: Christ the first-fruits; afterward they that are Christ's at his coming.

Then cometh the end, when he shall have delivered up the kingdom to God, even the Father; when he shall have put down all rule, and all authority, and power.

For he must reign, till he hath put all enemies under his feet.

The last enemy that shall be destroyed is death.

For he hath put all things under his feet. But when he saith, all things are put under him, it is manifest that he is excepted which did put all things under him.

And when all things shall be subdued unto him, then shall the Son also himself be subject unto him that put all things under him, that God may be all in all.

Else what shall they do, which are baptized for the dead, if the dead rise not at all? why are they then baptized for the dead?

And why stand we in jeopardy every hour?

I protest by your rejoicing which I have in Christ Jesus our Lord, I die daily.

If after the manner of men I have fought with beasts at Ephesus, what advantageth it me, if the dead rise not? let us eat and drink; for to-morrow we die.

Be not deceived; evil communications corrupt good manners.

Awake to righteousness, and sin not; for some have not the knowledge of God. I speak this to your shame.

But some man will say, How are the dead raised up? and with what body do they come?

Thou fool, that which thou sowest is not quickened except it die:

And that which thou sowest, thou sowest not that body that shall be, but bare grain; it may chance of wheat, or of some other grain:

But God giveth it a body as it hath pleased him, and to every seed his own body.

All flesh is not the same flesh; but there is one kind of flesh of men, another flesh of beasts, another of fishes, and another of birds.

There are also celestial bodies, and bodies terrestrial: but the glory of the celestial is one, and the glory of the terrestrial is another.

There is one glory of the sun, and another glory of the moon, and another glory of the stars; for one star differeth from another star in glory.

So also is the resurrection of the dead. It is sown in corruption, it is raised in incorruption:

It is sown in dishonor, it is raised in glory: it is sown in weakness, it is raised in power:

It is sown a natural body, it is raised a spiritual body. There is a natural body, and there is a spiritual body.

And so it is written, The first man Adam was made a living soul, the last Adam was made a quickening spirit.

Howbeit, that was not first which is spiritual, but that which is natural; and afterward that which is spiritual.

The first man is of the earth, earthy: the second man is the Lord from heaven.

As is the earthy, such are they also that are earthy: and as is the heavenly, such are they also that are heavenly.

And as we have borne the image of the earthy, we shall also bear the image of the heavenly.

Now this I say, brethren, that flesh and blood cannot inherit the kingdom of God; neither doth corruption inherit incorruption.

Behold, I shew you a mystery: We shall not all sleep, but we shall all be changed,

In a moment, in the twinkling of an eye, at the last trump: for the trumpet shall sound, and the dead shall be raised incorruptible, and we shall be changed.

For this corruptible must put on incorruption, and this mortal must put on immortality.

So when this corruptible shall have put on incorruption, and this mortal shall have put on immortality, then shall be brought to pass the saying that is written, Death is swallowed up in victory.

O death, where is thy sting? O grave, where is thy victory?

The sting of death is sin; and the strength of sin is the law.

But thanks be to God, which giveth us the victory, through our Lord Jesus Christ.

Therefore, my beloved brethren, be ye steadfast, unmovable, always abounding in the work of the Lord, forasmuch as ye know that your labor is not in vain in the Lord.

Bishop Simpson, of Philadelphia, then offered the following opening prayer:

Almighty God, our Heavenly Father, as with smitten and suffering hearts we come into Thy presence, we pray, in the name of our blessed Redeemer, that Thou wouldst pour upon us Thy Holy Spirit, that all our thoughts and acts may be acceptable in Thy sight. We adore Thee for all Thy glorious perfections. We praise Thee for the revelation which Thou hast given us in Thy works and in Thy Word. By Thee all worlds exist. All beings live through Thee. Thou raisest up kingdoms and empires, and castest them down. By Thee kings reign and princes decree righteousness. In Thy hand are the issues of life and death. We confess before Thee the magnitude of our sins and transgressions, both as individuals and as a nation. We implore Thy mercy for the sake of our Redeemer. Forgive us all our iniquities. If it please Thee, remove Thy chastening hand from us; and, though we be unworthy, turn away from us Thine anger, and let the light of Thy countenance again shine upon us.

At this solemn hour, as we mourn for the death of our President, who was stricken down by the hand of an assassin, grant us also the grace to bow in submission to Thy holy will. May we recognize Thy hand high above all human agencies, and Thy power as controlling all events, so that the wrath of man shall praise Thee, and that the remainder of wrath Thou wilt restrain. Humbled under the suffering we have endured, and the great afflictions through which we have passed, may we not be called upon to offer other sacrifices. May the lives of all our officers, both civil and military, be guarded by Thee; and let no violent hand fall upon any of them. Mourning as we do, for the mighty dead by whose remains we stand, we would yet lift our hearts unto Thee in grateful acknowledgment for Thy kindness in giving us so great and noble a commander.

Thou art glorified in good men, and we praise Thee that Thou didst give him unto us so pure, so honest, so sincere, and so transparent in character. We praise Thee for that kind, affectionate heart, which always swelled with feelings of enlarged benevolence. We bless Thee for what Thou didst enable him to do; that Thou didst give him wisdom to select for his advisers, and for his officers, military and naval, those men through whom our country has been carried through an unprecedented conflict.

We bless Thee for the success which has attended all their efforts, and victories which have crowned our armies; and that Thou didst spare Thy servant until he could behold the dawning of that glorious morning of peace and prosperity which is about to shine upon our land; that he was enabled to go up as Thy servant of old upon Mount Pisgah, and catch a glimpse of the promised land. Though his lips are silent and his arm is powerless, we thank Thee that Thou didst strengthen him to speak words that cheer the hearts of the suffering and the oppressed, and to write that declaration of emancipation which has given him an immortal reward; that though the hand of the assassin has struck him to the ground, it could not destroy the work which he has done, nor forge again the chains which he has broken. And while we mourn that he has passed away, we are grateful that his work was so fully accomplished, and that the acts which he has performed will forever remain.

We implore Thy blessing upon his bereaved family, Thou husband of the widow. Bless her who, broken-hearted and sorrowing, feels oppressed with unutterable anguish. Cheer the loneliness of the pathway which lies before her, and grant to her such consolations of Thy spirit, and such hopes, through the resurrection, that she shall feel that "Earth hath no sorrows which Heaven cannot heal."

Let Thy blessing rest upon his sons; pour upon them the spirit of wisdom; be Thou the guide of their youth; prepare them for usefulness in society, for happiness in all their relations. May the remembrance of their father's counsels, and their father's noble acts, ever stimulate them to glorious deeds, and at last may they be heirs of everlasting life.

Command thy rich blessings to descend upon the successor of our lamented President. Grant unto him wisdom, energy, and firmness for the responsible duties to which he has been called ; and may he, his cabinet, officers and generals who shall lead his armies, and the brave soldiers in the field, be so guided by Thy counsels that they shall speedily complete the great work which he had so successfully carried forward.

Let Thy blessing rest upon our country. Grant unto us all a fixed and strong determination never to cease our efforts until our glorious Union shall be fully re-established.

Around the remains of our loved President may we covenant together by every possible means to give ourselves to our country's service until every vestige of this rebellion shall have been wiped out, and until slavery, its cause, shall be forever eradicated.

Preserve us, we pray Thee, from all complications with foreign nations. Give us hearts to act justly toward all nations, and grant unto them hearts to act justly toward us, that universal peace and happiness may fill our earth. We rejoice, then, in this inflicting dispensation Thou hast given, as additional evidence of the strength of our nation. We bless Thee that no tumult has arisen, and in peace and harmony our government moves onward; and that Thou hast shown that our republican government is the strongest upon the face of the earth.

In this solemn presence, may we feel that we too are immortal! May the sense of our responsibility to God rest upon us ; may we repent of every sin ; and may we consecrate anew unto Thee all the time and all the talents which Thou hast given us; and may we so fulfil our allotted duties that finally we may have a resting-place with the good, and wise, and the great, who now surround that glorious throne! Hear us while we unite in praying with Thy Church in all lands and in all ages, even as Thou hast taught us, saying:

Our Father which art in heaven; hallowed be Thy name. Thy kingdom come. Thy will be done in earth as it is in heaven. Give us this day our daily bread. And forgive us our trespasses, as we forgive those who trespass against us. And lead us not into temptation, but deliver us from evil. For Thine is the kingdom, and the power, and the glory, forever. Amen!

DR. GURLEY'S SERMON.

As we stand here to-day, mourners around this coffin, and around the lifeless remains of our beloved chief magistrate, we recognize and we adore the sovereignty of God. His throne is in the Heavens, and His kingdom ruleth over all. He hath done, and He hath permitted to be done, whatsoever he pleased. Clouds and darkness are round about him; righteousness and judgment are the habitation of his throne. His way is in the sea and his path in the great waters, and his footsteps are not known. Canst thou by searching find out God? Canst thou find out the Almighty unto perfection? It is as high as Heaven, what canst thou do? Deeper than hell, what canst thou know? The measure thereof is longer than the earth, and broader than the sea. If He cut off and shut up, or gather together, then who can hinder him? for He knoweth vain men, He seeth wickedness: also, will he not then consider it? We bow before His Infinite Majesty, — we bow, we weep, we worship.

> "Where reason fails with all her powers,
> There faith prevails and love adores."

It was a cruel, cruel hand, that dark hand of the assassin, which smote our honored, wise, and noble President, and filled the land with sorrow. But above and beyond that hand there is another, which we must see and acknowledge. It is the chastening hand of a wise and a faithful Father. He gives us this bitter cup, and the cup that our father has given us shall we not drink it?

> God of the just, thou givest us the cup,
> We yield to thy behest, and drink it up.

Whom the Lord loveth he chasteneth. Oh, how these blessed words have cheered and strengthened and sustained us through all these long and weary years of civil strife, while our friends and brothers on so many ensanguined fields were falling and dying for the cause of liberty and union. Let them cheer and strengthen and sustain us to-day. True, this new sorrow and chastening has come in such an hour and in such a way as we thought not, and it bears the impress of a rod that is very heavy, and of a mystery that is very deep, that such a life should be sacrificed at such a time, by such a foul and diabolical agency; that the man at the head of the nation, whom the people had learned to trust with a confiding and a loving confidence, and upon whom more than upon any other were centred, under God, our best hopes for the true and speedy pacification of the country, the restoration of the Union, and the return of harmony and love, — that he should be taken from us, and taken just as the prospect of peace was brightly opening upon our torn and bleeding country, and just as he was beginning to be animated and gladdened with the hope of ere long enjoying with the people the blessed fruit and reward of his and their toils, care and patience and self-sacrificing devotion to the interests of liberty and the Union. Oh, it is a mysterious and a most afflicting visitation. But it is our Father in Heaven, the God of our fathers and our God, who permits us to be so suddenly and sorely smitten; and we know that His judgments are right, and that in faithfulness He has afflicted us. In the midst of our rejoicings we needed this stroke, this dealing, this discipline and therefore He has sent it. Let us remember our affliction has not come forth of the dust, and our trouble has not sprung out of the ground.

Through and beyond all second causes, let us look and see the sovereign permissive agency of the great First Cause. It is his prerogative to bring light out of darkness, and good out of evil. Surely the wrath of man shall praise him, and the remainder of wrath he will restrain. In the light of a clearer day, we may yet see that the wrath which planned and perpetrated the death of the President was overruled by Him, whose judgments are unsearchable and His ways past finding out, for the highest welfare of all those interests which are so dear to the Christian patriot and philanthropist, and for which a loyal people have made such an unexampled sacrifice of treasure and of blood. Let us not be faithless, but believing.

"Blind unbelief is prone to err, and scan His work in vain;
God is his own interpreter, and he will make it plain."

We will wait for his interpretation; and we will wait in faith, nothing doubting. He who has led us so well, and defended and prospered us so wonderfully during the last four years of toil and struggle and sorrow, will not forsake us now. He may chasten, but he will not destroy. He may purify us more and more in the furnace of trial, but he will not consume us. No, no. He has chosen us, as he did his people of old, in the furnace of affliction; and he has said of us, as he said of them, this people have I formed for myself; they shall show forth my praise. Let our principal anxiety now be that this new sorrow may be a sanctified sorrow; that it may lead us to deeper repentance, to a more humbling sense of our dependence upon God, and to the more unreserved consecration of ourselves, and all that we have, to the cause of truth and justice, of law and order, of liberty and good government, of pure and undefiled religion. Then, though weeping may endure for a night, joy will come in the morning. Blessed be God. Despite of this great and sudden and temporary darkness, the morning has begun to dawn, the morning of a bright and glorious day, such as our country has never seen. That day will come and not tarry, and the death of a hundred presidents and their cabinets can never, never prevent it. While we are thus hopeful, however, let us also be humble. The occasion calls us to prayerful and tearful humiliation. It demands of us that we lie low, very low, before Him who has smitten us for our sins. Oh that all our rulers and all our people may bow in the dust to-day beneath the chastening hand of God, and may their voices go up to him as one voice, and their hearts go up to him as one heart, pleading with him for mercy, for grace to sanctify our great and sore bereavement, and for wisdom to guide us in this our time of need! Such a united cry and pleading will not be in vain. It will enter into the ear and heart of Him who sits upon the throne, and He will say to us, as to his ancient Israel, "In a little wrath, I hid my face from thee for a moment, but with everlasting kindness will I have mercy upon thee, saith the Lord, thy Redeemer."

I have said, that the people confided in the late lamented President with a full and a loving confidence. Probably no man since the days of Washington was ever so deeply and firmly imbedded and enshrined in the very hearts of the people as Abraham Lincoln Nor was it a mistaken confidence and love. He deserved it; deserved it well; deserved it all. He merited it by his character, by his acts, and by the whole tenor and tone and spirit of his life. He was simple and sincere, plain and honest, truthful and just, benevolent and kind. His perceptions were quick and clear, his judgments were calm and accurate, and his purposes were good and pure beyond a question. Always and everywhere he aimed and endeavored to *be* right and to *do* right. His integrity was thorough, all-pervading, all-controlling, and incorruptible. It was the same in every place and relation, in the consideration and control of matters great or small, the same firm and steady principle of power and beauty, that shed a clear and crowning lustre upon all his other excellences of mind and heart, and recommended him to his fellow-citizens as the man, who, in a time of unexampled peril, when the very life of the nation was at stake, should be chosen to occupy in the country, and for the country, its highest post of power and responsibility. How wisely and well, how purely and faithfully, how firmly and steadily, how justly and successfully he did occupy that post, and meet its grave demands, in circumstances of surpassing trial and difficulty, is known to you all, — known to the country and the world; he comprehended from the first the perils to which treason had exposed the freest and best government on the earth, — the vast interests of liberty and humanity that were to be saved or lost forever in the urgent impending conflict. He rose to the dignity and momentousness of the occasion, saw his duty as the Chief Magistrate of a great and imperilled people, and he determined to do his duty, and his whole duty, seeking the guidance and leaning upon the arm of Him of whom it is written, "He giveth power to the faint, and to them that have no might He increaseth the strength." Yes, he leaned upon his arm. He recognized and received the truth, that the kingdom is the Lord's and He is the governor among the nations. He remembered that God is in history, and he felt that nowhere had his hand and his mercy been so marvellously conspicuous as in the history of this nation. He hoped and he prayed that that same hand would continue to guide us, and that same mercy continue to abound to us in the time of our greatest need. I speak what I know, and testify what I have often heard him say, when I affirm that that guidance and mercy were the props on which he humbly and habitually leaned; that they were the best hope he had for himself, and for his country. Hence, when he was leaving his home in Illinois, and coming to this city to take his seat in the Executive Chair of a disturbed and troubled nation, he said to the old and tried friends who gathered tearfully around him, and bade him farewell, I leave you with this request, — pray for me. They did pray for him, and millions of others prayed for him. Nor did they pray in vain. Their prayers were heard, and the answer appears in all his subsequent history. It shines forth with a heavenly radiance in the whole course and tenor of his administration, from its commencement to its close.

God raised him up for a great and glorious mission, furnished him for his work, and aided him in its accomplishment. Nor was it merely by strength of mind, and honesty of heart, and purity and pertinacity of purpose, that He furnished him. In addition to these things, He gave him a calm and abiding confidence in the overruling providence of God, and in the ultimate triumph of truth and righteousness, through the power and the blessing of God. This confidence strengthened him in all his hours of anxiety and toil, and inspired him with calm and cheering hope, when others were inclining to despondency and gloom. Never shall I forget the emphasis and the deep emotion with which he said, in this very room, to a company of clergymen and others, who called to pay him their respects in the darkest day of our civil conflict: "Gentlemen, my hope of success, in this great and terrible struggle, rests on that immutable foundation, the justice and goodness of God; and, when events are very threatening, and prospects very dark, I still hope, that in some way which man cannot see, all will be well in the end, because our cause is just, and God is on our side." Such was his sublime and holy faith; and it was an anchor to his soul, both sure and steadfast. It made him firm and strong. It emboldened him in the pathway of duty, however rugged and perilous it might be. It made him valiant for the right, for the cause of God and humanity; and it held him in steady, patient, and unswerving adherence to a policy of administration which he thought, and which we all now think, both God and humanity required him to adopt. We admired and loved him on many accounts; for strong and various reasons. We admired his childlike simplicity; his freedom from guile and deceit; his stanch and sterling integrity; his kind and forgiving temper; his industry and patience; his persistent, self-sacrificing devotion to all the duties of his eminent position, from the least to the greatest; his readiness to hear and consider the cause of the poor and humble, the suffering and the oppressed; his charity for those who questioned the correctness of his opinions and the wisdom of his policy; his wonderful skill in reconciling differences among the friends of the Union, leading them away from abstractions and inducing them to work together and harmoniously for the common weal; his true and enlarged philanthropy, that knew no distinction of color or race, but regarded all men as brethren, and endowed alike by their Creator with certain inalienable rights, amongst which are life, liberty, and the pursuit of happiness; his inflexible purpose, that what freedom had gained in our terrible civil strife should never be lost, and that the end of the war should be the end of slavery, and as a consequence of rebellion; his readiness to spend and be spent for the attainment of such a triumph, a triumph, the blessed fruits of which shall be as wide-spreading as the earth, and as enduring as the sun. All these things commanded and fixed our admiration, and the admiration of the world, and stamped upon his character and life the unmistakable impress of greatness. But more sublime than any or all of these, more holy and influential, more beautiful and strong and sustaining, was his abiding confidence in God, and in the final triumph of truth and righteousness, through him, and for his sake. This was his noblest virtue, his grandest principle; the secret, alike of his strength, his patience, and his success. This, it seems to me, after being near him steadily, and with him often, for more than four years, is the principle by which, more than by any other, he being dead yet speaketh. Yes, by his steady, enduring confidence in God, and in the complete, ultimate success of the cause of God, which is the cause of humanity, more than in any other way, does he now speak to us, and to the nation he loved and served so well. By this he speaks to his successor in office, and charges him to have faith in God. By this he speaks to the members of his Cabinet, the men with whom he counselled so often, and associated with so long, and he charges them to have faith in God. By this he speaks to all who occupy positions of influence and authority in these sad and troublous times, and he charges them all to have faith in God. By this he speaks to this great people, as they sit in sackcloth to-day, and weep for him with a bitter wailing, and refuse to be comforted, and he charges them to have faith in God; and by this he will speak through the ages, and to all rulers and peoples in every land, and his message to them will be, Cling to liberty and right, battle for them, bleed for them, die for them if need be, and have confidence in God. Oh that the voice of this testimony may sink down into our hearts to-day, and every day, and into the heart of the nation, and exert its appropriate influence upon our feelings, our faith, our patience, and our devotion to the cause, now dearer to us than ever before, because consecrated by the blood of its most conspicuous defender, its wisest and most fondly trusted friend!

He is dead. But the God in whom he trusted lives,— and he can guide and strengthen his successor as he guided and strengthened him. He is dead. But the memory of his virtues, of his wise and patriotic counsels and labors, of his calm and steady faith in God, lives as precious, and will be a power for good in the country quite down to the end of time. He is dead. But the cause he so ardently loved, so ably, patiently, faithfully represented and defended, not for himself only, not for us only, but for all people, in all their coming generations till time shall be no more, — that cause survives his fall, and will survive it. The light of its brightening prospects flashes cheeringly to-day athwart the gloom occasioned by his death, and the language of God's united providences is telling us, that, though the friends of liberty die, liberty itself is immortal. There is no assassin strong enough and no weapon deadly enough to quench its inextinguishable life or arrest its onward march to the conquest and empire of the world. This is our confidence and this is our consolation as we weep and mourn to-day: Though our beloved President is slain, our beloved Country is saved; and so we sing of mercy as well as of judgment. Tears of gratitude mingle with those of sorrow. While there is darkness, there is also the dawning of a brighter, happier day upon our stricken and weary land. God be praised that our fallen chief lived long enough to see the day dawn, and the day star of joy and peace arise upon the nation. He saw it, and he was glad. Alas! alas! He only saw the dawn. When the sun has risen full-orbed and glorious, and a happy re-united people are rejoicing in its light, it will shine upon his grave, but that grave will be a precious and a consecrated spot. The friends of Liberty and of the Union will repair to it in years and ages to come, to pronounce the memory of its occupant blessed, and gathering from his very ashes, and from the rehearsal of his deeds and virtues, fresh incentives to patriotism, they will there renew their vows of fidelity to their country and their God.

And now I know not that I can more appropriately conclude this discourse, which is but a sincere and simple utterance of the heart, than by addressing to our departed President, with some slight modification, the language which Tacitus, in his life of Agricola, addresses to his venerable and departed father-in-law. With you we may now congratulate. You are blessed not only because your life was a career of glory; but because you were released, when, your country safe, it was happiness to die. We have lost a parent; and, in our distress, it is now an addition to our heartfelt sorrow that we had it not in our power to commune with you on the bed of languishing, and receive your last embrace. Your dying words would have been ever dear to us. Your commands we should have treasured up, and graved them on our hearts. This sad comfort we have lost, and the wound, for that reason, pierces deeper. From the world of spirits behold your disconsolate family and people. Exalt our minds from fond regret and unavailing grief to the contemplation of your virtues. Those we must not lament. It were impiety to sully them with a tear. To cherish their memory, to embalm them with our praises, and so far as we can to emulate your bright example, will be the truest mark of our respect, the best tribute we can offer. Your wife will thus preserve the memory of the best of husbands; and thus your children will prove their filial piety. By dwelling constantly on your words and actions, they will have an illustrious character before their eyes; and, not content with the bare image of your mortal frame, they will have what is more valuable, — the form and features of your mind. Busts and statues, like their originals, are frail and perishable. The soul is formed of finer elements, and its inward form is not to be expressed by the hand of an artist. With unconscious matter our manners and our morals may, in some degree, trace the resemblance. All of you that gained our love and raised our admiration still subsist, and will ever subsist, preserved in the minds of men, the register of ages and the records of fame. Others, who have figured on the stage of life, and were the worthies of a former day, will sink for want of a faithful historian into the common lot of oblivion, inglorious and unremembered. But you, our lamented friend and head, delineated with truth, and fairly consigned to posterity, will survive yourself, and triumph over the injuries of time.

PRAYER.

The Rev. E. H. Gray, D. D., of the E St. Baptist Church, closed the solemn services with prayer, as follows:

God of the bereaved, comfort and sustain this mourning family. Bless the new Chief Magistrate. Let the mantle of his predecessor fall upon him. Bless the Secretary of State and his family. O God, if possible, according to Thy will, spare their lives that they may render still important service to the country. Bless all the members of the Cabinet. Endow them with wisdom from above. Bless the commanders in our Army and Navy, and all the brave defenders of the country. Give them continued success. Bless the Embassadors from foreign courts, and give us peace with the nations of the earth. O God, let treason, that has deluged our land with blood, and desolated our country, and bereaved our homes, and filled them with widows and orphans, which has at length culminated in the assassination of the nation's chosen ruler, — God of justice, and Avenger of the nation's wrong, let the work of treason cease, and let the guilty perpetrators of this horrible crime be arrested, and brought to justice! O hear the cry and the prayer and the wail rising from the nation's smitten and crushed heart, and deliver us from the power of our enemy, and send speedy peace into all our borders. Through Jesus Christ our Lord. Amen.

REV. E. N. KIRK.

PSALMS XLVI. 10.

BE STILL, AND KNOW THAT I AM GOD.

ON Sunday, the 2d instant, our army was exultingly chasing the main army of the rebels from Richmond. On Sunday, the 9th, the Commander-in-chief of the rebellious forces capitulated to General Grant. On Sunday, the 16th, the voice of song has died in our streets. The triumphant banner of the Republic wears the weeds of widowhood. A word can start the tear in every eye. Arrangements for rejoicing are suspended. A nation is making preparations for a funeral; the greatest funeral but one it ever attended; yes, the greatest: for, the people never buried such a President at such a time, — a murdered President.

Which way shall we look? what shall we do? What becomes a people so afflicted, — so great a nation under so great a calamity? If we should catch and execute a thousand vile assassins, or their viler employers, would it bring back our lost? would it place our practised pilot at the helm again? Where are we? We had fondly hoped the experience of four such years as we have passed would give us guaranty for the four years to come.

But our hopes are blighted, our plans are frustrated We are stunned by the suddenness of the blow; confounded by the awful wickedness of the deed. Murder is abroad; murder, that seeks the highest mark; that dashes down one of the noblest of our race; that blots out the brightest star in our heavens; that strikes at the wisest, kindest, gentlest of us all; that strikes at the life of the nation in the man to whom the nation has intrusted that life.

We are sad, — we are sick at heart. We feel as if our globe had lost its course, and were drifting down toward the Botany Bay of the Universe. The reign of Justice, of Law, of Order, seems to be past.

We seem to be struggling like drowning men, — the black, chill waters are blinding our eyes, stiffening our limbs, stifling our breath.

What shall we do? Shall we fill the air with our clamors? Shall we put forth our strength in some mighty deeds of vengeance?

What is the work and duty of the hour, — of this holy Sabbath?

Thanks be to God! a voice sounds from behind the black cloud; a voice from the upper throne; a voice from the world where no assassin lifts his hand; where treason and murder never are known. "Be still, and know that I am God." That is just what our oppressed, aching hearts rejoice to hear. It is, in the Psalm, as really addressed to our enemies in their vain exultations, as to us in our sorrow. But we need now to hear it for ourselves.

This, fellow-citizens, is the great lesson of the day in which we live; of the horrid tragedy that makes a nation mourn; of the whole bloody plot of which this is the culmination. What is the lesson?

I. *Suppress or modify all natural impulses by the controlling power of religious feeling.*

1. *Distress must not be allowed complete control.* — Nature quivers in agony under such a blow. Who is this thus brutally murdered? The man who had won our love and gratitude beyond any of the living. Around him, the tenderest cords of our hearts were bound. We had placed in his hands the most sacred of earthly trusts. He had led us so wisely, so firmly, so kindly, through such a wilderness, and brought us out as God's minister into so large a place and so great a deliverance. We had seen in him so much of magnanimity, of sound judgment, of gentle kindness, of robust manliness, of tender sympathy, of lofty principle, we could not but love him, strongly, tenderly. We have slept securely, we have dismissed anxiety and fear, because our father was at the helm. But he is gone, — dead; murdered; basely assassinated; with no last words, no time to tell us where his hope was anchored, and whither he was going.

Our hearts are weary with the dull pain of repeating to ourselves — he is gone, gone from us forever.

Hark, suffering hearts! a voice from the upper world, —

"Be still, and know that I am God. If Abraham Lincoln is dead, I live. If you loved him, love me, and trust him in my hands. Mourn for yourselves, but rejoice for him. His work was finished, nobly finished. And I have removed him from the turmoil and confusion of earth to the peace and rest of heaven."

2. We are liable to indulge in *murmurings*. Why should such wickedness be permitted to break in upon the order of society? Why should a wretch like the leader of this rebellion be endowed with such executive power and the ability to employ, directly or indirectly, the black-hearted assassin to invade so noble a life, and rob a nation of its polar star? "Be still, and know that I am God. Suppress all murmurs. Suffer, weep, but do not murmur. Clouds and darkness are round about him, but justice and judgment are the pillars of his throne. My thoughts are not your thoughts, neither are your ways my ways. For, as the heavens are higher than the earth, so are my ways higher than your ways, and my thoughts than your thoughts." Wisdom, rectitude, power, is the trinity of attributes on that eternal throne which presides over all human affairs. We not only should not complain of the divine government, we should cheerfully acquiesce in its decrees, and in its permissions; for it gives the Devil the length of his chain, and makes him, in doing his own work, accomplish the purposes that infinite wisdom and love had formed.

You remember that Job anticipated the very features of the divine government to perplex himself, that now perplex us. And you remember God's method of reply.

It was essentially just this, — Be still, and know that I am God. "Who is this that darkeneth counsel by words without knowledge? Gird up now thy loins like a man; for I will demand of thee, and answer thou me. Where wast thou when I laid the foundations of the earth? Declare, if thou hast understanding." If God walks on the waves of the sea, only faith can follow him there. Murmuring unbelief must remain on the solid shore, and lose sight of his footsteps. Faith alone can walk on waves, and sing amid the tempest, "In God is my salvation."

Look, for instance, at this fact. He informs us in his word that he chastens us for our good, though we cannot always see how the end is secured. Faith believes his statements and assurances. Sometimes it is obvious that his chastisements are directed expressly to removing that master-passion, the pride of our hearts.

If you are conversant with the history of Israel, you will have discovered that a very prominent aim of the Divine Providence is, to abase the pride of man. Man has an utterly false standard, which teaches him to admire most of the forms of pride in others, and all in himself. Just study that history with this clew in your hand; God's providence is rebuking the pride of men's hearts. That is what he is doing to-day among us. We had doubted Mr. Lincoln's ability at first. But now we have proved it, and trusted him. We placed him the second time at the head of our affairs, with the most unreserved confidence, and a fulness of joy and thankfulness to God. We felt secure when the decision was announced that he was re-elected. We were sure of four

4

years of wise administration, of integrity at the core of the government. But there was one thing we did not make sufficiently prominent; the uncertainty of human life. We forgot every morning when we arose that Abraham Lincoln's breath was in his nostrils. We forgot that his own clemency was harboring the villains that were plotting his destruction. But this was all virtually written in God's word; and we should have retained an humbler spirit had we kept that word in more vivid remembrance. It bade us not to put our trust in an arm of flesh, because, however strong to-day, to-morrow it may be crumbling back to dust. It bade us not to put our trust in man, for he is "crushed before the moth." A pistol-ball closes his history, annihilates his strength, turns him to dust. We were bidden not to put our trust in princes, for their breath is in their nostrils. Abraham was a prince, and we were proud of him, — so proud that we hid God behind him. And now we hear a voice in providence, echoing the voice in Scripture, Be still, proud heart, and know that I am God. Boast no more of thy strength, of thy generals, of thy brave defenders, of thy magnanimous leader; but "he that boasteth, let him boast in the Lord." This terrible event proclaims, Man is frail, God is eternal. There is another natural feeling now called into active exercise, but which we must attemper by the power of a higher religious sentiment.

3. *Revenge* is in man a perverted instinct, but as really an instinct as the love of life. It was placed in man as the sting was given to the bee, to resist aggression from superior force. But it has now become so

mingled with our selfishness, and so perverted we cannot properly exercise it at all in personal matters, and scarcely in public affairs. But it is impossible to look on a dastardly oppressor or an act of cruelty, on any wrong to another, without feeling an intense desire to make the wrongdoer suffer.

How intensely this feeling is working to-day in the length and breadth of this outraged country! But to that feeling to-day a voice from heaven speaks, — " Be still, and know that I am God. Vengeance belongeth to me, I will repay, saith the Lord." We have a duty to perform; a solemn duty, a stern duty. We are dealing with men who wear much of the image of their father, who was a liar, and a traitor, and a rebel, and a secessionist, and a murderer, from the beginning. The magistrate must deal with them by the stern decrees of law and justice, the soldier by the sterner decrees of military usage; but we, as men, as citizens, have no personal or party revenge to gratify. All we have to do in this matter is this; that as we are citizens of a republic, and the magistrate must be guided by two codes, the statutes, and the public sentiment that sustains or modifies them, we must form a correct public sentiment, which is with us the backbone of law. Let traitors carry personal revenge into their treatment of us. We must let our revenge hear that voice, — Be still, and know that I am God.

Another sentiment is outraged by recent events.

4. *Justice.* The outbreak was a high-handed act of injustice. The robbery committed on the government, the **robbery** not only of forts, and ships, and arms, but

of the territory purchased by our common treasury, and of the men the government had trained to the art of war at its own expense; the enlistment of the selfishness of foreign nations against us; the treatment of our brave soldiers, when made prisoners of war; the treatment of men who retained among them loyalty and allegiance to the government that had always blessed them,—all arouse the sense of justice more profoundly in this nation, than any events of our history. Yes, if there has been found in all that horrid region where rebellion has scorched the very air men breathe, and withered all the finer sentiments of the human soul, and turned the very fountains of religious life into poisonous springs; there, if an Abdiel has been found, "faithful among the faithless, among innumerable false, unmoved, unshaken, unseduced, unterrified," that one has been marked out for scorn and cruelty, for rapine and for murder, even though the reverend crown of age was on his brow.

A thousand times in this war has the sentiment of justice within us called for fire from heaven to fall upon the monsters. To-day it calls for the extermination of a miscreant race, that prove themselves unfit to breathe the air of heaven. But even that sentiment must be restrained; for we hear another voice. It proclaims to us, "Be still, and know that I am God. I will judge nations, communities, individuals, bringing them to my bar, to make every man answer for the deeds done in the body. Ask no more, wish for no more than that. When the time comes for your tribunals in my name to try each man by the laws of his country, then stand by your judiciary in its righteous decisions, and let no mawkish sentiment check the execution of them."

Another sentiment is now called into action.

5. *Fear.* A new pilot takes the helm. Mysteriously, he did not command our respect on the solemn day in which the nation put the crown upon his brow, and he took the solemn oath of office. He has repented: this is all we ask of him. Everything else in his history inspires hope, respect, and gratitude. But still, it is not the hand that held the rudder-wheel on those tempestuous nights in which we were running through those narrow channels where ruin lay on either side. Fear naturally arises in such circumstances. It would come up if you were in a steamship at sea, among icebergs, with a captain who had sailed only river-craft until now.

And we have another source of fear. The man who has held the powers of Europe at bay may also be removed. A new man there would naturally awaken solicitude.

And then, again: how do we know what new phase this assassination may put upon a yet unfinished war? what new demonstrations of sympathy with treason may spring up in the loyal States? But when these fears start up, we hear a voice saying to them, — "Be still, and know that I am God. I kill, and I make alive. Of whom hast thou been afraid, and hast not remembered me? Say to them that are of a fearful heart, Be strong, fear not. Behold, your God will come with vengeance; he will come and save you." "Fear not, thou worm Jacob, and ye men of Israel; I will help thee, saith the Lord thy Redeemer, and the Holy One of Israel." His aim is to produce in you that confidence which shall say: "God is my rock, my buckler. In God have I put my trust. I will not fear what man can do unto me. God is our refuge and strength, a very present help in trouble. Therefore will we not fear though the earth be removed, and though the mountains be carried into the midst of the sea."

"Be still, and know that I am God." Do nothing rashly, say nothing rashly. Wait until you see the pillar of cloud go before you; then move. Be still. Quiet the agitated sea of your heart. Feeling was not designed to hold the helm, but simply to fill the sails. When trouble comes, be still; so still that you can hear every syllable God is whispering. For, you remember, that when the prophet stood upon the mount before the Lord, and the Lord passed by, there was "a great and strong wind" that "rent the mountains, and broke in pieces the rocks before the Lord; but the Lord was not in the wind; and after the wind, an earthquake; but the Lord was not in the earthquake; and after the earthquake, a fire; but the Lord was not in the fire; and after the fire, a still small voice." There God was. The wind is raging and howling around us now, the earthquake shakes the solid globe; nay, our very hearts. The fire is raging. But if we listen only to them, we shall not hear the Lord. He is not in them. We must be still; for he comes in the still small voice, in a whisper within that soul which waits, above all things, to hear him speak.

Now when we are thus tranquillized, what does the Lord say to us? He says: "I am God."

II. *His existence, attributes, providence, grace, and glory are what he would have us to know and permanently recognize.* "Be still, and know that I am God."

1. *His personal existence* he would have us know. Just bring this test home to yourself. Imagine one of your neighbors to deny that you had a personal existence, to try to persuade others that you had not, to treat you as if you had not. Nay, let him affirm that you lack any one attribute of a rational being,— memory, judgment, conscience, affection,— how deeply he injures and offends you. And if he be your own beloved child, nurtured and cherished by you, how painful his treatment and estimate of you become! Judge from that how God regards pantheism, polytheism, atheism, theoretic or practical. This nation has manifested atheism very extensively. The Lord says— do so no more. Deny not, forget not my person, my attributes. Be not blind, amid the works of my hands, to my glory. Be not deaf when I speak to you in my word. Treat me as having a heart, an intelligence, a will, of which your own is an imitation. Come as children, and speak to me daily.

Oh! will this nation be still enough now to hear the Lord God Almighty assert his own existence, and declare that excellence which makes the command to love him supremely, infinitely reasonable?

2. *His providence he would have us know.* It is a providence of care: "upholding all things by the word of his power." States and families, like the individuals that compose them, "live and move, and have their being" in Him. It is a providence of forethought and

purpose, directing all events to one glorious issue, from the fall of a sparrow, or the shooting of an assassin's pistol, to the overthrow of an empire, — making the wrath of man to praise Him, and restraining the remainder. Look at the shortsighted wickedness of Joseph's brethren in sending him into what they supposed would be a lifelong bondage. Look at Pharaoh's oppression, aiming at the extermination of the sons of Jacob, resulting in their becoming the medium of salvation to the world. Look at these conspirators. They have now sealed the verdict of the world; the Confederacy is a conspiracy of assassins. It began with attempted assassination of the chief citizen, the representative man of the nation. It ended in securing his murder. They have murdered their strongest friend, and broken down the last bulwark that kept the popular will from being executed on them. A dark destiny is now before them. And woe to the man that now comes between them and the preparing blow! They have united the loyal citizens more completely in that purpose which will leave in some places no vestige of them but the desolation their wickedness has wrought. They have now made the issue. Die they, or the nation must.

Is it not wonderful how God secures his ends by the aims and endeavors of those who are attempting to thwart his purposes! See Him, fellow citizens; recognize his purposes concerning us, and his employment of his and our enemies to execute them. His time has come to bring Israel out of bondage, and Pharaoh must do it. His time has come to release our African brethren, but the masters must do it. His providence is one of moral judgment. He does not make up the full issue for any individual until death occurs. But communities He judges here. He declares by his servant Malachi: "Then shall ye return, and discern between the righteous and the wicked; between him that serveth God, and him that serveth him not. For, behold, the day cometh that shall burn as an oven; and all the proud, yea, and all that do wickedly, shall be as stubble."

What a development have the slaveholders made of their character! Some thought it severe, some untimely, for a senator to utter that sentence of judgment on them, pronouncing slavery barbarous. But the burning day of judgment has now come, and they are witnesses on the stand to the truth of the indictment, — arrogance, treasons, perjury, breach of trust, brow-beating, cruelty, assassination; these are the epithets history will apply to their conduct. The great white throne is set, and black appears black before it. Davis and Stevens, Lee, Toombs and Floyd, Mason and Breckenridge, every naval and military officer that left our service, every member of their Congress, every gaol-keeper that guarded our soldiers in their prisons, every act of violence to our negro soldiers in their hands, every loyal man of the South that they robbed and murdered, the corpse of Abraham Lincoln, the mangled frame of William Seward are their witnesses. Truly there is a Nemesis. They have gone like Judas to their own place in history.

To know God in his providence we must become familiar with his treatment of the Jews. The Old Testament must enter into our education. He made his providence more marked and distinct with them than with any other people. He blessed them when they recognized his presence, and treated Him as their benefactor and ruler. But see what terrible displays of his displeasure followed their disobedience. Their various captivities, of a duration of from five years to seventy, and their final dispersion show Him to be a holy God, holding nations and communities responsible to Him under terrible penalties.

3. *His grace is the other form of manifestation He has employed.* We must know Him as holy, requiring an expression of the evil of sin as great as can be made through the cross, in extending mercy to sinners. We must know Him as merciful, ready to be reconciled to us in Christ; as ready to make a covenant or compact of friendship with us, a covenant containing the richest promises of which the mind of man can conceive; as a hearer and answerer of prayer.

And this is the end at which He principally aims. All the real value of nations recognizing Him is, that it implies the personal knowledge of Him by individuals. And He counts no knowledge of Him satisfactory and complete, except that which leads us individually to repent of sin, and believe in the Lord Jesus Christ, and follow Him in the regeneration. Nations perish; individuals live forever. Hence God attaches a supreme importance to the personal faith of each individual. So it is said: " God so loved the world that he gave His only begotten son that *whosoever* believeth in Him might not perish, but have everlasting life. As many as received Him, to *them* gave He power to become the sons of God, even to them that believed on his name."

This is, then, the great issue to which the events of providence are pointing. The rebellion, this series of victories filling the nation with joy and thankfulness, this horrible crime filling the nation with grief and dismay, are all revelations of God. His language in the events which cheer and gladden you is, "I beseech you by the mercies of God that you present" yourself "a living sacrifice, holy and acceptable unto God." The language of an event which arouses the turbulent emotions of the heart, exciting grief or fear or anger, is. — Be still: hold that feeling in check, and observe me. I have come forth from my hiding place, to show you I am God.

Fellow-Christians, we never occupied such a vantage-ground as now, for bringing a revolted race to its allegiance to God. Our neighbors are beginning to see his presence, to recognize his will and power in passing events. For his sake, for their sakes, let us help them onward in this direction. Filled with adoration, submission, confidence, and love to Him, let us speak of Him in the convincing and persuasive words the quickened heart can always supply. Oh, may this nation to-day hear that voice as distinctly as it was heard from Sinai!

Fellow-citizens, make this a religious day, a day of thought, of such deep reflection as becomes you as rational beings brought into a wilderness of rugged rocks and frowning cliffs, of desolation and death, where you can, undiverted, hear the voice of God. Be still.

REV. CYRUS A. BARTOL.

ADDRESS.

I AM unable to give, and you perhaps indisposed to receive any regular preaching to-day. If I can but tell you what is in the air; if I can voice your feeling and my own, still more that spirit of God which is ready to be voiced by human lips, the real end of our meeting will, however informally, be reached. I lay aside therefore my written discourse. Though it be ecclesiastically a festival this morning, no Romish or other rubric has a right to prescribe our theme. I take no text save from the Bible of providence, the great book of events, God's finger is still writing in burning words every hour. I accept his subject, and defer my own.

I need not even tell the youngest of you what has occurred. How all too suddenly it was known! How on the wires it flashed, how in the atmosphere that overhangs, and in every wind that sweeps across our borders, it brooded and was borne! The craped and drooping flag, the slow-sounding bell, the minute-gun told it; and had the ocean-telegraph, yet to succeed, only served, the brain and heart of the world would be trembling with one sympathy. California, from our farthest bounds, is with us in the same sensation to-day.

I shrink from naming the deed by which we are so stirred. An actor in a theatre performs a part, in a scene of real life, which extinguishes all the interest of the mimic stage. What a contrast the last tragedy to our late jubilee! God seems to have chosen sacred days for his messages,— on two successive Sundays appointing celebrations of victory, — and now giving to Good Friday and Easter a new association indeed in Christian minds!

But, on this dark day, my purpose with you is not a lament, but comfort. Let me try to mention some consolations.

First, though our chief magistrate — all of him that could die — is dead, THE NATION LIVES. "What is your first impression?" asked a brother clergyman, adding that his was, — *the line must be drawn stricter between the friends and enemies of this country.* A second said his first impression was, that *an era of misrule had come.* I said, my first impression, after the shock of grief, was, — *though the President is gone, the nation lives, and will live more vital and vigorous for this blow.* What did the madmen, that struck at the Chief and the Secretary, so meanly — at the one from behind and the other in his bed — think to do? To kill the nation, to assassinate liberty, to cut the throat of law? What a mistake! This blow will hurt, not our cause, but only the hand that struck it; and no mischance to the truth be suffered by Him without whom not a sparrow falleth.

It is one consolation, too, that slavery died more swiftly and surely by this very stroke. Most important is it, that the act should be traced. We should not connect it with any quarter without proof. But we know its general and most authentic origin. It is not from any individual alone, but from the barbarism of slavery. That demon whispered in the actor's ear! That dragon fired his passion, and nerved his arm! His birth and breeding were in the hot-beds and centres of slavery, slave-breeding, and slave-trading. With indignation for the crime, mingles in my mind infinite pity for the criminal, whose personal guilt has what palliation depravity so deep can find in early nurture, bitter prejudice, or constitutional bias. He impersonated slavery itself in that theatre, which will hang henceforth, one of the most terrible pictures of history, on the walls of time forever. The horror affords this solace; that it hints the death-agony of the deadly foe of our republic. The monster, pursued in northern seas, is never more dangerous than in his dying struggles. Let the boat beware, that approaches him, lest the last lashing of his tail mix the blood of its crew with his own! With a worse monster than ever swam the deep, this new evidence of malignity should move us to keep no terms. Let this last precious life-current it has caused to flow be the *mordant* to set and seal the color of our eternal hatred, not to its misguided supporters, but to itself! Now that the assassination, which has been for four years and more after our Head, has accomplished its end, let our consolation be in the slavery's own unsparing destruction.

But still another consolation is in the power of justice returning to our hands. If we were going to be too lenient; if, to a lax and vicious good-humor, we were sacrificing the law and honor of God, we have learned that indulgence is not equity, and leniency is not love. Not revenge should be our object; for, spite of the text that ascribes it to him, I do not believe it is *God's!* Nor can we compass the absolute justice which God alone can measure out. But, for the protection of society, for the reformation of the criminal, for the guarding and nursing of the national life, we must watch every motion, and strain every nerve. Such atrocities of crime as can be traced should have condign sentence. Those who are responsible for the starving, in Southern pens and prisons, of our captured soldiers, should have due penalty. We cannot mete out the fair desert to all who have committed treason. We cannot hang a community. But the wicked leadership, the official malice, should feel our express displeasure, in the solemn sentence of the law. Let us convert what we can, disfranchise what has sinned basely, and banish with the mark of Cain what can never belong to us! We are gathering power to do this. The wild beast, which we have fought so long in the wilderness and the woods, we are getting under. Quickly as possible let us set up everywhere the civil and criminal courts! What the national stomach cannot assimilate it must vomit; and not keep it in the system, an indigestible and poisonous lump.

The last consolation is, that God can sanctify to us our supreme earthly ruler's death. He would not have permitted his life to be taken, had he not done his work. He has finished it, how well and nobly! Perhaps he would have been too gentle with evil-doers in the time to come. "Sic semper tyrannis," shouted the tragic actor, after discharging his pistol, as he brandished his blade. A strange motto for a slave state! For a murderer, as he slew the softest-hearted of men, a marvellous cry! *Sic semper tyrannis!* What! for him, Abraham Lincoln, the mildest among all he was set over, mild as May, into whose soul, from others' opposition or ridicule, no resentment could get; who never knew, in the way of authority or manner, how to get up to the dignity of his office; whose fault, if he had one, was, that he was not sufficiently stern with the vileness he could not comprehend; a man of the people, who waited before he struck at crime; a waiter on the people, who also waited on the Lord, and harkened for the harmony, yet to the coming of God's and the people's voice, — *he*, among whose last accents were words of kindness to the rebellious South, HE a tyrant! The speaker on the stage was *playing* indeed, though in a ferocious way. He feigned or fearfully mistook the side tyranny was on. Davis and Benjamin and Wigfall and Mason and Slidell not the tyrants? Nay, if such as they have not fallen by any privy blow, the reason is not that they are not tyrants, but we not assassins. Ah! could the agents and plotters of this ghastly crime have themselves only *waited* a little while, the measureless toils of our beloved one, more our servant than captain, might have worn him out. They need not have been so eager to anticipate the fate for him, toward which he was so rapidly consuming his own strength.

But be it our consolation, that the chariot of the Lord goes forward. He that takes hold of the spokes of its wheels, shall not stop it. What were the gentlest lips, that ever spoke, parted to say? "He that falls on this stone shall be broken; but on whom it shall fall, it will grind him to powder." Truly "the wrath of man shall praise him," and "the righteous shall be in everlasting remembrance." The "blessed martyr," that bore himself so meekly in the greatest station on earth, has gone to his harp and crown in heaven.

> After toil,
> To mortals rest is sweet.

REV. J. M. MANNING.

DEUTERONOMY XXXIV: 4, 5.

And the Lord said unto him, This is the land which I sware unto Abraham, unto Isaac, and unto Jacob, saying, I will give it unto thy seed; I have caused thee to see it with thine eyes, but thou shalt not go over thither. So Moses, the servant of the Lord, died there in the land of Moab, according to the word of the Lord.

"According to the word of the Lord." Sweet announcement to a broken-hearted nation, to-day! "Abraham Lincoln died this morning at twenty-two minutes after seven o'clock." That was the message which the wires, heavy-laden with their tidings, sobbed forth yesterday in all our pleasant places. And we awoke from our troubled sleep this morning, and, lo! it was not a dream! "According to the word of the Lord." "Even so, Father, for so it seemed good in thy sight." We look above all human agency. We recognize the will that never errs nor falters, and that worketh all things, in Heaven and on earth, after its own perfect counsel.

"So Moses, the servant of the Lord, died there." He had brought us through the "great and terrible wilderness," unto the borders of our goodly heritage; but was himself forbidden to enter. May the same God, who made him so much better than our fears, — such a *father* to us all, — do even greater things for the Joshua who succeeds him as the leader of our Israel! To this petition, every heart devoutly responds *Amen!* New responsibilities sober men oftentimes. Possessing real goodness of heart, they bend their shoulders loyally to the unexpected burden, and display great qualities of which they were thought destitute before. Thus a bereaved nation prays and hopes.

How incomplete, how complete, the dear life that has passed on! The surroundings, the hour, the instrumentality, — how painful! Why could not the name of one whom we so loved, whom we so tenderly revered, have a seemlier passage to its immortality? Thou, Lord, knowest! Thou dost not respect the person of any man. "Wise men die, likewise the fool and the brutish person perish." "Man being in honor abideth not." "Like sheep they are laid in the grave; death shall feed on them." We had traced a resemblance, often, between our beloved President and the great Prince of Orange, — called William the Silent. The same devotion to country, the same trust in a Divine Providence, the same cautious and persevering wisdom, the same tender regard for the people who confided in them. Oh, could not the parallel have been left imperfect? Must it be carried on to the bitter end? We loved to think that they were alike in their patriotism; but — poor, blinded mortals! — we did not foresee the dreadful event that was to make them so much alike in their death! Both slain with wife and friends around them, in the moment of social freedom and unconcern, by the assassin who long had been waiting for his chance to strike.

Let me quote from history, " On Tuesday, the 10th of July, 1584, at about half-past twelve, the Prince, with his wife on his arm, and followed by the ladies and gentlemen of his family, was going to the dining-room. William the Silent was dressed upon that day, according to his usual custom, in very plain fashion. He wore a wide-leaved, loosely-shaped hat of dark felt, with a silken cord round the crown,— such as was worn by the Beggars in the early days of the revolt. A high ruff encircled his neck, from which also depended one of the Beggar's medals, while a loose surcoat of grey frieze cloth, over a tawny leather doublet, with wide, slashed underclothes, completed his costume. Gérard (the murderer) presented himself at the doorway and demanded a passport. The Princess, struck with the pale and agitated countenance of the man, anxiously questioned her husband concerning the stranger. The Prince carelessly observed that it was merely a person who came for a passport; ordering, at the same time, a secretary to prepare one. The Princess, still not relieved, observed in an under-tone that she had never seen so villanous a countenance. Orange, however, not at all impressed with the appearance of Gérard, conducted himself at table with his usual cheerfulness, conversing much with the burgomaster of Leewarden, the only guest present at the family dinner, concerning the political and religious aspects of Friesland. At two o'clock the company rose from the table. The Prince led the way, intending to pass to his private apartments above. The dining-room which was on the ground-floor, opened into a little square vestibule, which communicated, through an arched passage-way, with the main entrance into the court-yard. This vestibule was also directly at the foot of the wooden staircase leading to the next floor, and was scarcely six feet in width. Upon its left side, as one approached the stairway, was an obscure arch, sunk deep in the wall, and completely in the shadow of the door. Behind this arch a portal opened to the narrow lane at the side of the house. The stairs themselves were completely lighted by a large window, half-way up the flight. The Prince came from the dining-room, and began leisurely to ascend. He had only reached the second stair, when a man emerged from the sunken arch, and, standing within a foot or two of him discharged a pistol full at his heart. Three balls entered his body, one of which, passing quite through him, struck with violence against the wall beyond. The Prince exclaimed in French, as he felt the wound, "O my God, have mercy upon my soul! O my God, have mercy upon this poor people!"

Such was the death, and such the last exclamation of the great and good father of modern liberty, the son and sire of illustrious princes, the wise subverter of despotisms, the champion of popular rights, to whom, more than to any other man perhaps, the world is indebted for free institutions and free ideas. Who can doubt, if strength had been left our good President when the fatal bullet struck him, that he also would have exclaimed, "O my God, have mercy upon my soul! O my God, have mercy upon this poor people?"

So alike, in the circumstances of their departure, how doubly consoling now to trace the previous parallel between their lives.

Listen. "His constancy in bearing the whole weight of a struggle as unequal as men have ever undertaken, was the theme of admiration even to his enemies. The rock in the ocean, 'tranquil amid raging billows,' was the favorite emblem by which his friends expressed their sense of his firmness." Can you not, as you hear these words, almost see the calm figure of Abraham Lincoln in his cabinet, quietly meditating his wise plans of deliverance, while the nation was quaking with fear, and some were wildly urging him to take the archives and flee? That rock, "tranquil amid the raging billows," has sunk to re-appear in another Sea where. as we would fain hope, only the billows of peace shall kiss it forever more. Hear, again, of the immortal Prince, whom our chief magistrate so closely resembled. "The supremacy of his political genius was entirely beyond question. He was the first statesman of the age. The quickness of his perception was only equalled by the caution which enabled him to mature the results of his observations. His knowledge of human nature was profound. He governed the passions and sentiments of a great nation as if they had been but the keys and chords of one vast instrument; and his hand rarely failed to evoke harmony even out of the wildest storms." Strange that this man should have lived three hundred years ago! It seems to us that we saw him but yesterday, laying his patient hand upon a sea of warring interests and opinions, and soothing them to peace and loyal co-operation;

moving so evenly that neither extreme was pleased at first, though both were satisfied at last; now seeming to go beyond, and now to come short of our eager wish. Yet true to his great duty, as the North-star to its eternal vigil, high and calm and clear, always in his place, shining with still and equal beam until our morning began to dawn, then wrapping his mantle of light about him, and joining the mighty host of the invisible.

"God alone knows the heart of man. He alone can unweave the tangled skein of human motives, and detect the hidden springs of human action; but, as far as can be judged by a careful observation of undisputed facts, and by a diligent collation of public and private documents, it would seem that no man, not even Washington, has ever been inspired by a purer patriotism." That was said of Orange, after all the history of his public and private life had been carefully summed up. But there is much in Abraham Lincoln — the sweetest and tenderest traits in his character — of which we have seen but glimpses yet. Still we feel no hesitation to-day in placing him, so far as patriotism and honesty of motive can go, on the same pedestal with Washington. And then, beyond what we now accord him, how his name will brighten as it rises out of present conflicts into the serene sky of history, as all his little, half-forgotten acts of love come welling up into the memories of us all; as prejudice and passion cease clouding our vision, and we see him "travelling in the greatness of his strength," one of the choice company of imperial souls, garmented and crowned with the gratitude of the ages, along the starry pathways of the immortal!

"His temperament was cheerful. At table, the pleasures of which, in moderation, were his only relaxation, he was always animated and merry, and this jocoseness was partly natural, partly intentional. In the darkest hours of his country's trial, he affected a serenity which he was far from feeling, so that his apparent gayety, at momentous epochs, was even censured by dullards, who could not comprehend its philosophy. He went through life bearing the load of a people's sorrows on his shoulders with a smiling face. Their name was the last word upon his lips, save the simple affirmative with which the soldier who had been battling for the right all his lifetime, commended his soul, in dying, 'to his great captain, Christ.' The people were grateful and affectionate, for they trusted the character of their 'Father William,' and not all the clouds which calumny could collect ever dimmed to their eyes the radiance of that lofty mind, to which they were accustomed, in their darkest calamities, to look for light. As long as he lived, he was the guiding-star of a whole brave nation, and when he died the little children cried in the streets." How apt the characterization! The Hollanders never said "Father William" more affectionately than we shall say "Father Abraham" henceforth. He did "bear the load of a people's sorrows on his shoulders with a smiling face." We do understand, at length, "the philosophy of that jocoseness" which troubled some of us at times while he lived. It was the oil lubricating the overtasked mechanism of that patient body and mind. It was the kind disguise, under which he concealed from us the deep anxiety of his heart, and bade us hope on, as though he were not himself almost ready to despair. It is plain to us now. We would not have his quaint stories one the less. Death has touched his unstudied manners, and lo! they are full of an immortal charm. Woe to the biographer who attempts to make him anything less plain than he was! Woe to the artist who tries to soften one feature, or to take one line out of his honest face! We love him, just as he was. We cannot spare one of his peculiar traits. He must be all there,—in history, in our memory, in imagination,—forever allowed to be just what God made him. And we will risk the verdict of the ages, for God's noblest work is an honest man.

In one point the parallel between Mr. Lincoln and the Prince of Orange fails. The Prince made a tour through the provinces, "honoring every city with a brief visit. The spontaneous homage which went up to him from every heart was pathetic and simple. There were no triumphal arches, no martial music, no banners, no theatrical pageantry,—nothing but the choral anthem from thousands of grateful hearts. "'Father William has come! Father William has come!' cried men, women, and children to each other, when the news of his arrival in town or village was announced. He was a patriarch visiting his children, not a conqueror nor a vulgar potentate displaying himself to his admirers. Happy were they who heard his voice, happier they who touched his hands; for his words were full of tenderness, his hand was offered to all. There were none so humble as to be forbidden to approach him, none so ignorant as not to know his deeds."

"None so humble as to be forbidden to approach him." Is there any but one man alone, of whom we can think to-day, as we hear those words? the tall, swaying form rising to welcome the poor freedwoman into his own family circle, — bidding her sit down in his own arm-chair, the tears gathering in his eyes as he listened to her simple story of sufferings and wrongs, — introducing her to his wife and friends, and waiting upon her as carefully as though she had been a queen. "His words were full of tenderness." That we might know by looking into his deep, sad, almost tearful eyes. "He was very pitiful, and of tender mercy." And the tones of his voice, falling on the ear of distress and wretchedness, will linger, in sweet benedictions, until the ears that heard them are dull and cold as his own. "A patriarch visiting his children." Such he would have been, no doubt, had he lived to indulge his goodness, and to please the ardent wish of thirty millions of people. We know what our welcome would have been. But we cannot conceive the great love which would have gushed up unto him out of the soft hearts of a disenthralled and enfranchised race. His first concern was to save "his children," then he would have leisure to "visit" them. Thank God, we are permitted to believe that he fulfilled the main purpose: may he receive, in the streets of the Golden City, the offerings of love which are due him from his delivered "children!"
"No triumphal arches, no martial music, no banners, no theatrical pageantry," but a voice, as the voice of many waters, saying unto *him*, next *after* the Lamb

that was slain, "THOU HAST REDEEMED US BY THY BLOOD!"

How incomplete, yet how complete!

> " No waning of fire, no quenching of ray,
> But rising, still rising, when passing away !
> Farewell, and all hail ! thou art buried in light !
> God speed thee to heaven, O star of our night !"

How complete! Would he not say so, as to all that concerned his country, if his spirit could stoop for a moment, and touch those cold lips which are sealed forever? Would it not have filled out the utmost stretch of his ambition and earthly hope, when he came from his simple home in the West, had he known,—*that* the State across which he was borne *secretly and in disguise*, would come first, singing the pæans of freedom, to lay its offerings of thanksgiving at his feet; *that* he should live to issue, in the providence of God, a proclamation giving manhood and womanhood to four millions of slaves; *that* he should hear of his own plain name, tenderly spoken all over the earth wherever goodness is revered and liberty loved; *that* he should be permitted, by his wise counsels, seconded by the able captains whom he drew to his cause, to make his distracted country feared and respected throughout the civilized world; *that* the very day on which his summons to eternity should come, would be but the fourth anniversary of the day on which the Starry Banner stooped to the dust at Fort Sumter; and that on that day the same banner, by the same hand which surrendered it, should be lifted up to its ancient height, but covered with more than its ancient glory,— had he foreknown all this, would he not have said, "Lord, that will be enough: then let thy servant depart, for mine eyes will have seen thy salvation?"

> "Follow now, as ye list! the first mourner to-day
> Is the nation, — whose Father is taken away!
> Wife, children, and neighbor may moan at his knell,
> He was lover and friend to his country as well!
> For the stars on our banner, grown suddenly dim,
> Let us weep, in our darkness, — but weep not for him!
> Not for him, — who, departing, leaves millions in tears!
> Not for him, — who has died full of honor and years!
> Not for him, — who ascended fame's ladder so high,
> From the round at the top he has stepped to the sky!
> It is blessed to go when so ready to die!"

I will not attempt to scan the counsels of the Most High, and to say why it is that we are thus bereaved. Perhaps it is better for us that we should be orphans to-day, than that he whom we loved to call "Father" should have been spared. His paternal heart, had it still throbbed in life, might have proved too tender for the stern work we are yet to do. He disliked the sight of blood. He was melted by tears. He was made soft as woman by the tones of pleading wretchedness. We do not know; but there is One who does know. The Eye which looks through all things, may see, in the feeble man whom He now chooses, a strong, innate sense of justice. That man, upheld by our sympathies and prayers, and inspired by God's special grace, may prove to be the sword of divine justice, executing wrath upon the evil-doers. Those who naturally exult over the tragedy, may find that only *mercy* is slain, while *vengeance* yet lives! Lives, did I say? ah, yes! and roused up to an intensity of fury which will require all our might to restrain! "Traitors! would you have forgiveness? go seek it of him whom your bloody hands have slain!" — that is the voice which now rises up and rolls over the land, from shore to shore. But God's way is "far above." It is his glory to conceal a thing. "Who hath known the mind of the Lord, or who hath been his counsellor?" It seems to us, even in this bitter hour, that we see the trailing splendors of the inner light which he inhabits; "but how little a portion is known of Him? the thunder of his power who can understand?"

We have one occasion of thanks, in this hour of agony, in the fact that our departed ruler was not a king. Had he been the sovereign, who can tell what anarchy might now ensue? But the people are the sovereign, and he was their minister. We may thank God that our "king never dies." He is myriad-handed and myriad-eyed. We look for no disturbance, no bewilderment, for no wandering up and down, as of sheep not having a shepherd; but for a full and clear comprehension of the exigency of the hour; for a calm wisdom, and prompt energy, on the part of a great people, which has successfully grappled with so many dangers in the past. Perhaps God is giving us our grand opportunity to show to an incredulous world, that we are indeed a government by the people. Had not our beloved President been taken from us, had he lived until we were clearly out of all our troubles, it might have been pleaded that his personal wisdom carried us through. Not so now. That cavil against free governments cannot be made. We may solve the problem on its own ground now, with no helping element to throw uncertainty around the result. We, by our steadiness to duty and firm resolve, may now prove, that, whoever dies and whoever lives, while the people live the government cannot be overthrown, or falter in its course.

But ah! poor human reason, be still. I seem to hear, "Be still, and know that I am God. Shall I not do what I will with mine own? And may I not choose my own instruments, with which to rule in the armies of heaven, and among the inhabitants of earth?" O my brother mourners! let us take refuge in the thought that "the Lord God omnipotent reigneth." Not a sparrow falleth on the ground without your heavenly Father. The Lord gave, and the Lord hath taken away, and blessed be the name of the Lord. When father and mother forsake me, the Lord shall take me up. He careth for us in the day of our orphanage and grief. His arm is stronger than any arm of flesh,— an everlasting arm, and it is underneath us all. He saves us from the terror by day, and the fear by night. All events, and the passions and outfoaming wrath of men, are subject unto Him. He holds them and us, and our nation and the world, all the living, and the departed whom we mourn, in the golden net-work of his purposes of love. And He will show us, when He unrolls that web to the eye of "the incorruptible," that all its threads are mercy and judgment; and that the hand which has woven it through the ages, and wrapped it around all the interests of all the children of men, has never been stretched out or withholden, nor lifted up in seeming displeasure, but to fulfil some kind and wise design.

"AND THE CHILDREN OF ISRAEL WEPT FOR MOSES IN THE PLAINS OF MOAB THIRTY DAYS: SO THE DAYS OF WEEPING AND MOURNING FOR MOSES WERE ENDED.

AND JOSHUA, THE SON OF NUN, WAS FULL OF THE SPIRIT OF WISDOM; FOR MOSES HAD LAID HIS HANDS UPON HIM: AND THE CHILDREN OF ISRAEL HARKENED UNTO HIM, AND DID AS THE LORD COMMANDED MOSES."

REV. JOHN E. TODD.

PRESIDENT LINCOLN.

The Lord reigneth. — *Psalms* xciii : 1.

God cannot die. Beyond the reach of the fatal dart of disease, or the withering touch of creeping age, or the breath of the pestilence, or the missiles of battle, or the arm of the cowardly assassin, He lives and reigns; and His throne, girt with justice and judgment, mercy and truth, is forever and ever, and the thoughts of His heart are unto all generations. This is our only consolation to-day.

It would be in vain for me to attempt to speak to you at this time on any other subject than the one which fills every mind and heart; and yet I have nothing to offer but the confused and bewildered thoughts of a mind which is still too much under the influence of the excitement and horror of the recent shock, to be able to act clearly and collectedly.

The tidings were too terrible to be comprehended or credited at once: the President foully assassinated in the very presence of the people, with deliberate forethought; the Secretary of State stabbed while lying on a sick bed, and his attendants killed and wounded. Other important officers of government, — the Secretary of War, the Lieutenant-General of the United States Army, — escaped only, without doubt, in consequence of unexpected detention from the President's side. Such was the dreadful story. It was ticked off at first, at midnight, to a few blanched faces, and was rejected. It came again with stronger authority. It stared out in grim and terrible lines from the morning papers, making the brain of the reader to reel, and the heart to grow sick It was told in husky and frightened tones by one to another, and with voices choked with tears. It leaped from face to face, pale and livid, as we never saw the faces of the people before. It began to fringe the flags, and darken the streets which were but recently so gay. It began to create gloom, and a hush and loneliness in business haunts, which, but a few days since, were filled with crowds and processions and cheers and music. It began to wail from steeple to steeple. It broke at last from the cannon's mouth in solemn thunder. And, at length, we begin to realize to-day, that our beloved President is no more.

It is a terrible national calamity, such as has not fallen upon us since we became a nation. It is an atrocious crime such as is almost unparalleled in history. It is universally regarded as such by the people. Never have they been so moved. No tidings of victory or defeat, not even the intelligence of the first assault upon the flag at Sumter has so stirred the depths of popular feeling. The country is swept to-day by a storm of silent but intense and very dangerous passion.

The feelings which these heavy tidings have universally excited, are — I mention them in the order in which they naturally arise — horror, grief, rage, anxiety. The country is convulsed with these emotions.

The first emotion experienced by every one upon learning of this terrible event was one of unmitigated horror, and it is a feeling from which we have not yet recovered. There were various things fitted to intensify it. We had not yet recovered from the ecstasies of delight occasioned by victories unprecedented in modern warfare, and which gave promise of speedy peace. The horrible tidings found us on the heights of exultation, and the fall in our feelings, and the shock, were proportionally tremendous. It was of all things the least expected. At an earlier stage in our national troubles, grave apprehensions were entertained of attempts upon the President's life. But for four years the enemy had forborne to resort to assassination; and, among the people of the loyal States, the President had been steadily gaining in the confidence and esteem and love of all. It was hardly imagined that he could have a personal enemy. The crime seemed horrible, because perpetrated upon a person of such high position, the head of a powerful nation, the equal of a king, or rather the superior; for kings rule by birthright, Presidents by the people's choice. It seemed horrible, because it was committed upon a man of such unoffending goodness. It seemed horrible, because it was committed from such a motive. Assassination is a new weapon in politics in this country. It seemed horrible, because it was a part of a conspiracy against a *number* of the heads of government, and was executed, so far as it was executed, with such brutal and blood-thirsty ferocity. It seemed horrible from the circumstances of its commission. With that confidence in his fellow-citizens which has distinguished every President, and led him to dispense with a body-guard, — a confidence which President Lincoln had especial right to feel, he had gone with a part of his family, unattended, to the theatre; not that he cared to go, but that he did not care to disappoint the people. He had been received with unusual demonstrations of enthusiasm and affection. Seated in a rocking-chair by the side of his wife, and with a multitude of his people around him, and regarding him as a father, he rested from the cares of office. Suddenly a man, — a *man!* — availing himself of the President's confidence, approached him stealthily from behind, and, without a word of warning, with a coward's hand and eye, fired at his head; then, rushing to the front, dropped upon the stage, brandished a knife, and uttered a tragic exclamation in his last role, disappeared behind the scenes, threaded the familiar passages, emerged into the open air, and escaped. Escaped? Ah, no! he should have committed his crime among some people less unitedly devoted to their Chief Magistrate; he should have done it in the empire of some other God. He will not escape. He may take the wings of the morning and fly to the uttermost parts of the sea; he may make his bed in hell; but he will not escape.

The first feeling of uncontrollable horror is succeeded by one of profound grief. It is not merely sorrow that such a crime should have to darken the annals of American history. It is not merely disappointment in being, after all, cheated out of the ruler of our choice. It is not merely the gloom which a great crime always throws upon a community. It is not merely a regret for the uncertainty which this event throws upon our future. There is in the heart of the people a profound grief arising from a sincere and very strong attachment to President Lincoln. And well he deserved our attachment. This is not the time to enter upon any extended or thorough examination of his life and character; but I cannot omit this opportunity to add my humble tribute to his worth to those of my countrymen.

President Lincoln assumed the reins of government when the whole country was in confusion, when whole States were in rebellion, when the hands of the government were paralyzed. He was bitterly hated and opposed by a great minority, even in the States by which he was elected. He was ridiculed and hooted, not only by the press of the enemy, but by that of all Europe. During his administration he has felt compelled to employ not a few measures which have created very great discussion and feeling. And yet, after four years of unprecedented difficulties and trials, he has come forth, I need not tell you with what triumphant successes for our country; — I need not tell you with what enthusiastic admiration of his countrymen, even of many who once opposed him; with what admiration and respect in foreign lands, and among the enemy. Such a record is one of which to be proud, and proves that he had greatness.

He was never a leader, he always *followed* public sentiment; but he followed it with the accuracy and fidelity of a stag-hound. Some of us would have preferred a bolder and fiercer leader; but, on looking back, we can see that such an one would either have ended our strife prematurely before its results were accomplished, or more probably would have divided us so that we never could have done anything. Some of us have disapproved of some of his measures, but the result has generally shown that he was more sagacious than we. He may sometimes have erred, in the opinions of some, from the strict line of prerogative, but his sterling principle and noble purposes kept such aberrations, if there were any, from doing harm. He was a man of the purest and highest motives, and the strongest principle. His chief aim was the welfare of his people, and with the heart of a true statesman he loved all, even his rebellious people. He was willing to sacrifice himself to any extent. He never used his office and power to enrich himself or his family. He did not allow himself to be governed by his party, or to become a tool in the hands of his political friends. He never espoused theories, but was governed by experience. He never took any notice of abuse,—never lost his self-control. He could not be brought to a hasty decision; could not be turned when once decided. He endured the mistakes and disobediences of his civil and military officers with a patience which was marvellous. The people had learned to have *confidence*, not only in his honesty of purpose, but in his strength and sagacity of mind. His personal character was without a stain. His manners were plain, but unaffected and hearty. His benevolence was unbounded. Many are the hospitals which he has visited, the soldiers whom he has grasped by the hand, the widows and mothers to whom he has sent a word or line of sympathy, the personal appeals from the humblest individuals which he has answered. Nothing is more remarkable than his kindness toward the colored race, and the earnest and determined purpose with which he set about their emancipation, and yet the subordination in which he kept this sovereign purpose to the work of extinguishing the rebellion.

His faults, for grave faults undoubtedly he had, were principally those of over-leniency and generosity, deliberation and patience,—faults which would have been excellences in less desperate times, and which even in these times have probably been our salvation. His virtues were such as would have adorned a king. There is another bond between President Lincoln and many of us, a bond which not even death can sever. He was, to all appearance, a *Christian* man, and in the sense in which *we* understand the term. If a conversation which has been reported really occurred, he professed to have consecrated himself amid the graves of Gettysburg to the Lord Jesus Christ, and to be endeavoring to live by the faith of Him who loved us and gave Himself for us. The public documents which have issued from his pen have certainly been remarkable, especially of late, for their religious tone. This trait in President Lincoln's character, so distinguishing him from all his predecessors, rendered him especially interesting to the Christian mind, and will irradiate his grave with a peculiar and glorious hope. We have, at length, a President who " sleeps in Jesus."

President Lincoln was remarkably a man of the people, and not merely in having traits which won popular confidence. He was *one* of the people. He rose from the humblest class; he had a popular way of talking and writing; he could get hold of the popular heart. It is doubtful whether any of our Presidents, even Washington himself, was so thoroughly in the sympathies and affections of the people as President Lincoln was. The people themselves did not know how much they loved him, till he was stricken down. There have been many bitter tears shed in every city and hamlet of the North, within the last few hours, over the tidings of his fall. Strong men have wept, and been convulsed with grief, as if they had lost a father or a brother. Oh, if votes could raise him from that bier to that chair of state, what a ballot would the North cast now! The *nation* mourns, with a sincere and sacred grief. No such sorrow has ever touched the national heart. These draperies, in which the land is dressed to-day, these solemn-tolling bells, which speak to one another from valley to valley, from hill-top to hill-top, give expression to no formal mourning; they tell of a real, profound, and mighty grief.

There is a consolation in the midst of this grief; in the return of a day suggestive to very many minds of a triumph over death. We do not follow our noble chief-magistrate to the grave with the feeling that this is the last. We are spared the sadness with which we are too often compelled to witness the end of earthly greatness. Gloom has no place around the grave of the Christian. How sublime and comforting those words which seem to float to-day over the whole land, echoing through its numberless cemeteries and battle-fields, and lingering to touch alike the bier of the Christian President and the sod that covers the Christian slave, " I am the resurrection and the life; he that believeth in me, though he were dead, yet shall he live"!

There is another feeling which naturally succeeds the emotions of horror and grief; it is *rage*. I would not say a word to inflame the passions and exasperation which are already filling the public mind. I would rather say that which may soothe excited feelings. It is a time for every man to lay upon himself a strong control. It is easy at such a time to be ungenerous and unjust. Let us discountenance all violence and passion, and seek the punishment of evil-doers only through the legally constituted channels. Let us not be violent even in our defence of the fallen. Let us remember that there is one thing more sacred than even friendship, and that is liberty. The contemptible creatures who profess to rejoice in the work of an assassin are not worth spending rage upon; there is nobler game afoot. Let us not waste too much passion upon the perpetrators of this dastardly crime;— not that they are not deserving of indignant condemnation, and condign punishment; they *must* receive it. But their importance is not commensurate with the mischief which they have done. To lavish indignation upon them is to misuse and waste it.

Let us not jump hastily to the conclusion that the perpetrators of this vile deed were in the employ or the counsels of the enemy. For one, I do not believe that the Southern leaders are too honorable to stoop to such a deed; I do not believe that they are too shrewd to see that it would injure rather than serve them. But let us not come to conclusions without proof. We can wait for the light of evidence.

But there is one direction in which the general indignation may be properly turned, — always in lawful ways and the appropriate channels, — and that is against the rebellion, and all who uphold it. The real spirit of secession, the kind of men who are most devoted to it, the conduct which it inspires, are made obvious in one more notable instance. If, in the providence of God, this last utmost stroke of malignity shall be the means of opening the eyes of this people to the real character and spirit of secession and secessionists, the calamity will not have been sent altogether in vain. It will begin to be found out at last, that the men who are rabid with secession, the leaders, or rather, the mis-leaders of the South, are not men to be paroled, and let off with political disabilities, and shaken by the hand, and feted: they are men to be hunted down like wild beasts, and sent to the prison and the gallows; that secession is not to be vanquished by leniency and kindness, but is to be stamped out with the iron heel. This is said, not in any spirit of vengeance and wrath, but from a solemn conviction that the true interests of the country, and true humanity and religion, require the prosecution of a vigorous policy of extermination and utter subjugation.

The spirit of secession has at last shown itself in every possible variety of form. It is the spirit of hate, the spirit of murder, the spirit of cowardly cruelty and treachery, the spirit of barbarism, the spirit of hell. If men will not renounce it now, and all connection with it, and all sympathy with it, let them be, by the proper authorities of course, cut down without mercy. Let our indignation take the form, not of frantic and revengeful passion, but a stern and united determination that this rebellion, with its leaders, and with all who persist in upholding it, shall be wiped out, so that no one will ever be able to find the stain where it was.

There is one other feeling which fills almost every mind, — it is anxiety.

President Lincoln's life was one on which much seemed to be depending. He had won the confidence of the people; he was meeting with triumphant success; his policy was somewhat apprehended; his plans seemed to be working well. But now a cloud is suddenly fallen upon the future. What kind of a man the new President will prove himself, — who will be his friends and advisers, — what policy he will pursue, and what the results will be, — how well he will succeed in uniting the people in himself, — and what is before us, are matters of blind conjecture. I might present to you some considerations of a subordinate character, calculated to afford hope and encouragement; I might point you to the cheering features in the past career of the new chief magistrate; I might remind you of the overwhelming successes already achieved, and how little in the way of conquest remains to be done; I might show you, that the union and strength of feeling which this very calamity has caused is auspicious: but of the worth of such considerations, you are better able to judge than I. I prefer only to remind you that we are under the rule of a wise and benignant God, who disposes and ordains all things for the best. What He does we do not always know now, but we shall know hereafter. The event which has crushed our hopes and spirits seems to be one of those mysterious and inscrutable permissions, with which He is wont to remind us, that His ways are not as our ways. To us it seems a terrible and irreparable calamity. I confess, that as I look at it from one side and another, I can hardly find a single bright spot to relieve its darkness. But let us have faith in God; I doubt not that He has some wise purpose to serve, some great end in view, though it is now hidden from us. I cannot fathom His motive in allowing this awful crime; perhaps this was needed to bring the people to some desired point; perhaps He had a work to be done fitter for some other hands than those which have done so much noble work, and are now forever still; perhaps He found that we were not humbled enough, and has more trouble in store for us; I will not pretend to explain the enigma, but I am very sure that there is wisdom and mercy in it all; and wisdom and mercy for *us*. I do not believe that God intends anything but that which in the end will be best for our beloved but unhappy country; the prayers and tears of our fathers will not permit Him to give us up to ruin. I do not believe that the safety and prosperity of this country are dependent upon the life of any one man, however great and good; much less can I believe that they are in the hands of an infuriated and probably drunken actor. God is able to raise up other instruments instead of those that he lays down. Moses may lie down to die, on the very borders of the promised land, but a Joshua shall be raised up to lead the people in to possess it. And it is remarkable how often it happens, in the providence of God, that the Moses dies. It is seldom granted to the same man to guide through the desert, and to enter into the land of promise.

For President Lincoln *himself*, perhaps there was no better time to pass away. He fell in the very height of glory. Just re-established in the Presidential chair by the overwhelming choice of his countrymen, risen into the profound respect of the civilized world, permitted to see his long watchings and toils crowned with success, to rejoice in stupendous military achievements, in the prospect of speedy peace, and in the assured approach of universal freedom, to fall honored by all men, wept by a nation, in the bosom of his family, with his cabinet around him, with a nation waiting in tears, in the hope of the gospel, was a death becoming a Christian patriot,—a glorious death to die. It may be that he could not, in a hundred years, have found a moment in which to fall so lamented, or leave behind him such a memory. Henceforth a humble tomb in the capital of Illinois will divide with Mount Vernon the homage and pilgrimages of our countrymen. Perhaps if these mighty dead, the leaders in the two wars for freedom, are permitted to revisit their resting-places, the murdered President will experience the greater joy, in finding not only his head-stone worn with the kisses of his own race, but the sods of his grave sprinkled with the tears of eyes that used to weep in the house of bondage.

God bless the memory of Abraham Lincoln!

God bless the President!

God in his mercy bless and save these United States of America!

REV. JAMES FREEMAN CLARKE.

8*

2 *TIM. 1* : 10.

WHO HATH ABOLISHED DEATH.

[Indiana-Place Chapel was decorated on Easter with appropriate and symbolic ornaments. The entire chancel was covered with a rich purple fabric looped to the wall at different points with wreaths of white flowers. Over the chancel, fixed to the wall, was a large cross surmounted by a crown, and at the side appeared the words "He is Risen," each worked in foliage and flowers. There were also numerous bouquets and single specimens of choice flowers and plants placed at different points in the chapel, which, with the national colors draped in mourning drooping from the gallery, heightened the general effect.]

When Jesus died, it seemed as if the last hope of the world had perished. It seemed as if God had left the earth alone, — it seemed as if there was no Providence left. It was the blackest hour in the history of the human race. The power of darkness was at its height. Satan had conquered God. One man had at last appeared capable of redeeming mankind; he had given himself to that work, — one man teaching and believing a religion spiritual, humane, free; above ceremony, above dogmas, above all fanaticism, enthusiasm, formality.

He was here; the one being who knew God wholly and human nature exactly; who could say, "I and my Father are one," "I and my brother are one." No sin terrified him, for he was able to cure the foulest diseases of the human heart and soul. From him flowed a *life*, a vital power, which strangely overcame diseases of the body and the soul. He was young: he had just begun his work. A world dying of weariness, an exhausted civilization, a worn-out faith, longed to be regenerated. The great auroral light of Greek intelligence had died away. The stern virtue of Rome had ended in effeminacy and slavery. The world, prematurely old, asked to be made young again; and here was the being who could do it. And then men took him and murdered him. They assassinated their best friend. BLACK TREASON, in the form of Judas; COWARDLY DESERTION, in his disciples; SHAMEFUL DENIAL and FALSEHOOD, in the person of Peter; TIME-SERVING SELFISHNESS, in Pilate; CRUEL POLICY, in the priests; BLIND RAGE, in the people; COLD-BLOODED BARBARISM, in the Roman soldiers, — all these united in one black, concentrated storm of evil, to destroy the being so true, so tender, so gentle, so brave, so firm, so generous, so loving. It was the blackest day in the history of man.

And yet we do not call it Black Friday or Bad Friday; we call it GOOD FRIDAY. We call it so, because the death of Christ has abolished death; because evil that day destroyed itself; sin, seeming to conquer, was conquered. And so we see, in the death and resurrection of Jesus, the great law revealed, that we pass through death to life, through sorrow to joy, through sin to holiness, through evil and pain to ultimate and perfect good.

We dress our church in flowers to-day in token of this triumph. Nature, every spring, renews her miracle of life coming out of death. The little, tender buds push out through the hard bark. The delicate stalks break their way up through the tough ground. The limbs of the trees, which yesterday clattered in the wind, mere skeletons, are now covered with a soft veil of foliage. Earth clothes itself with verdure, and these spring flowers come, the most tender of the year. They come, like spirits, out of their graves, to say that Nature is not dead but risen. Look at these flowers,—living preachers! "each cup a pulpit and each bell a book," and hear from every one of them the word of comfort: "Be not anxious, be not fearful, be not cast down; for if God so clothe us, and so brings our life out of decay, will He not care for you and yours evermore?"

On this day of the resurrection we commemorate the subjugation of the last enemy,—Death. "He has abolished death," says our text. Abolished it; or, as the same word is elsewhere translated, "made it void"; that is, emptied it of reality and substance; left it only a form; "*made it of no effect; destroyed it; brought it to nothing; caused it to vanish away.*" Death to the Christian ought not to be anything. If we are living in terror of death, if we are afraid to die, if we sorrow for our friends who die as those who have no hope, then we are not looking at it as Christians ought. We ought to be, and we can be, in that state of mind in which death is *nothing* to us.

For what makes death terrible? First, it is terrible because it ends this life, and all the enjoyment and interest of this life. We are made with a love of life, and God means we should love it.

We are made to be happy in the sight of nature; in this great panorama of sky and land, hill and plain, sea and shore, forest, mountain, rivers, clouds, day and night, moon and stars, work and play, study and recreation, labor and sleep. We are made to enjoy the society of friends, the love of the near and dear, the quiet of home, the march of events, the changes of the seasons, the vicissitudes of human and national life. Death seems to be the end of all this; and so we shrink from death. But that is because we do not see that all these things are the COMING OF GOD to us; that these are God's words and God's actions; that when surrounded by nature we are in the arms of God, and that all these things are from him, and through him, and to him. And as when we die we do not go away from God, so we shall not go away from all this beautiful variety and harmony, this majestic order and transcendent beauty of creation. We shall doubtless have more of it, know it better, enjoy it more entirely. And so, since Christ makes us realize the presence of God in nature, history, life, he abolishes thereby that death which seems to come to take us from them.

Another thing which makes death a terror is our own consciousness of sin. The sting of death is sin. But Christ removes this sense of sin, by bringing to us the pardon of sin. The conditions are simple and practicable: repentance and faith. If we turn from our sin and renounce it, and then trust in the pardoning grace of God, we are forgiven our sin. Then not only the mercy, but the truth and justice of God are pledged to forgive us. "If we confess our sin. God is faithful and just to forgive us our sin." No one need to remain with a sense of unforgiven sin in his heart. In his dying hour, as in his life, Jesus sought to lead mankind out of the feeling of sin into that of reconciliation. When he said to the sinful woman, "Go, and sin no more; neither do I condemn thee"; when he said of the other sinful woman, "Her sins, which are many, are forgiven; for she loved much"; when he told the story of the prodigal son, to show how God sees us when a great way off, and receives us back at once into the fulness of his love; when, at his death, he said, "This is my blood, which is shed for you, and for many, for the forgiveness of sin," he sent into the soul of men the conviction that they could be at one with God notwithstanding their evil.

And the resurrection of Christ has abolished death, because it shows us that death, instead of being a step down, is a step up. It shows us Christ passing on and up, through death, to a larger life. It shows that when he died he did not close his work for man, but began to do it more efficiently. The resurrection of Jesus was the resurrection of Christianity; the rising up of human faith and hope. Jesus rose into a higher life, and his disciples then rose into a higher faith. They became strong, brave, generous, true. Their weaknesses and follies fell away from them. Christianity broke the narrow bands of Jewish ceremony, and became the religion of humanity and of all time. The world seemed to have lost everything when Christ died; but it really gained everything. His followers, "risen with him," "sitting in heavenly places" with him, sought and found deeper, higher, larger views of Christianity. And so his word was fulfilled: "I, if I be raised up, shall draw all men unto me."

When the awful news came yesterday morning of the assassination of our President and of Mr. Seward, and the other murders which accompanied those acts, it seemed impossible to dress this church with flowers, impossible to keep Easter Sunday with joy to-day. As on Thursday we changed a Fast into a Thanksgiving, so it seemed to be necessary to-day to change this feast of joy into a day of fasting and sorrow. Yet, after all, the feelings and convictions appropriate to Easter are what we need to-day. When we say "Christ is arisen," we are lifted into that higher faith which is our only support and comfort in calamities like these.

Perhaps the crime committed last Friday night, in Washington, is the worst ever committed on any Good Friday since the crucifixion of Christ. It was not only assassination, — for despots and tyrants have been assassinated, — but it was parricide; for Abraham Lincoln was as a father to the whole nation. The nation felt orphaned yesterday morning, when the black tidings came; for during these four years we had come to depend on the cautious wisdom, the faithful conscience, the shrewdness, the firmness, the patriotism of our good President. We have all quarrelled with him at times; we wished he would go faster; we wished he had more imagination, more enthusiasm: but we forget all our complaints to-day, in the sense of a great and irreparable calamity. Had he been a tyrant and despot, there would have been the excuse for the act which we make for Brutus and Cassius; but the chief fault of Abraham Lincoln was that he was too forgiving to his enemies, too much disposed to yield to those from whom he differed, and to follow public opinion instead of controlling it. He could not bear to punish those who deserved it; and the man who will suffer the most from his death is his murderer, for had Lincoln lived, he would have forgiven him. Simple in his manners, unostentatious, and without pretence; saying his plain word in the most direct way, and then leaving off; he yet commanded respect by the omnipresence of an honest purpose, and the evident absence of all personal vanity and all private ends. Since Henry IV. fell by the dagger of Ravaillac, no such woe has been wrought on a nation by the hand of an assassin. Good Friday was well chosen as the day, — a day dedicated to the murder of benefactors and Saviours. We shall miss him often in the years to come, for when shall we find among politicians one so guileless; among strong men one with so little wilfulness; among wise men one with so much heart; among conservative men one so progressive; among reformers one so prudent? Hated by the South from that instinct which makes bad men hate the goodness which stands between them and their purpose, he never hated back; reviled by the most shameless abuse, he never reviled again. Constant amid defeat and disaster, he was without exultation in success. After the surrender of Lee, he caused to be written on the Capitol the words, " *Thanks be to God, who giveth us the victory.*"

And so we find him mourned equally by the conservative and the progressive wing of the loyal people, because he was in reality a thoroughly conservative and a thoroughly progressive man. Both could depend on him as truly their own leader. For his moderation was not the negative moderation of a compromise which balances between two extremes, but the positive moderation of the large sincerity which accepts the truth on both sides. The Conservatives knew that he was sincerely cautious, and were sure he would never act rashly. The Progressives knew that he was sincerely ready to reform evils; and though he might move slowly, certain to move forward.

Fortunate man! who thus exhausted the experience of life, beginning as a splitter of rails and ending in a chair higher than a monarch's throne; studying his grammar by the fire-light of a log-cabin when a boy; when a man, addressing the senate and people from the capitol of a great nation; tried by hardship, hardened by labor, toughened by poverty, developed by opportunity, trained by well-fulfilled duties, chosen by God to be the emancipator of a race, and the saviour of a nation's life; and then, having finished his work and seen the end near, crowned with the martyr's halo, to be made immortal through all history and all time as the chief actor in the greatest drama of modern days. Happy in life; happy also in the opportunity of death, for when could death come more welcome than on that day, when, having emancipated the slave, having conquered the rebellion, having walked into Richmond and written a letter at Mr. Jefferson Davis' desk, and having directed the flag to be restored on Fort Sumter, he commanded recruiting to cease throughout the land, and declared to Europe that the blockade was at an end, and the war over as far as foreign nations were concerned? Macaulay says of Hampden: "Others could conquer, he alone could reconcile. It was when, to the sullen tyranny of Laud and Charles had succeeded the fierce conflicts of sects and factions, ambitious of ascendency, and burning for revenge; it was when the vices and ignorance which the old tyranny had generated endangered the new freedom, that England missed that sobriety, that self-command, that perfect soundness of judgment, that perfect rectitude of intention, to which the history of revolutions furnishes no parallel, — or furnishes a parallel in Washington alone."

"The history of revolutions has furnished another parallel in Abraham Lincoln." So says a late London journal; for even London journals have learned to look through the rough shell to the rich kernel. Abraham Lincoln is essentially of the same type as Washington. Washington was born and bred a patrician, — the lord of slaves and of broad acres. Lincoln was born and bred a plebeian, — a man of the people. But subtract these surface-differences and they were radically the same; each built up of CONSCIENCE and of COMMON SENSE. Neither of them had imagination; but that was a blessing: it saved their lives. For if, in addition to the heavy weight of real responsibilities, there had been added the sleepless anxiety of a mind which constantly pictures to itself all possible contingencies, they would both have died, worn out by exhaustion. In the gallery of the world's great men our good Abraham Lincoln will stand hereafter by the great shape of Washington, having as great a work to do as he, and having done it as well.

But what shall *we* do without him? What shall become of us, in this doubtful Present around us, this dark Future approaching us? We thought our trials over; they seem about to begin anew. But we have learned in these years to see the hand of God in all things, and how He makes the wrath of the wicked to praise Him. Still let us believe that He knows what we need, and that this black event will also turn to good. Let the day on which he fell teach us a lesson — saddest day in the history of men. The death of Jesus, at the beginning of his work, seemed the direst calamity that could befall mankind. It was the loss of the one being whom the world could not afford to lose, — the one perfect soul the race had produced; cut off, with his word apparently half uttered, his work seemingly half done, his life half lived, leaving only a few half-taught disciples behind him.

But as out of that evil came so much good, so out of this God will educe the blessings and discipline we want. We thought our trials over; but perhaps we need more. The people of the North, always hopeful and good-natured, needed perhaps another example of the spirit of barbarism which has grown up in slavery, in order not to trust again with power any of this existing race of rebels. Always audacious, they were just about to come together to tell us how the Union was to be reconstructed. Having been beaten in the field, they were quietly stepping forward to claim the results of victory. But this murder has probably defeated their expectations. As Abraham Lincoln saved us, while living, from the open hostility and deadly blows of the slaveholders and secessionists, so, in dying, he may have saved us from their audacious craft, and their poisonous policy. We are reminded again what sort of people they are.

It is idle to say that it was the work only of one or two. When the whole South applauded Brooks in his attempt to assassinate Charles Sumner; when, during these four years, they have been constantly offering rewards for the heads of Lincoln and of Butler; and when no eminent Southern man has ever protested against these barbarisms, they made themselves accessories before the fact to this assassination. Throughout the South, to-day, there is, probably, very general exultation. FOOLS AND BLIND! Throughout the North, this murder will arouse a stern purpose, not of revenge, we trust, or only such a revenge as will consist with the memory of Lincoln. The revenge we shall take for the murder of Lincoln will be, to raise the loyal black population of the South not only to the position of freemen, but of voters; to shut out from power forever the leaders of the rebellion; to re-admit no Southern State into the Union until it has adopted a free-state constitution, and passed that anti-slavery amendment so dear to Abraham Lincoln's heart.* We might not have insisted on these

* See, at the end of this discourse, an extract from the sermon preached by the writer on Fast Day, the day before this assassination, in regard to these points.

conditions, — perhaps it was necessary for Lincoln to die, to bring the nation to the point of demanding them.

I suppose that since the beginning of the world, there never was an hour in which a whole nation experienced at the same moment such a pang as was felt from Maine to San Francisco yesterday morning. The telegraphic wires sent a thrill of horror into every city and every large town on the Atlantic and Pacific, on the Kennebec and the Missouri, at the same time. It was like the blow of a hammer descending on the heart of the nation. But such a hammer and fire welds together the soul of a people into a strong, righteous purpose. As the attempt of Guy Fawkes to destroy the British Parliament united all England for two centuries against the Papacy; as the attempt of Brooks to murder Sumner united the free States against slavery, so this crime will unite the whole North to make thorough work with the rebellion, and put it down where it can never stir itself again.

The word "assassin," it is said, was introduced into Europe by the crusaders, and took its name from that mountain chief whose followers devoted themselves to murder any of his foes. He was named Ha-shish-in: so named from hashish, the intoxicating herb, which they took to give themselves the energy of madness. Assassins are always madmen, — they destroy the cause they mean to help.

To-day, then, amid our grief and tears, let us not lose that trust in Providence which the past four years have been teaching to this nation, — and which every Good Friday and Easter Sunday, during eighteen centuries, have been teaching to mankind.

"Bear him, brothers, to his grave;
  Over one more true and brave
    Ne'er shall prairie grasses weep
  In the ages yet to come,
  When the millions in our room,
    What we sow in tears, shall reap.

"One more look of that dead face,
  Of his murder's ghastly trace!
    One more kiss, O widowed one!
  Lay your left hands on his brow,
  Lift your right hands up, and vow
    That *his* work shall yet be done.

"Patience, friends! The eye of God
  Every path by murder trod
    Watches, lidless, day and night;
  And the dead man in his shroud,
  And his children weeping loud,
    And our hearts, are in his sight.

"We, in suffering, — they, in crime,
  Wait the just award of time,
    Wait the vengeance that is due;
  Not in vain a heart shall break,
  Not a tear for Freedom's sake
    Fall unheeded: God is true.

"Lay the earth upon his breast,
  Lay our slain one down to rest,
    Lay him down in hope and faith.
  And above the broken sod,
  Once again to Freedom's God
    Pledge ourselves for life or death."

NOTE.

The following extract from a sermon preached by the writer, two days before, gives a further explanation of the points touched on our page :—

No doubt much remains to be done. The gravest questions rise before us. There loom up now the questions, " what shall be done with the rebels ? Shall the leaders of the rebellion be punished, and how ? What shall be done with the conquered States ? How shall they be governed ; by military or civil power ?

In answering these questions it is evident, that, first of all, we need guarantees that the substantial results of the war shall not be lost—that the cure of the South shall be radical—that there shall be no more treasons, no more rebellions. Any leniency that overlooks this necessity is not moderation, is not generosity —it is folly, cruelty, and crime. We may forgive ; but we have no right so to forgive as to leave the old conspirators with power to conspire again.

What guarantees, then, do we need? Plainly, the first is the utter abolition and destruction of slavery in the South. We must not have it in any form or shape. We must not allow it to remain as apprenticeship, or as serfdom, or as pupilage. But can this be done if we give back the power over the Southern States into the hands of the old disloyal leaders, now made ten times as bitter as before their defeat ? I see by the prints that distinguished citizens of Virginia are on their way to Washington to arrange terms for the reconstruction and re-admission of Virginia into the Union. What do we want of distinguished citizens of Virginia ? We want them all to keep out of the way. We are to deal now with the real people of the South, colored and white, not with the old slaveholding aristocracy. We do not want any Hon. Mr. Hunters or Breckinridges ; no Governor Wise, no Governor Foote, to arrange terms with.

It seems to me that the question of punishment may be entirely set aside. We do not wish to punish any one. " Vengeance is mine, I will repay, saith the Lord." They will be punished enough, no doubt of that. If defeat, disgrace, and utter ruin are punishments, if contempt at home and neglect abroad are punishments, if to have shown a want of statesmanship and ignorance of history, to have destroyed the peace and prosperity of these States is punishment, they have it. We have, no doubt, a right to punish them to any extent. The crimes of rebellion, treason, and waging civil war without a cause, are the blackest which can be committed by man. To lose life, property, and all, is not too severe a punishment. But what we wish is not to punish them, but to protect ourselves. And the most moderate punishment which is adequate is the best, because it is the most certain to be inflicted. And therefore I say, that, in my opinion, what we want is to keep all the old rebel leaders, and old slaveholding aristocracy out of the way, until the States of the South can be re-organized on the basis of freedom. We want to keep them from having anything to do with the government or control of the South until every Southern State is as loyal as Massachusetts. Now, every eminent Southern man is liable to be tried, convicted, and put to death for treason under the law of 1790. It is true that he can only be tried within the State where the act of treason was committed. But when Lee invaded Pennsylvania, he committed treason there, and so did the whole rebel government, for in treason all are principals — and the purpose of overthrowing the government of the United States by arms is a treasonable purpose — and every one who deliberately aids in any way that purpose, even by furnishing supplies, is held by the Courts to be a principal.

The punishment of death for treason is therefore hanging to-day over the head of every man concerned in the rebellion. They may be very grateful if allowed to escape by exile, confiscation, and disqualification. But looking, not at vengeance or punishment, but simply at self protection, it is my opinion that we might agree to waive the trial for treason, and substitute for it these penalties: 1st. In the case of Jefferson Davis, and his government, and all the chief conspirators, we might substitute for death, exile for a term of years, — say ten years. This would be so moderate a punishment that it would pretty certainly be carried out. 2d. Then for those who have left the service of the United States to fight against it, and for the civil officers of the rebel States let the punishment be disqualification for any office, and inability to vote during ten years. So fast do things move in this country, that in ten years, when the exiles return, they will find no opening left for them, all their influence gone, others in their places, the whole machinery of state re-organized, and they all sent into obscurity and oblivion. 3d. Let all those who have committed specific crimes, such as murdering citizens, starving to death our prisoners, and killing colored persons in cold blood, be tried and punished for those crimes under the laws. 4th. Let all the common people who have been forced and cheated into rebellion be pardoned on taking the oath of allegiance and keeping it. 5th. Let no rebel State be re-admitted into the Union till its Legislature has passed the Constitutional amendment abolishing slavery in the United States.

This is my plan for reconstruction. Let the military government of the U. S. be continued over the States, and let garrisons of colored troops be kept in all the large towns. Let no State be re-admitted till a convention of the people has met, revising its Constitution and abolishing slavery, and till its Legislature has passed the Constitutional amendment. Let the Federal Courts for the District of Pennsylvania find indictments for treason against every member of the rebel government, rebel Congress, and every head officer in the rebel army. Let the Federal Courts in Ohio, Maryland, and Missouri, do the same. Then let Congress be called together, and modify the law, substituting exile for a term of years, and disqualification for office, under certain conditions. So that by accepting and submitting to the lesser punishment, they may escape the greater.

REV. GEORGE H. HEPWORTH.

MATTHEW IX: 15.

"CAN THE CHILDREN OF THE BRIDE-CHAMBER MOURN AS LONG AS THE BRIDEGROOM IS WITH THEM? BUT THE DAYS WILL COME WHEN THE BRIDEGROOM SHALL BE TAKEN FROM THEM, AND THEN SHALL THEY FAST."

BRETHREN, last Thursday morning I read to you the first part of the verse which I have chosen for my text. It was a day appointed for fasting, humiliation, and prayer; but so signal had been the victories of the few preceding days, that this people, with one accord, united their voices in a great chorus of thanksgiving. Little dreamed we then, that so soon the latter clause of my text would call this mourning nation to the saddest duty of its life.

Who can measure the great grief of this people? The blow came so unexpectedly, that we hardly yet know how to express our feelings in fitting words. Each man weeps for a friend in the loss of this our Foremost American Citizen. When the dreadful tidings first flashed upon our hearts, it seemed too appalling to be credible. We struggled against it. The wires have played us false, we said, and we almost grew indignant with the tamed lightning which but a few hours before had thrown the whole North into such a bewilderment of joy as it told us the story of the fall of Richmond, and which now changed our joy into the very bewilderment of woe as it wrote upon the bulletin, " The President is dead ! " We did not know how much we loved that good man, nor how much confidence we had reposed in him, until the fearful certainty of our loss assured us. Was ever public officer so sincerely mourned before ? Every home of the North will drop its tear of genuine sorrow upon his grave, for mothers sent their boys to do the dreadful work of war all the more willingly because our commander-in-chief was so prudent, careful, and thoughtful; every hamlet will learn the lesson of the hour from its draped pulpit when the preacher shall tell how fell the unsullied patriot from the affections of the whole people into the bosom of immortal life; every city, from where the Atlantic wave moans its sorrow to the rising sun to where the Pacific sighs out its grief to the sinking orb, testifies its respect and love for the great man, by those emblems which sadly decorate every public building, if not every private residence, and which always tell us that the people's heart is heavy.

Brethren, it is not merely a brave warrior whom America mourns. No battle chieftain, however great his exploits in the field of danger and of conquest, could ever rouse such love as this we bear to Abraham Lincoln. It is not merely the clearness and sagacity of his mind that most we miss. No philosopher, however gifted, ever rested so securely in the affections of the whole community. No: these tears are shed for one, who, standing on an eminence so high that few would not be made dizzy by it, walked humbly, honestly, and faithfully, doing the greatest work of many a century, as a servant of the people and a servant of God. We felt that the Republic was safe while he stood at its head. In those seasons of intense public excitement when great and important questions were to be decided, — questions affecting our welfare in the distant future, and our relations to foreign powers, — he was the calmest man in the country; and many and many a time, when we have rebelled against his judgment, and given way to passionate criticism, we have learned to regret our own heat, and wonder at his serenity. Ah! where shall we not miss him? His influence was potent within the halls of Congress, shaping the legislation which is to affect the country when the glad morrow of peace comes; it was felt in all the ramifications of our foreign and domestic policy, tempering all decrees by a statesmanship not more remarkable for its sagacity than for its kind consideration of all parties; and it will be felt by every soldier in the field in whose heart the destinies of his native land and the name of Abraham Lincoln have been so intimately interwoven.

In 1809, in a little village in Kentucky, beneath the thatched roof of a poor man's cottage, was born a child, whose prospects for the future seemed very limited. He received from his parents nothing but poverty and a good name. His childhood was in no degree remarkable. There were no foreshadowings of the greatness to be achieved, and very few of those traditions of wonderful precocity, which, in some mysterious way, cluster about every eminent name. His library consisted of a well-thumbed Bible, and his fortune of an empty purse. He spent the first thirty years of his life upon that monotonous plane on which every poor farmer's boy lives. He spent his days in driving the team afield, in caring for the little flock as it wound slowly o'er the lea, and in the common drudgery which marks the lowly position he occupied.

When he was on the threshold of middle life, a resident of a village in Illinois, he was intrusted with some slight responsibility by his fellow-citizens. He was regarded with kindness because he had been something of a traveller, and an observer of men and things — having made a voyage down the lordly Mississippi — and because he had given his services to the Government in the Black Hawk war, and shown no lack of courage, but rather a quiet persistency and fearlessness which added to the lustre of the shoulder-straps which made him a captain. Having served his constituents faithfully in a minor position, he began that slow and toilsome journey of promotion, which is marked at every step by honesty of purpose; and which ended, when, obedient to the will of the North, he assumed the position of President of the United States.

Never have I been more proud of my country than when, gazing upon the lowly spot on which he was born, and the straitened circumstances of his youth, and then upward to the proud position he won for himself. I remembered that in America we have no royal circle from whose narrow limits the rulers of the kingdom are chosen, while the gaping multitude look on in open-mouthed wonder; but that every boy on the continent has royal blood in his veins, and, if he but will it, he shall rise, forgetful of his humble origin, — nay, nay, forgive me, *proud* of his humble origin, — to the most responsible positions in the land. Happy country, which sees the brilliant light of promise and of hope in the eye of every boy! Blessed institutions, which instead of veneering the top of society, sends the school-book and the prayer book to the lowliest, and electrifies the great body of the people with an honorable ambition!

If a stranger were to offer his criticism upon Mr. Lincoln, I think the first characteristic of which he would speak would be the extreme and charming Simplicity of the man. This is so marked a peculiarity, that no one can have failed to notice it. It is to be observed not only in his daily talk, and in his always courteous bearing, but also in his public speeches, and in those documents, some of which are to become a part of our national literature. He is the most truly Republican President we have ever had. Occupying a position as important and as influential as that of the Emperor of France, he carried to the White House the rigid simplicity of his Illinois home; and in his endeavor to do the work, — the arduous work of the hour, — he forgot to put on any of the trappings or pomp of royalty.

So noticeable was this peculiarity, that many of us regretted what we called a certain want of refinement. *We* would have had him keep in remembrance that he was President of the United States; but *he* could never ignore the fact, that he was simply Abraham Lincoln. To say what he meant, was his ambition; and to mean what he said, was a matter of honor. Perhaps he did not always indulge in court language; perhaps he was not as graceful as some lesser men have been; but he always acted the wise, prudent, and manly part. He claims our forbearance for telling an apt story; for wit and sarcasm, which sometimes seem out of place; but he has no need to seek our forgiveness for connivance against the honor of the Republic. Grace of bearing is a good thing; but unswerving integrity is sublime, even when it is awkward. For my own part, I am glad that we have at last had a President who scorned to use the privileges of his position for the study of the rules of politeness; and who, a yeoman, would not ape the courts of Europe, but set himself at work to do a real service for his country, at a time when she had been robbed by so-called gentlemen of the first families, and must be set right, if at all, by the great mass of the common people and their representative.

If you should look this broad continent over to find a man who came from the people, who knew their wants and their troubles by experience; who had been educated only in the schools of the people; who possessed their confidence; who was proud of his ability to do them good; who had been led neither by scholarship nor ambition to a forgetfulness of their exact condition: in other words, if you should search this nation through to find a man who should be a true type of the America of to-day, you could not discover one so fit for the purpose as Abraham Lincoln. In his earnestness and in his wit; in his persistency and in his good humor; in all the angles of mind, character, and life, he was the best man of this generation to show the strength and the peculiarities of the American.

He was pure-minded, seeking not for himself with unhallowed ambition of conquest, but rather for his country, with the holy ambition of the patriot. He was pure-hearted, governed in all his dealings by a pervading sense of moral responsibility. He was unsuspicious,— alas, alas, brethren, he was *too* unsuspicious! he believed too *much* in the honor of those around him, and for this reason he sleeps upon his bier, while a nation bends in tears because his slumber knows no waking.

Another marked characteristic of the man was his Religious Faith, his often avowed belief that this people are in the especial keeping of Providence, and that it was his duty as President to await the expressed will of God, and then to act. He was not of that company of heroes who win the sympathy of many by electing themselves men of destiny; but he firmly believed that this nation is a nation of destiny, and was modest enough, aye, humble enough to forget himself in his honest endeavor to obey the people's will. I delight to linger on this part of our great leader's character; for our public men have so often been mere politicians, winning their way to position by those various arts which are recognized as legitimate in the circles where they are used, but hardly looked upon with favor by an impartial religion, that it is exceedingly refreshing to know that in the time of our country's dire necessity the highest officer of the nation was the humblest of us all, and sought to know the will of God before he listened to the will of man. I verily believe that the religious view of the war, — and this seems to me to be the sublimest fact of the war, — which has pervaded every class in the community, and shown itself in the subdued manner in which, for the last two years, we have received the tidings of every great victory, is greatly due to the position assumed by Mr. Lincoln. How easily he could have stirred this people to acts of revenge, — acts which we might never cease to regret, — had he but issued a series of documents filled with revolutionary rhetoric. But instead of this, America has often been quieted in the hour of intensest excitement by the moral weight of our President's character and words.

I do not speak thus as one who blindly praises the dead. I have no desire to lift Mr. Lincoln into the upper region of a faultless manhood. I have no wish to forget the fact that he had faults, — ay, even grave faults, — in speaking of his virtues. At a more appropriate time, I may give you an estimate of his relation to, and influence upon, the age; but now our sorrow and our love are our only eloquence, and in reckoning the qualities which so endeared him to us, we will not forget that the tone of simple trust in God, which gave depth and beauty to nearly all his public documents, and which in private intercourse made so lasting an impression upon those who were privileged to take his hand, did much, very much, — even more than we knew at the time, to direct public opinion into those channels through which the popular feeling and excitement naturally flowed towards a religious view of our national affairs. And who can tell the benefit of such a tendency? Who knows how much of the moral strength of this people to-day comes from this fact?

Many a time have delegations from various organizations gone to this First Citizen of America, and said: "Mr. Lincoln, this people believe that you have been providentially placed in this position for the salvation of the nation. Every village church in the land lifts its fervent petition in your behalf, and every loyal man feels that he may trust you to vindicate and establish his dearest rights;" and the old man, instead of drawing himself up to his full height, and, in courtly fashion, receiving this language as homage done to himself, has bowed his head as in the presence of sublime duties, and consecrated the memory of the interview with tears. Brethren, these things are not often written in the biography of great men.

One other characteristic of which I must not fail to speak was his Firmness. Justice has never been done to Mr. Lincoln in this respect. He was not one of those boisterous men who herald the fact that they have strong wills, and who seem to act as though an unbending will was the chief element of heroism. He had his own way very quietly, yet he generally *had* his own way. He knew the value of advice when given by his peers, and was always courteous and deferential while it was being bestowed. But he held it in about the same estimation in which others of the world's best men have regarded it, — a something which it is very necessary to receive, but not always necessary to heed.

It is rather a peculiar fact in the history of his administration, that while so many have blamed him for lagging behind the people, nearly all have thrown the odium of such sloth upon him personally, as though it were the natural tendency of his character, and not the result of any outside influence. The future historian will give him credit for a degree of determination in the establishment and execution of his public policy which may surprise us all. He made but little noise, yet he is more responsible for the acts of his administration than any President we have had for many a year.

And now he is gone. Alas! a good man and a true man has been taken away. Steadily our love and respect for him has increased since 1860. He early won, and has steadfastly kept our confidence in the progress of this tremendous struggle; and now we may say, without fear of contradiction, that no man ever wielded such power, and made so few enemies. I repeat it, *no man ever wielded such power during four successive years of blood and sacrifice, of tears and death, and made so few enemies.*

> "He was a man, take him for all in all,
> We shall not look upon his like again."

And now he is gone: gone when we seemed to need him most, and when we loved him best: gone from a good life to a better; from the soldier's home on earth to the soldier's home in heaven; from his triumphs to his reward: gone to the blessed company of great men, who, in times past, have led the people on from sin to liberty, and laid down their own lives as a willing sacrifice on the altar of progress. To-day, while we mourn, he sits in the council-chamber where martyrs and heroes are convened; where are Washington, and Adams, and Hancock, and Warren; and he is their peer in the love he bore his country, and the love his countrymen bore to him.

O, exalted spirit! if you can spare a single moment to look from those heavenly realms which have so lately burst upon your enraptured vision upon our bereaved homes, you shall see how dear was the place you held in all our hearts. You have been the people's friend, and they put the evergreen of gratitude about your name. Calmly you have led us, wisely, tenderly, and yet firmly, through four times twelve months of woe. You have gone with us into the valley of defeat, where we have reckoned the fearful cost of life which was marking the uncertain progress of the war. You have been with us when the glad tidings of victory came, and we have always found you our friend, faithful and true; our leader, just and wise.

You need no monument to tell your worth. These tears are better than the marble shaft. These grateful hearts, which will tell the children who sleep in the cradle the wondrous story of the times through which we have lived, will not forget to say that all the nation trusted, and all the people loved you. You shall live in the new America that is to be, and your best monument shall be your Redeemed and Free Country. You were with us, with kindly word of counsel, when with one voice we cried, "Our country shall be one and indivisible," and when a million men, the flower of the generation, stood side by side to battle and to die for the

Union: you were with us when the voice of the people was heard all over the world, saying, "Never more shall there be slave upon this soil; hereafter all beneath the protecting folds of our flag shall be freemen;" and when in gratitude two hundred thousand dusky braves sprang to arms, and fought for the honor of the country that dared to proclaim that they were men: you were with us when the weak and worn enemy flew panic-stricken from their last defences; when the arch traitor fled the avenging hand of justice, and hid himself in the swamps of the South and the depths of his own crime; and when the commander-in-chief of organized rebellion gave up his blood-stained sword to the noble chieftain who was the representative of order, union, and liberty, — and now you have gone! Nay, nay, we will not believe it. You are still with us, and you will be with us unto the end.

Brethren, we still trust in God. The meaning of this event we cannot read. We are not robbed of our faith; and who shall dare deny, that *Lincoln dead may yet do more for America and Americans, than Lincoln living?*

In my mind's eye, I see a stout and well-built ship, lying a wreck upon hidden rocks. Bravely she has breasted the storms of a score of winters. She has battled with the tornadoes of Indian seas, bending her proud masts until the frenzied wave threw its furious spray upon the highest sail; she has confronted Atlantic tempests; and, when she came into port at last, was just enough defaced to prove the terrible character of the struggles from which she had come in triumph. She has brought her rich cargo of hope and faith, of good laws and liberty; and, but yesterday, her cargo safely landed upon the wharf, she slipped her moorings and playfully unbent her sails for an hour's enjoyment. But, alas! there were rocks, hidden rocks, in the way,— rocks not laid down upon any chart except the chart of Satan. She struck; and tears filled our eyes as we saw the noble vessel that had done her duty so well, lying there, the victim of a mischief that could not have been foreseen. So is it with our country to-day.

W. R. NICHOLSON.

AT ST. PAUL'S CHURCH.

The Rev. Dr. Nicholson spoke as follows: —

My Brethren, in the extraordinary circumstances in which we meet together this morning, I feel unwilling to begin our joyous Easter services without a brief word of introduction. I am sure you will pardon me for this one moment's digression from our usual course.

Easter is the synonyme of joy and triumph, and Easter-day has come. How sweetly its blessed light has dawned upon us this morning. And yet it has brought with it the saddest tidings, — yes, in an important sense, the saddest tidings, — which have ever concerned us since we were a people. To-day, our whole land is filled with sorrow and mourning; not only so, but with the keenest sense of national shame and mortification. It is a dreadful public calamity, — in every point of view a dreadful public calamity; and certainly it is God's call to us for a yet deeper self-humiliation. The instinct of my heart would be to observe this, the first Sunday after so grievous an affliction, with such outward expressions of sorrow in our public worship as might befit a worshipping congregation. Were it *another* Sunday, the irrepressible grief of our hearts would require us to do so. But it is Easter, — the Queen Festival amongst all the glories of Gospel Truth. Oh, we cannot shove aside the grandeurs, the heavenly grandeurs, of our Saviour's resurrection! It is the culmination of all saving truth; the only light for our darkness, the only joy for grief, the only solace in our deepest troubles. Were it the festival of an earthly joy, instinctively we should keep silence; but our Easter joys are the only medicine, as well for our national wounds, as for the individual heart.

If properly looked at, then; if these services are not construed as an æsthetic show, a mere parade; if we bear in mind that it is God's own truth which here concerns us; surely nothing could be more appropriate, even for so direful a calamity, than are these Easter services. Let our hearts be chastened; let us sink in self-humiliation deep and sincere; let us lift our eyes to Jesus in faith strong and simple, — then, all the more because of our present national grievance, oh, all the more, strike the very highest notes of Easter joy and triumph!

And may the benediction of our God descend and brood over us, in these our precious services!

REV. WILLIAM HAGUE.

2 SAMUEL III: 38.

And the King said unto his servants, Know ye not that there is a Prince, and a Great Man fallen this day in Israel?

We have come into our sanctuary to-day, with heavy hearts and weary step. We are "bowed down to the dust" beneath the weight of a calamity that has thrilled a nation with anguish too deep for tears.

We are all mourners at one funeral; not a funeral that leaves a vacant place in any one of our households, nor simply the funeral of a father, son, or brother, of a personal friend, champion, or protector; but of him who combined the interests and endearments of all these relations in one, and whose sudden loss a nation bewails as inexpressible and irreparable.

The hand of the assassin that smote down our President achieved its fiendish aim, and in that mortal stroke inflicted a pang that throbs in the hearts of more than twenty millions; and though these all beat in unison, yet as the Prophet Zachariah said of Judea in a time of trouble, "The land mourneth, every family apart."

Every one bemoans the affliction as a sorrow of his own.

There is sorrow in the crowded streets; sorrow in the marts of trade; sorrow in the council-rooms of States, in the school-rooms of children and youth, and at every hearthstone of the Commonwealth: but more than that, there is sorrow in every solitude, even in the closet of prayer, "the secret place" where emotion is quickened by no sympathy except sympathy with God, who knoweth the heart's bitterness better than it knows its own.

Never, we believe, since the death of Washington, did the countenance of every man, every woman, and every child, over the broad area of the republic, express a sentiment of grief so profound and keen as that which greets us now, whithersoever we may turn.

We have heard of monarchs honored as benefactors, of kings loved as fathers; but it is only in a free republic that you can ever see such signs of love and devotion as those which now glisten in the eyes, or quiver in the tones of stalwart men, of war-worn soldiers, of mirthful youth, of venerable matrons; or such as rise to heaven in the prayers of the vast masses who kneel at their domestic altars in the mansions of merchant-princes, in the tenant-houses of poor laborers who differ from each other as to color and complexion, in the rough cabins of backwoodsmen, and in the huts of emancipated slaves.

All these, spread abroad over the breadth of a continent, make it one expanded "house of mourning," where one bereaved family are prostrate in the expression of a common woe; unto all these voices the ear of God is open, and over all these He watches with sympathetic care, waiting to fulfil in the experiences of this afflicted, storm-tossed nation that benign promise which gleamed of old through the reft cloud of many a portentous night in the history of Israel, "Call upon me in the day of trouble; I will deliver thee, and thou shalt glorify me."

That word is as true to-day, and as apposite to our condition as if an angel were uttering it for the first time in the ears of the people, as a fresh message from the throne of the Eternal King. We are still in the keeping of our fathers' God, to whom, in the fiery trials of the revolutionary era, Washington was wont to pray in forest solitudes. As the ancient Psalmist said, we say, "He that keepeth us shall neither slumber nor sleep." The assassin's dagger cannot reach Him. And though the deadly stroke aimed at our chief ruler hath pierced the nation's heart, He liveth to parry the force of the blow, to heal the wound, to bring good out of evil, strength out of weakness, life from death, to make the wrath of man to praise Him, and its remainder to restrain.

All the events of our history, from the beginning even until now, tally with the hopes which these promises inspire. As a faithful woman in Israel said to her desponding husband when he trembled before the manifestation of the Divine Majesty, "If the Lord had been pleased to kill us, He would not have received such offerings at our hands, nor would He have showed us such things as these."

Think of it. Can we, as a people, in this hour of trial, recall to memory the last four years of devastating war, the superhuman malice of cunning foes acting in concert with the educated craft and wealth of the aristocratic powers of Europe, the era of successful treachery and intrigue, of victories over us on bloody battle-fields, the taunts of triumph like those of old Philistia's daughters in Gath and Askelon, rehearsed and wafted back from beyond the sea, and all the terrible scenes of national agony through which we have passed, along the verge of an unfathomable abyss, under the chosen leadership of Abraham Lincoln, without being assured to the utmost depth of our heart's capacity of grateful feeling, that God raised him up, "made him great," and then, at the set moment, GAVE him to us as an angel of deliverance, in order to work out for us that "great salvation" which has just now become the most amazing and hopeful spectacle of the nineteenth century in the sight of the whole civilized world?

No, never: these years are "years of his right hand," the remembrance of which has called forth over the rice-fields and cotton-fields of the emancipated South, and in the open streets and marts of Boston and New York alike, songs of praise that rolled in all the lyrical majesty of "Old Hundred," and sounded forth the joy of millions as in the deep thunder tones of ocean waves.

These grand anthems, God himself extemporized for us; He made the "logic of events" vocal with prophecies of our glorious future, as sure to us as any that ever came from Isaiah's lips, that were touched by fire from Heaven; and shall we now, in this hour of sudden gloom, be tempted to yield for a moment to doubt or fear or dark forebodings, like those who adore no God but chance or fate, or blind, inexorable law ? Oh, no! truth, love, faith, honor, gratitude forbid it.

I know how hard it is, at times, for the stricken heart, under the shock of terrible and scathing bereavement, to school itself (I will not say into submission, or resignation, for these are, comparatively, tame words) into joyous, hopeful, filial trust.

I know what extraordinary and mighty reasons there are to tempt us, in spite of all the signs of wise design and overruling Providence in the past, to treat this event as being too *ill-timed* to furnish occasion for the exercise of these Christian graces, or to be regarded as anything else than a bad chance-stroke, full of disastrous portent to the fortunes of our country.

I know how prone are the shocked sensibilities of some to arouse the fear of strange evils that throw their shadows before, (as a patriotic woman and mother expressed it yesterday,) of a Reign of Terror like that which racked revolutionary France in the days of Robespierre.

I know what a dreadful depression of spirit is likely to be produced by the contrast between the tone of the last public service in this sanctuary and the tone of the present; between the glowing scene of Thursday, when a Fast was turned into a Festival by that last triumph of our arms, which seemed like a new proclamation from the Supreme Governor of the world, and the more than funereal gloom that overcasts our lurid sky at this hour, and turns the greatest Festival of Christendom into a Fast, to the sickened heart of Christian patriotism. I know this, and I feel the oppressiveness of the murky air laden with rumors of coming trouble.

In view of all these things of sad significance I know how hard it is for some to interpret an event, that seems so mysteriously *ill-timed*, into harmony with a cheerful, hopeful view of those kind designs and wise forecastings of Divine Providence that insure our national welfare, and our progress in a bright national career of honor, glory, strength, freedom, and prosperity.

Nevertheless, I know at the same time what are the rocky grounds of our trust, and adopt the words of a French statesman, explanatory of his own conduct, amid the moral earthquake in his own country in 1848 : " I believe in God ! "

All these portents of evil are but as foil to the diamond.

I welcome the hope with which Moses inspired Israel when he said " God made him to suck honey out of the rock, and oil out of the flint."

I remember the machinations of assassins against the life of the President that were strangely baffled in those times when success would have been fatal, and turned the trembling scale of national destiny in favor of armed treason with a force that would have mocked resistance ; when an announcement like that which flashed over the wires yesterday would have been the signal for the rallying of treacherous cabals, not only in the capital, but throughout all the North, from the St. Lawrence to the Potomac, and from the Great Lakes to the Mississippi.

In those days of disaster, despondency, and weakness, the faith of the people in our President was our great bond of union, and the bulwark of our safety against the complicated plots of open and secret foes. But now he is gone; and who fears them now? Think of it: who fears them now, when the rebel power is crushed, its fortresses and cities and capital captured, its government dissolved, and its armies flying like chaff before the storm?

Surely, I know the answer that your hearts indite. What a difference between now and then! What a cheerful light gleams out from this comparison of the past and the present, spanning the dense cloud of our sorrow with the bow of promise, the sign of a covenant of hope, well ordered in all things and sure!

The death of those we love, honor, and trust, at the first sight, never seems *well-timed;* the parting pang is ever painful; —

> "The flesh will quiver where the pincers tear;
> The blood will follow where the knife is driven";

the tear will gush from the depths of nature where the cherished ties of life are broken: but there is a time of separation set, and that time is adjusted to a perfect harmony with those far-reaching purposes of our Heavenly Father, which, as Jesus teaches in the Sermon on the Mount, take within their scope the fall of a sparrow as well as the fall of an empire.

O, it is a consoling truth, "Our times are in his hand";

> "The voice that rolls the stars along
> Speaks all the promises."

And yet, in the sweep of a great calamity like this which we now bewail, where the immediate cause is not some mighty agency of nature, but a mere play of human passion, or a mere freak of some perverse human will, or some untoward thing which it was within a man's power to have avoided, the troubled mind will often stagger, through unbelief in providence, and lose sight altogether of a divine, overruling wisdom.

In the view of many, the rough edge of the evil would have been taken off, and the sense of fitness would have been less shocked, if the President had died by disease, or died in battle. In that case, the sorrowing heart more readily bows before the inevitable, more devoutly acknowledges the majesty of the Supreme Arbiter of destiny. But death by the hand of an assassin that might have been so easily arrested, or death following a certain step that might have been so easily omitted, seems like a malign agent jarring against the order of the universe, trampling God's law in perverse wantonness, provoking exasperation rather than submission.

But then it must be remembered that this is a mere seeming.

For God's comprehensive purposes are realized by the free actions of men, and devils too, as well as by the blind forces of material nature. The moral element of free will may have ample play, without being able to baffle the divine will any more than does the planet which is never allowed to fly one hair's breadth from its appointed track.

The grandest *programmes* of inspired prophecy have often been pivoted upon some trifling act of man which might have been easily avoided. The conquest of Old

Babylon, the oppressor of Israel, was predicted by Isaiah two centuries before the birth of the conqueror, whom God called by name, and said to Cyrus, "I have guided thee, though thou hast not known me." Not only was the event announced, but the funeral dirge of the empire was written by the Hebrew seer, and the night-scene of the overthrow described with as much of graphical minuteness as if the prophet had lived to muse amid the ruins of the imperial city. At the set time her fall shook the world; and yet one obscure man might have prevented it. A single hand of an humble official might have baffled the Persian and his army, if the guard at the brazen gate had attended to his duty, and moved the bolt to its place.

So, too, within the memory of living men, the grand crisis of European history turned upon the action of a single will, — and that, too, the will of a man whose name we should never have cared to mention but for that one inexplicable decision. When General Blucher, with his Prussians, appeared on the field of Waterloo, to join the Duke of Wellington, and turn the tide of battle, Napoleon was still confident of victory; because, as he said, "General Grouchy *must be* behind them." In vain did he reason out the case; in vain did he watch. "Why does not Grouchy come?" He *might* have come; he had gained the bridge at Wavre; the way was open to him; but he *did not* come. Instead of marching forward with his counterpoise to Blucher's force, he decided to wait for news from the field; and that decision, which even the sagacity of Napoleon could not anticipate as being within the bounds of probability, gave the day to England, and brought down the empire that had ruled the continent.

All this is after the manner of God in the evolutions of history; and therefore, let none of us, O friends, in our melancholy musing upon the loss which we mourn as the strangest catastrophe of our times, interpret the fatal effect of the assassin's stroke as a sign that the fortunes of our country are abandoned of Heaven, or regard the deadly play of perverse will and maddened passion, in the removal of the nation's ruler, as a sort of proof that it was, in the view of right reason, an *ill-timed* event, and that the overruling wisdom of God is no longer guiding our affairs to a happy and glorious consummation.

Rather, O friends, amid the sorrows of the hour, the stormy excitements of the public mind, and the extraordinary combination of events racking the land like the vibrations of an earthquake, let our weakness grasp the hand of Omnipotence, like the royal Psalmist of old, who, when his timid advisers said to him, "Flee like a bird to your mountain, for the wicked make ready their arrow upon the string, and righteousness amounts to nothing," answered them in those living words of religious trust, "The Lord's throne is in the heavens; his eyes try the children of men; he will rain upon the wicked, fire and brimstone, and a horrible tempest: this shall be the portion of their cup; the righteous Lord, loveth righteousness, and his countenance doth behold the upright."

It is to us a fact of great significance that this nation has a history, which the leading minds of the Old World, in courts, camps, and universities, are studying now as never before. Hitherto they have never believed that our republican government had enough of coherent strength to withstand the shocks of a great rebellion. Its strongest bonds have seemed to them but as flaxen cords, that "sunder at touch of fire." The poor emigrant, who has purchased a voyage across the Atlantic with the hard earnings of many years, and come to build up the fortunes of his family on these shores, could see where our great strength lay; but the princes, dukes, earls, the educated statesmen and diplomatists could not see it. Nevertheless, He who raised Abraham Lincoln from the farm and forest to the chair of state, and called him to exchange the woodman's axe for the sceptre of authority, has revealed to them, through him, new ideas of the nature of real power. They have seen his sterling character put into the crucible to be brought forth like gold from the refining flame, and they have learned, through him, as the ruler of free men and the representative of free labor, how great a work this nation has to do. The story of his life is the guarantee of our national immortality. And thus to-day, our fathers' God, who hath wrought out our national emancipation by this "chosen instrumentality," teaches them as well as us, that his resources are not stinted, that "his arm is not shortened that it cannot save"; and that, as the exiled prophet of Patmos said, He is "Alpha and Omega, the First and the Last"; the beginning is the surety of the end.

And let it be observed in this connection, that the event which engrosses the nation's thought at this hour will ever stand forth as a salient point of American history. Its full effect, no human being can foretell; but it will surely accelerate the progress of the republic upon its new career of a free, Christian civilization. More than ever the millions of our land, whether of Caucasian or African, of Teutonic or Celtic blood, are fused into one vital nationality. "The day of the Lord hasteth greatly," said the prophet Zephaniah to the people of his time. Even the workers of mischief help it forward, though not after the manner they intend. Since the death of Julius Cæsar in the Roman senate-house, no assassination of a public man has exerted an influence so profound and far-reaching. The murder of Cæsar was perpetrated in the name of freedom; but it established imperialism, and brought forth a race of emperors, most of whom were unsurpassed as monsters of wickedness; the assassination of our President has been accomplished in the interest of the slave-power; but will it subserve, think you, the behest of that base, barbarous despotism? No. Although the joy of victory may have disposed the hearts of many to favor the invitation extended to some of the rebel champions to take their places in the halls of legislation as the architects of reconstruction, the loyal masses of the people will be more wary now, and will not rest until the last fibre in the heart of the slave-power shall have been crushed, and its last "vital spark" of infernal flame extinguished.

True, indeed, our enemies still exult, — Gath and Askelon are yet merry; they rejoice in their secret cabals, in their haunts of violence, in their guerilla dens, in their resorts of revelry and song. They say Abraham Lincoln is dead, "Aha, so would we have it." But we believe in the resurrection, — yea, more; we believe that Abraham Lincoln " still lives," that he is " marching on," and time will soon teach them " What this rising from the dead doth mean." Time shall soon furnish a fresh commentary, a new unfolding of the far-reaching sense of that saying which Jesus uttered on the first day of the first " passion-week," in the year 33 : " Verily, I say unto you, except a corn of wheat fall into the ground and die, it abideth alone ; but if it die, it bringeth forth much fruit." The world will see this truth realized in our history. " By wicked hands " the President " hath been slain ; " but the harvest of moral fruitage from his death will be the garnered legacy of the nation through the ages to come. The dark Saturday of the Passion-week of 1865 will be the harbinger of a brighter day, " whose sun shall no more go down."

As we trace the hand of God in history, it is a source of comfort and strength to call to mind the proofs evolved by the last five years, that God raised up Abraham Lincoln, and " made his name great" for us ; that the singular combination and balance of forces that distinguished his character was a special gift to this nation for its " time of need ;" and the cheering truth that gleams forth from this retrospect, inspiring fresh hope touching the veiled future is, that there was the same divine wisdom in the *withdrawal of the gift* that there was in its bestowal.

Over the lifeless form of our murdered leader, therefore, let it be ours to worship and adore, in the spirit of the afflicted patriarch, " the greatest of all the men of the East"; who, as he sat in sorrow amid the ravages of his fields, the desolations of his home and the corpses of his children, exclaimed in those memorable words, more than ever weighty with an emphasis of meaning for us to-day, "the Lord GAVE, and the Lord hath taken away, blessed be the name of the Lord."

Shall we, as a favored people, acknowledge the greatness of the gift, the munificence of the giver, and then fail to see and acknowledge the wisdom that hath determined the time of its continuance? Thanks be to God, that the President lived to see the rebel power broken by the surrender of its general-in-chief, and to walk the streets of its capitol. Thanks be to God, that he lived to see the close of the day that witnessed the restoration of our insulted flag over the ruins of Fort Sumter by the same hand that had unfurled it there, amid many prayers, in an hour of peril, and then had withdrawn it without dishonor! Thanks be to God, that the last announcement of the President to the nation that he loved more than life was, that he was drafting a proclamation of national thanksgiving, calling upon all to unite in anthems of praise unto Him who hath given us the victory. That call a grateful people will answer in due time; and in the anthems of that festival he will join in concert with the heavenly choirs that hailed the advent of our Messiah over the plains of Bethlehem, when they sang: "Glory to God in the highest, peace on earth, and GOOD WILL TOWARD MEN!"

REV. E. B. WEBB.

ISAIAH XXI: 11, 12.

He calleth to me out of Seir, Watchman, what of the Night? Watchman, what of the Night?

The Watchman said, The Morning cometh, and also the Night.

These words seem to me strikingly appropriate to our present circumstances. Last Sabbath morning it was my privilege to place before your minds some reasons for thankfulness, — thankfulness to God. Then the streets were decked with symbols of joy; gladness in welcome accents broke from every lip. Men's countenances were bright, as if reflecting the coming of the morning. We clasped each other's hands with a jubilant pulse, and every eye answered back hope, inspiration, to the eye that looked into it.

But how changed is all in a moment! Yesterday morning flags were set at half-mast. Even Sumter's flag is but half raised. As the day advanced, emblems of mourning drooped from the highest windows to the sidewalk. *The President is assassinated!* Men hold their breath, and turn pale at the appalling words. Citizens meet, and shake hands, and part in silence. Words express nothing when uttered. All attempt to express the nation's grief is utterly commonplace and insignificant. An eclipse seems to have come upon the brilliancy of the flag, — a smile seems irrelevant and sacrilegious. Even the fresh, green grass, just coming forth to meet the return of spring and the singing of birds, seems to wear the shadows of twilight at noonday. The sun is less bright than before, and the very atmosphere seems to hold in it for the tearful eye a strange ethereal element of gloom. Surely "*the night cometh.*" And as we gather here this morning, after an absence of only two days, how appalling, in this cheerful home of our religious affections, are these wide-hung emblems of grief and anguish! It is manly to weep to-day. The coming of the morning, and also the night, are strangely mingled.

Had death overtaken any one of our brilliant military leaders in the field, we should have said it was a thing to be expected. Had any sudden reverse in the fortunes of war visited one of our armies, it would have been a terrible grief, but still a kind of calamity to which we have become accustomed. Had the President fallen by a chance shot in Richmond, or by the hand of some lurking assassin, as he passed the fortifications through which our hearts did not consent to his going, we should but have realized some of our transient forebodings. But after his safe return, and the triumph of our arms, which he took so much pleasure in telegraphing to the people, we had almost dismissed from our minds any fears for the safety of his life. And hence the telegram announcing the death of the President at such a time, in such a way, falls upon us like a crash of thunder from an unclouded sky.

Wearied with the duties of his high position, and the persistent annoyance of petty office-seekers, and unwilling to disappoint the people even in their unreasonable expectations, he sought an hour's recreation in the theatre. And what a horrible tragedy! The actor, having thoroughly prepared his part, and being often defeated in one way and another from the fiendish acting of it, finds his opportunity at last. With the stealthy step of a base, brutal coward, with a damning lie on his tongue, and the heart of a demon in his breast, he approaches the generous, unsuspecting man in the rear of his seat, and, aiming the fatal weapon with practised hand at the back of his head, puts the ball directly through his brain, and then makes his escape through the screens and drapery and doors with which his calling had made him acquainted. There are no last words for wife or children, — no word for the people's heart to which he always spoke, — no parting counsel for a bereaved and almost bewildered nation. The hand that signed the *emancipation proclamation* hangs helpless in death: the mind which had borne so evenly the tremendous strain of four unparalleled years is hurled from its throne: the great, good, magnanimous heart is stilled: those generous lips which have spoken *mercy* so often, and would perhaps, like the martyred Stephen's, have said in their last articulate speech, "Lord, lay not this sin to their charge," are sealed forever. The nation has lost a father; the human race a sincere, devoted, and able leader!

I have had no time to analyze the character, or choose out words to express our sense of the worth of the late Abraham Lincoln. But I may employ, with your approbation I am sure, the words used by Daniel Webster concerning Zachary Taylor: "He has left on the minds of the country a strong impression; first, of his absolute honesty and integrity of character; next, of his sound, practical good sense; and, lastly, of the mildness, kindness, and friendliness of his temper towards all his countrymen."

Yes, "towards all his countrymen." He was, on the very day of his untimely death, exerting all the kindness of his unselfish nature, and prepared, it is believed, to peril all his great popularity in inaugurating a policy *most lenient, most forgiving* towards those who had forfeited everything except the right to be hung. They have put aside their friend. They have murdered the new-born mercy which waited to bless them. No man could if he would, and no man was disposed to do so much for them as Abraham Lincoln.

And how the loyal people confided in him; how implicitly the common people trusted him! The world has scarcely seen the like. He came to the chair of the chief magistrate from the rough experience of frontier life. He owed his election, and the favor with which he was received, to the belief in the minds of the people, that he was an honest man.

And did he disappoint that confidence? Did he show himself unworthy? Did he ever incur the suspicion of dishonesty, or corruption? Or did he ever swerve from what he conceived to be the path of duty to win popular applause? Never. On the other hand, so impartial was he in selecting men from all parties to fill the high offices of government, so artless was he in all that he did, so transparent were his deeds, and his motives, that by a popular vote scarcely paralleled, the people called him a second time to guide the nation for another four years. He knew nothing of tricks, or double dealing, or party shifts, or crooked policies. He was a sincere, impartial, straightforward, honest man. And the people saw it and felt it, and were glad of an opportunity to honor him with an overwhelming repetition of their well placed confidence. What a noble example is he to all young men looking to office, or popular regard. With no military reputation, with no brilliant oratory, with no winning grace of manners, he was the foremost man for the highest office in the gift of a great, free, and intelligent people, once and again because he was a man of absolute honesty and integrity of character.

And besides these unselfish, impartial, upright elements of character, there was a masterful common-sense, a genial mother-wit, and a practical statesmanship, which showed themselves in some of the most compact specimens of argument, happy avoidances of difficulty, and a thorough apprehension of popular instincts and judgments.

He was unpolished in style, but he was profound in thought. He was pithy in his sentences, but original and patient in investigation: rough on the exterior but a jewel within, —

"Rich in saving common-sense."

How much we owe to his unambitious example; how much to his far-reaching discernment; how much to his good-natured hearing of all sides; how much to his steady calm judgment which held the scales, in the fury and gusts of the storm, as equally poised as if in the atmosphere of peace and calm; how much to his great forbearance under stinging reproach; how much to his knowledge of, and unwavering confidence in the people and the people's cause, God knows, but we know not as yet. May the day never come when by bitter contrast we shall learn how wise and safe was the confidence which we reposed in him.

This nation mourns to-day as it never mourned before. The statesmen of the land had learned to trust him in the greatest exigencies; the impatient were restrained by his moderation; the immovable and morose were moved and almost brought into time by his steady, sympathetic step forward; the one-eyed were made ashamed of their ignorance by an hour in his society; the revengeful learned magnanimity from his deeds. The soldiers loved him, and the soldier's mother loved him, and confided in him. The negroes loved him; oh how they will mourn for him! Moses was not allowed to lead the children of Israel into the land of peace and plenty, neither was he allowed himself to enter it, but only to survey its broad prospect from Pisgah's top. And so *their* deliverer and *ours* is only permitted to come to the border, and in these last few days catch pleasing glimpses of the glorious, opening future. And, as when Moses died, his eye not dim and his natural force not abated, there was mourning throughout all the camp till the plain of Moab resounded with the cry of sires and sons, mothers and maidens, so now there will be mourning in the camp, and mourning on the prairies, and far away over the mountains; but nowhere keener anguish and disappointment than among the sable hosts whom his noble heart and hand has freed. All men unconsciously speak of him as our beloved President. And the hand of the assassin has embalmed him with all his virtues and greatness, and made him sacred and sublime in our fond, loving hearts, and in the heart of the world forever.

Were I to select some one thing by which to characterize Abraham Lincoln, I should name his profound apprehension and appreciation of the popular instinct; that instinct which is true to the right as the needle to the pole, in all storms, and on every sea. He believed in God; he believed God was to be recognized in this war. He believed that the *set* of the loyal masses, — the deep, silent current, which bears on events is in the line of God's advance. And, thus believing, he governed himself by his apprehension of the people, and of God as manifest in their silent set or drift. As the philosopher learns the plans of God from an unprejudiced study of nature, so he learned the purposes of God from the instincts of the people. As the naturalist discovers from the structure of the animal what its mode of life and habits must be, so he saw from the essential peculiarities of our government whither our future must tend. He did not mean to be ahead of the popular feeling, for then there would be a re-action against his policy. He did not mean to be much behind it, for then some other agent might be sought through which to give it expression. And so regarding the voice of the loyal people in this great crisis of the republic as the voice of God, he kept his ear open and his eye attent, and marshalled his policy not quite abreast of the divinely led masses. He sought not to control an age thus moved and inspired, but to be controlled by it.

Herein was his wisdom; herein his greatness; herein his power. This was the secret of his success, the source of that light which, in all coming time, shall gild with unfading splendor the name of Abraham Lincoln.

As the Netherlands mourned for William, Prince of Orange, as France mourned for Henry IV., "we have lost our father,— we have lost our father!" so America mourns to-day.

> "Such was he, his work is done;
> But while the races of mankind endure,
> Let his great example stand
> Colossal, seen of every land,
> And keep the soldier firm, the statesman pure;
> Till in all lands and thro' all human story,
> The path of duty be the way to glory.
> But speak no more of his renown,
> Lay your earthly fancies down;
> And in the vast cathedral leave him,
> God accept him, Christ receive him."

1. And now, my friends, what are the lessons of this great calamity? *First of all, submission.* God reigns; we are absolutely dependent and sinful. The Emperor Mauritius seeing all his children slain before his face at

the command of the bloody tyrant, and usurper, Phocas, himself expecting the next stroke, exclaimed aloud, in the words of David: " Righteous art thou, O Lord, and upright are thy judgments." This event takes us by surprise, but the origin, maturity, and perpetration of this awful crime was all under the sleepless eye of God. For reasons which we cannot fathom now, nor find, He has permitted it. Perhaps when this day, *the 14th of April,* forever marked in our calendar; marked by the humbling of the flag at Sumter; marked by the exaltation of the flag four years after, — perhaps, when the 14th of April comes round four years hence, we shall know more of God's designs in permitting this foul murder of our beloved President. There is ONE whom the hand of violence cannot reach; and He has not led us thus far to desert and destroy us now. Meanwhile, as becomes us, let us bow our heads in meek submission to the divine will. Surely his footsteps are in the great deep; his designs are hidden from us in the dark: but let us trust him; let us cleave unto him. Submitting penitently to the rod of affliction, let us put our hand in his, and say, Father lead, Father spare and bless.

2. A second lesson is this : *Execute justice in the land.* What is the foundation of our confidence in God? Is it not that he will do right? Is it not what David says, over and over again, in all his trials, — *justice* and *judgment* are the habitation of his throne? And just these — *justice* and *judgment* — are the foundation of every throne, and of every government. I spoke on Thursday, as far as it was appropriate to my theme, of the tremendous mistake and folly and sin, for the

people of a great nation to think that they can neglect or violate the laws of God with impunity. Just here has been our danger. There has been a miserable, morbid, bastard philanthropy, which, if it did not make the murderer's couch a bed of flowers, and set his table with butter and honey, made him an object of sympathy, and, after a while, of executive clemency. We are weak in our sense of justice. Why, how long is it since a man was pursued in the streets of Washington, and, though begging for his life, shot to mutilation? He was guilty of a foul crime? Yes. But did that give the injured man a right to murder him? Are there no courts, no ministers of justice in the land? But the murderer was acquitted, with applause in the court-room. Only this very spring, a young woman shot one of the clerks dead in the hall of the Treasury-building. To be sure, she said that he had broken his vow to marry her. And when I was in Washington, a few weeks since, it was confidently expected that she too would be acquitted. And here in Massachusetts, not to speak of other States now, where the punishment of murder is death, the guilty wretch, who could brood over his infernal plan for weeks, and finally, after several attempts on the same day, execute it upon an innocent, unsuspecting young man, and all for the sake of a few hundreds, or, at the most, thousands of dollars, is allowed to live, and become an object of sympathy. To shield his forfeited life imperils that of every young man who stands behind a counter in Massachusetts. Living, he is an encouragement to all persons like-minded to do likewise. Yea, saith the Governor, ye shall not surely die.

And so in regard to the leaders of this infernal rebellion; the feeling was gaining ground here to let them off really without penalty. They are our brethren, it is said. Then they have added *fratricide* to the enormity of their other crimes, and are unspeakably the more guilty.

The punishment which a nation inflicts on crime is the nation's estimate of the evil and guilt of that crime. Let these men go, and we have said practically that treason is merely a difference of political opinion.

I do not criticise the parole which was granted, though, for the life of me, I cannot see one shadow of reason for expecting it will be kept by men who have broken their most solemn and deliberate oath to the same government. It was not kept by the rebels who took it at Vicksburg. Nor will I criticise, for I cannot understand, the policy which allows General Lee to commend his captured army for " devotion to country," and " duty faithfully performed." But I considered the manner in which the parole was indorsed and interpreted as practically insuring a pardon; and to pardon them is a violation of my instincts, as it is of the laws of the land, and of the laws of God. I believe in the exercise of magnanimity; but mercy to those leaders is eternal cruelty to this nation; is an unmitigated, unmeasured curse to unborn generations! It is a wrong against which every fallen soldier in his grave, from Pennsylvania to Texas, utters an indignant and unsilenced rebuke. Because of this mawkish leniency, four years ago, treason stalked in the streets, and boasted defiance in the halls of the Capitol; secession organized unmolested, and captured our neglected forts and starving garrisons. Because of a drivelling, morbid, perverted sense of justice, the enemy of the government has been permitted to go at large, under the shadow of the Capitol, all through this war. God only knows how much we have suffered for the lack of justice. And now to restore these leaders seems like moral insanity. Better than this, give us back the stern, inflexible indignation of the old Puritan, and the *lex talionis* of the Hebrew Lawgiver. Our consciences are debauched, our instincts confounded, our laws set aside, by this indorsement of a blind, passionate philanthropy.

Theodore Parker has a passage in his work on religion, in which he gathers into heaven the debauchee, the swarthy Indian, the imbruted Calmuck, and the grim-faced savage, with his hands still red and reeking with the blood of his slaughtered human victims. And the idea, to me, of placing the leaders of this diabolical rebellion in a position where they might come again red-handed into the councils of the nation, is equally revolting and sacrilegious. It makes me shudder. And yet I think there was an *indecent* leniency beginning to manifest itself towards them, which would have allowed to these men, by and by, votes and honors and lionizing. The soldiers did not relish this prospect. They are not to be deceived by the misapplication of the term magnanimity to an act that turns loose into the bosom of society the men who systematically murdered our prisoners by starvation, and again and again shot prisoners of war after they had surrendered,

— shot gallant officers, even in these last battles, after being told that they were mortally wounded, and strung up Union men in North Carolina because they had enlisted in the federal army.

And now *we* see and feel just as the soldiers do. The spirit that shot down our men on the way to the capital, the spirit that shot Ellsworth at Alexandria, the spirit that organized treachery, treason, and rebellion, the spirit that armed those leaders to strike at the life of the government, is the same hell-born spirit that dastardly takes the life of our beloved President, — is the same atrocious spirit that seeks the bed-chamber of a sick and helpless man, and cuts his throat, and strikes the murderous dirk at the heart of every attendant. We see its malignant, fiendish nature now!

And what shall be done with these secessionists, if we succeed in arresting them before they get out of the country, with the blood of the President, and of the Minister of State on their hands? Pity them as insane? parole them as prisoners of war? Doubtless, like the St. Albans raiders, they have their commission from Richmond! Does this make your blood boil? is this too shocking to suppose? Well: shall we hang them, — hang the less guilty, and let the more guilty go free? hang the miserable, worthless hirelings, and let the principals and chiefs live? To do that is to arm men, and goad them to take vengeance into their own hands. The instinctive justice of the human conscience must be satisfied by the action of government, or it will have private revenge. There is a consciousness of right in the masses, that will not be tampered with, in such a time as this. Not the branches of this accursed tree, but the trunk and the roots must be *exterminated* from the land. Hear me, patriots, sires of murdered sons, weeping wives and orphans, — I say *exterminated!* "Ye shall take no satisfaction for the life of a murderer, and ye shall take no satisfaction for the life of him that is fled, that he come again to dwell in the land; for blood it defileth the land, and the land cannot be cleansed but by the blood of him that shed it." And when David died, he charged Solomon to fulfil this divine command in regard to Joab and Shimei, who had been too strong for him during his life.

3. One thing more: *Let us face the future, and all the solemn responsibilities of these uncertain hours with courage.* We have God on the throne that no violence can reach, — the God who has always been with us. "Why art thou cast down, O my soul? and why art thou disquieted in me? Hope thou in God, for I shall yet praise him who is the health of my countenance and my God."

And then, such is the happy structure of our government that no assassination can arrest its wheels. A terrible calamity has overtaken us, but it will only the more exhibit the inherent vitality of our institutions, and the greater strength of the people.

Andrew Johnson, who now becomes the chief magistrate, by the mysterious providence of God, is unquestionably an able man. He has been much in public life, and never failed — except in his speech on inauguration day — to meet the exigencies of his position. Besides, he has had a schooling in Tennessee which may have prepared him to lead at this very time. When I was in Washington, four years ago, I heard much in his praise. He told the secessionists, who were just then leaving their seats in the Senate to inaugurate the rebellion, — told them to their faces, for substance, — " were I President of the United States, I would arrest you as traitors, and try you as traitors, and convict you as traitors, and hang you as traitors." And judging from the speech which he made at Washington after the news of the fall of Richmond, he has not changed his mind.

We want no revenge : we will wait the forms and processes of law. We want justice tempered with mercy. We want the leaders punished, but the masses pardoned. Let us confide in him as our President. And do you make crime odious; disfranchise every man who has held office in the rebel government, and every commissioned officer in the rebel army; make the halter certain to the intelligent and influential, who are guilty of perjury and treason, and so make yourself a terror to him that doeth evil, and a praise to him that doeth good, — and we will stand by you, Andrew Johnson.

Another ground of courage is, that the nation is a unit against rebellion to-day as it never was before. It is too much to hope, I suppose, that any traitor will have his eyes opened to see the true character of the awful work in which he has been engaged, though it seems as if such an atrocious butchery were enough to make him see it; but of this be sure, that all loyal men are united now; and woe be to the secessionist who does not instantly sue for mercy, or fly the country. I have seen them launch a great ship. The ways are laid, solid and secure. And then the workmen split away, one after another, the blocks from underneath the keel. Gradually the huge structure settles upon the slippery ways, and glides majestically into her future element. The two ways under our ship of state are *justice* and *mercy*. In the providence of God, block after block has been knocked away; prop after prop removed, till now, just ready to glide into the new future, she is settling all her weight upon her ways, — ways made slippery by the blood of the murdered chief magistrate, and minister: *woe, woe, woe* to him who puts himself in the line of her course. Infinitely better for him, had he been strangled at the birth.

Be sure, this people will mourn from sea to sea: but be sure, also, that any provocation will bring out the indignant, instant, sympathetic cry from every lip, "Die, traitors, assassins, all; live, the republic, liberty, and law."

The God of infinite justice and mercy be our helper. Amen.

NOTE. — Preached Sunday morning, April 16, after the news of the assassination of President Lincoln.

REV. R. H. NEALE.

MATTHEW, IX: 15.

AND JESUS SAID UNTO THEM, CAN THE CHILDREN OF THE BRIDE-CHAMBER MOURN AS LONG AS THE BRIDEGROOM IS WITH THEM? BUT THE DAYS WILL COME WHEN THE BRIDEGROOM SHALL BE TAKEN FROM THEM, AND THEN SHALL THEY FAST.

I QUOTED the first part of this text last Thursday, as a reason for turning the annual fast into a day of thanksgiving. They were used by the Saviour to show that it was not required of his disciples to mourn on joyous occasions, and we were then full of gladness. Sad looks would have been sheer hypocrisy. So universal was the feeling of gratitude for the recent victories of our armies, that it would have been inconsistent and unnatural on that day to have put on sackcloth and sat in ashes. It seemed more befitting to improve the day, as I believe it generally was improved, in songs of praise, and by the voice of melody. How little did any imagine that the occasion for sorrow, for appropriate fasting and universal weeping, was so near at hand!

So great was my joy on Thursday, that, as I then said, I did not feel in a sermon-like mood of mind, though religious considerations were never nearer, more vivid and sublime, than then. They appeared, however, not in a mere clerical form, but as they presented themselves to the whole community, and I wanted to throw off professional restraint and speak out freely, as a citizen and a man; and so I went on, speaking from the heart, and you obviously responding with equal fulness of soul, of the great things the Lord had done for us; we were grateful and glad, and sang praises to the God of our fathers, who had defeated the enemy and broken the spear asunder.' But how soon has our joy been changed to sorrow! I feel that there is a leaden weight upon every heart. How can I preach to-day? It would seem more natural to do as did our citizens yesterday, when news of the dreadful tragedy first came. They took one another by the hand, pressed it in silence, and " wept the grief they could not speak." Oh, it is hard to think, and must I utter the unwelcome thought, that the President, the good President, is dead! that Abraham Lincoln, *our* Abraham Lincoln, whose name is fraught with so many endearing associations, is gone! He has been with us during all this war; the thought of him, his sagacity, his fidelity, his buoyant hope, has cheered us in seasons of despondency. We felt secure while he was at the helm, and were confident so long as he was not afraid. We leaned upon him as our stay and staff. Alas! and is the dear man to be with us no more! What familiar memories come sadly up at this hour! It is painful to think of pleasant things, his looks, his anecdotes, the way in which we called him, not disrespectfully, but lovingly, by his first name. He was one of us, a member of the family, a parent and brother, toward whom reverence and love were sweetly intermingled, — and must we part?

He has gone, too, at such a time! Just as the bright period long looked for had come, — the war ended, slavery dead, the rebellion put down, the long-conflict over. The good President, we thought, will now have some rest. He will need no disguise at Baltimore, no military guard at Washington. He can rest upon his laurels, and walk the streets when and where he pleases. Everybody will be his friend. No one, surely, will wish to hurt him, he is so kind-hearted himself. When did he ever knowingly harm anybody? It was a comfort to him, he said recently, that he had never said a word or done an act that was designed to inflict a wound upon any heart. Anger and revenge were no part of his nature. Like his Master, when reviled, he reviled not again, but committed himself to Him that judgeth righteously.

But while we are oppressed with bereavement, while a nation mourns, and the people are in tears at their loss, it is consoling to think that he is safe. He is where no sorrow can reach him. As you have just sung:

> "No mortal woes
> Can reach the peaceful sleeper here,
> While angels guard his soft repose."

He was a good man, a truly pious man: he did not wish to go to the theatre. The etiquette of public life required him, sometimes, to sacrifice his individual preferences; besides, as General Grant had been advertised to be there, and could not go, he was afraid the people might be disappointed. How much was this like Abraham Lincoln, erring, if at all, always on the side of kindness! He was a man of strong religious feeling. How impressive was the scene at Springfield, Illinois, when he was about to leave home for Washington! He stood on the platform of the cars, his friends and neighbors around him, and thinking as he did of the responsibilities he was to assume, the trials and dangers that were before him, it was no mere formal request that he made, that christians would remember him in prayer. The same request he has often made of the different religious bodies that have called upon him at the Presidential mansion.

I remember the interview which he had with the Christian Commission at our first meeting in Washington. He received us cordially, and spoke warmly of the enterprise. "Nothing," he said, " is better for the soldiers than to be followed with Christian influences," and seemed grateful for the privilege of giving to the cause his official sanction. " Whatever the government could do to give to our agents free access to camp and hospital should be done."

In referring, on Thursday last, to the many good things we should be grateful for, I mentioned the re-election of our present noble Chief Magistrate. It was an occasion of gladness to the loyal people that he who had been raised up of God to conduct us safely through the wilderness had not been left like Moses to die upon Mount Nebo, but had crossed the Jordan and entered the promised land. It may seem now as if the congratulation was premature. I do not think so. He has in the highest sense entered upon the inheritance of true patriotism and christian hope. Gladly would we have honored him here on earth. We would have carried him in triumph through our streets. But God saw fit to bestow upon him a higher reward than we could give. A more brilliant assembly than ever was convened on earth shall hear his approbation pronounced, and he shall be crowned, not with fading laurels, but with immortal honor.

It is consoling to think, also, that not only no war, but no political animosities shall reach him more. No shafts of calumny shall enter his breast. I am told that the war is not half over; that the process of reconstruction will be attended with more difficulty and excitement than the conflict of arms. And I confess, that, warmly attached to the President as I am, I still felt afraid that party divisions and party rancor might hereafter arise that should disturb his peace. Whatever else might happen, I wanted that there should be, in reference to him, only kind words and kind thoughts. Such, I doubt not, was the universal feeling of the loyal people. This wish, at least, is gratified. His name and fame are secure. There will be hereafter as now, and through all time, and amid all controversies, a unanimity of profound respect for the honesty, the moral integrity, the lofty patriotism, the well balanced mind, and the administrative ability of Abraham Lincoln, not surpassed, if even equalled, by that which is paid to the memory of Washington. No man in the history of the nation has had greater responsibilities, and it will be the united voice of future generations, that no public man has ever sustained them more satisfactorily.

How will the soldiers mourn this death! Mr. Lincoln was not a military man, but no officer of the government, no military chieftain, not even the Lieutenant-General himself, was more beloved by the army. The President often visited them in the field. He went to the hospitals, and was sure to take every soldier by the hand, and say some comforting words to him. O, how their bosoms will heave, and their heads bow in sadness, at news of his death.

In the recent battles about Petersburg and Richmond he was near to the scene of action, and his great heart throbbed with joy at the successes that were achieved. He seemed to forget that he was President of the United States, in the pleasure he felt of forwarding telegrams to the rejoicing people. He was happy in making others glad. With what childlike simplicity he speaks of the honor the commanding general had conferred upon him, in allowing him to tell the good news! Noble hearted man! thy disinterested patriotism and sublime goodness of soul shall be a treasure to this nation and to humanity forever.

And the negroes. What a blow this death will be to them? He wrote the proclamation of their freedom, and enjoyed the comfort of doing it, more than all the honors which the nation or the world can confer. He stood against the combined influence of love and hatred, political opposition and partisan friendship, the unfaltering advocate of African freedom, and the stern defender of human rights. How those oppressed and grateful ones welcomed him in his recent visit to Richmond! And how the good man enjoyed it! He wished for no prouder ovation. Men, women, and children, poor, ragged, and black, met him at the wharf and attended him through the streets, weeping, laughing, praying, singing, shouting, and dancing for very joy. And he the happiest of them all. I hope the scene will be photographed. It will be an honor to our republic, and cause a thrill of pleasure in the breast of benevolence and humanity the world over.

Mr. Lincoln had strong domestic attachments. His bosom was full of warm affection. He was so from boyhood. He almost worshipped his mother. His young heart was filled with grief when she died. He was sorry, that, owing to the privations of pioneer life, there could be no regular religious services at her funeral. No church was nigh. No preacher could be obtained in season. But he remembered his mother's favorite minister in Kentucky; and, having learned to write, he gladly employed his newly acquired accomplishment in sending a letter to him, requesting that he would, if possible, come to Indiana, and perform the rites of religion near the burial-place of his lamented parent. The preacher came. Abe, as he was called, built a platform, and the sermon was delivered as desired over his mother's grave. Some natural tears were shed; but filial love was gratified, and the boy's heart was at rest. As with the boy, so it was with the man. Home was his delight. His wife and children were his choice companions. Every honor he received, every joy that entered his own heart, he hastened to share with them. No wonder, when such a husband and father was suddenly smitten down, his family should be overwhelmed by the dreadful shock. They will have the sympathies of the nation, and our earnest prayers that God will support them at this hour, and impart to them, in future days of grief and loneliness, the consolations of our holy faith.

In the great calamity which has befallen us in the death of the President, it is an occasion of devout gratitude that the Secretary of State has been spared.

The nation is under great obligations to this officer, for the manner in which he has conducted our foreign relations during the perilous crisis through which the country has passed. He has neither involved us in complications with other governments, nor lowered the dignity of our own. He has been wisely forbearing, and, I doubt not, will be wisely firm. May he and his stricken son soon be restored to health and their country's service.

The fearful tragedy which has taken from us the head of the nation is so recent, and our grief so deep, that we are scarcely prepared to speculate upon its causes, or probable consequences in the future. The immediate perpetrator of the act will doubtless be arrested, and the motives which led to it be fully ascertained. If found to be in pursuance of a conspiracy on the part of slaveholders and secessionists, it will be one of the most signal instances of folly, as well as wickedness, ever known in the annals of crime. No event could occur, which, in the indignation it has aroused, could be more terrible to the conquered foe. If secession had been compelled to capitulate before, it will now be arrested, condemned, and executed. If slavery had received its apparent death blow, the work will now be made sure. It will be struck to the heart, and pierced through and through, nor left until it is annihilated to the smallest fibre. If this foul assassination has been done or countenanced by men under the bitterness of defeat, they will now find the cup filled to the brim with the water of gall. Mr. Lincoln was disposed to be lenient; but if, in their malignity, they dash the cup of kindness from his hand, they must not complain if the contents of the apocalyptic vial should now be poured out upon their land, till it shall consume every green thing, and turn a third part of the waters into blood. If they smite down their best friend, they must take the consequences. We can only say, Thou art righteous, O God, who wast and art, and art to come, the Almighty, because thou hast judged thus. They have shed the blood of saints and of martyrs, and Thou hast given them blood to drink, for they are worthy!

I do not doubt that the Lord God Omnipotent reigneth, that He will bring good out of evil, and that this tragedy, like all other events in human history, will be overruled for his glory. But his judgments are a great deep. His way is in the sea, and his path in the mighty waters, and his footsteps are not known. Some seem to think the President was in danger of consenting to an unrighteous compromise, and that this was a reason why God, in his wise providence, permitted his removal. This may be so. But I had no misgivings on this point. With all his good nature, he was firm.

Wherever principle was involved, no man was ever more immovable. His was the wisdom from above, — first pure, then peaceable, gentle, and easy to be entreated; full of mercy and good fruits; without partiality and without hypocrisy. He never would have consented to any civil disabilities because of color. The hand that signed the memorable proclamation never would have signed any document that did not contemplate the full citizenship of those who have proved themselves the worthiest portion of the Southern people. He was kind and forgiving, and I love and honor him all the more for it. There was not a particle of hate or revenge in his soul; and this is one of the glories of his character, and will be one of the brightest features in his enduring fame. In the dreaded process of reconstruction, I do not believe he would have been unjust to freedom, or have made the slightest sacrifice of principle for the sake of peace. In the settlement of difficulties, he would have been guided by truth and justice as well as mercy. On no occasion would he lose his temper; and this perfect self-control was his shield and buckler. He might have met representatives from the Southern people pleasantly, perhaps told a story or two, but there would have been no parley with treason, no yielding to secession; and the leaders of the rebellion would have been put down forever.

I have confidence in his successor. President Johnson's opinions and policy are known, and will be approved by the loyal people. There is now a roused but I believe a healthful public sentiment, which will not be satisfied until rebellion is exterminated and consumed, root and branch, and its blossoms go up as the dust.

Above all, let us have confidence in God. How wonderful are the ways of Providence! Who can fail to see the hand of the Lord, and to stand in silent and grateful adoration, as he goes forth to the accomplishment of his purposes, in a way which we know not, and by means which seem mysterious and awful? The assassination of the President occurred on the day which is usually observed in commemoration of the Saviour's death. The enemies of our Lord thought that by the cross Christianity would be destroyed. So the authors of this fearful tragedy thought thus to crucify and entomb our national life, and to crush freedom and humanity through that mangled form. But, my friends, to-day is the day of our Saviour's resurrection; and, as Christianity gathered fresh energies in the sepulchre, and rose to newness of life, so I believe that the spirit and principles which have been embodied in our beloved and lamented President shall come forth from his freshly-opened grave with greater vigor than ever. If any are weeping over the tomb of freedom, or of any of those principles for which our soldiers have fought, and for which our Chief Magistrate has been called to lay down his life, let me say to you, Dry up your tears. Ye that are walking to Emmaus, silent and sad, come back to Jerusalem. The angel of the Lord hath appeared, though in a strange form, and rolled away the stone from the door of the sepulchre.

The tragedy which has occurred is a most impressive warning of the nature and evil of sin. This assassin was a young man, but what a finish of depravity he has reached! Reckless of a wife's bereavement, of children's tears, of a nation's grief; reckless of God, and reckless of himself. Such recklessness is traceable in part to his diseased imagination. He lived on airy and depraved fancies. He was an actor, and craved for some tragic scene. He imagined it quite theatrical, no doubt, to utter the words, " Sic semper tyrannis," as he sprang, brandishing his dagger, from the scene of murder. It is traceable, also, to the excitement of liquor; but it all comes from sin. This is the root of the whole. The heart's depravity grows up sometimes in the form of treason, and sometimes shows itself in other forms, — profaneness, drunkenness, and murder; but it is itself the father of all evil. Whoever cherishes it in any form has the devil, and hell itself, in his own soul. Depraved passions within are sure to tear and rend their victim, or break forth in flames of unquenchable fire.

Let me, in conclusion, refer to one of the most interesting incidents in the history of our departed President. At the consecration of the Soldiers' Cemetery at Gettysburg, after the eloquent address of Mr. Everett (alas! that he, too, is gone), Mr. Lincoln made a few most impressive remarks. He said that the best way to honor the heroes that had fallen on that bloody field was to consecrate ourselves more fully to the cause for which they bled. There was another thought within, he afterwards remarked, in a private conversation; and it was, that he should himself consecrate his own heart to God. He hoped, he said, that through divine assistance he had done this; and thus had arisen in his bosom the sweet, precious, sublime emotions of a new and spiritual life. It is well, my friends, that we should manifest our grief under this great and oppressive bereavement: we cannot and ought not to restrain our tears. It is right that tokens of mourning should be hung out from every dwelling. The whole nation and foreign lands will unite in doing honor to the distinguished dead. But no higher honor can be paid to the memory of Abraham Lincoln than to imitate his example in giving ourselves more fully to the cause in which he fell a martyr, and individually in prayer, and on bended knee, to consecrate our own heart to God.

REV. HENRY W. FOOTE.

ADDRESS SPOKEN AT KING'S CHAPEL,

WEDNESDAY, APRIL 19, 1865.

WE are gathered here in this solemn service, that we may have the last sad satisfaction of joining with a whole nation in paying every rite of respect and honor and veneration to him whose mortal part is this day committed to the tomb. Our hearts, so recently, alas! throbbing with an exultant sense of security in the blessed assurance of approaching peace, have been quickly clothed again in the habit of anguish so familiar, but now in a sackcloth blacker than the loss of many battles could have brought, whose hues of mourning must hereafter darken all our lives. Not even victory can come with notes so triumphant as to hush the wail of our grief for the leader who gathered our armies and chose our generals, and with patient heart brought us to the very gates of entire triumph; nor even can God's whitest angel of peace return, save with tear-dimmed eyes, and the disquiet of a mighty sorrow. But the very greatness and permanence of our emotions forbid us from trying to put them into speech. In this hour, the sob of a nation's overwhelming bereavement fills our ears and our hearts, and best tells the story of our loss. And, under the shadow and horror of a gigantic crime, we would fain learn the mysterious lesson of Providence in silence. "*Be still*, and know that I am God." Yet these services of sacred commemoration would seem prematurely closed, did we not try to gather up their meaning into brief and simple words. We need to go out from this house of prayer into an atmosphere of faith and prayer; not into deeper and more hopeless grief. And he, — the good, the great man, whom we desire to honor by doing as he would have us,— could he open those lips forever silent, would bid us carry hence stronger and higher purposes with which to withstand the cloud of sorrow that has settled down over the land he loved so well. He would bid us say little of him, but much of the great cause. He would bid us forget the murderous deed by which one foul hand has brought darkness upon twenty million loyal hearts, and remember only that in this place we have been uplifted, by communion with God's Spirit, into a truer allegiance to the principles of freedom and justice, of mercy and peace, as whose embodiment and representative he stood before the world. We cannot, indeed, turn thus aside from the contemplation of those qualities which made him what he was. The man stands before us, whichever way we turn, so identified with these great and uplifting themes, that, when we mention *them*, we must perforce think of *him*. He stands forever in history their illustrious representative, giving them honor, and receiving honor from them.

Not here in the short space which remains for us ere we rise, and go in spirit with those who bear what was mortal of our President to his burial, — nor now, when we are in the very presence of death, can eulogies be spoken. *That* can be safely left for History, who will find time enough in succeeding generations, and room enough on the scanty roll of her greatest names, where his henceforward stands forever written.

But, even here and now, the thought of what he *did*, or had a part in, — of what he *was*, — and of what he *will* be in the influence of example, is in all our hearts. Out of the fulness of such thoughts, let us try to gather up the lessons which we wish to carry hence.

Abraham Lincoln, the sixteenth President of the United States, will be remembered as long as the annals of this nation endure, as the ruler, who, under God, guided us, through four years of a terrible civil war, to the very borders of the peaceful restoration of national unity, under the one lawful government of the land. How the heart goes back (as we think of this, his mighty work) over all the varying anxieties and misgivings, — the public calamities and the private sorrows, — the alternations of success and defeat, — the vast problems of public policy, — the intricate relations with foreign powers, — which have filled the years with a weary weight. They have been hard to carry, for us all. They have seemed longer to those who were in the fierce current and whirling eddies of the time — as who was not? — longer than a lifetime of peace. But *he* who was held responsible for everything which went wrong; who stood in the central place of all, and held all the countless threads in his hand; yes, who gathered them all up in his *heart*, — with what a crushing burden have the years rested upon *him!* No wonder that men said, the other day, at Richmond, that he looked utterly worn out. The wonder is, how with *twenty* lives he could have endured so long. The most responsible place in the gift of any people it devolved upon him to fill, when its responsibilities were increased five hundred fold; when friends were few, and hostile critics too many to be numbered, and all the way before us was dark with unknown perils. And he has filled it, through good report and through evil report, silencing his opponents, one by one, and changing them to friends, until, when he died, no tongue was mute to speak his praise. Has there ever before been a recorded instance of a man coming to power without experience, and almost unknown, guiding a nation through the shock and strain of a vast war, welding them continually into greater unanimity of purpose, and gaining constantly on their respect and affection? In all history, he is the first example. It will stand written against his name, that he was the means, through God, of arousing a great people to a real national life. Look at it beforehand, and we should have called it impossible. There was a time — and not so long ago — when men doubted whether, under our institutions, there *could be* a genuine loyalty. Surely *he* was a providential man, to whom it was given to wake that feeling in the public heart. He has waked it, and kept it living, because it was in the deepest place of his own heart. It spoke in that call, after the fall of Sumter, which made the nation spring to its feet. It held him up, when, through the watches of that July night, he heard the ceaseless tramp, across the Long Bridge, of the army retreating from Bull-Run. And through many reverses since, when hope deferred made the heart sick, (need I name the battles and retreats which are written on our remembrance in characters of blood?) it sustained him unfaltering.

The people wrought in him, and he again wrought in the people, a sublime faith in our national ideas. And that was work enough for any man. However men may differ about the wisdom or expediency of this measure or of that, — and it would be strange if in such a time a man had not committed grave mistakes again and again, — none can doubt that he has done this one transcendent work of strengthening the spirit of nationality, without which all else were vain; with which all else *must* in the end go well. This being granted, all the detail of questions about special acts can be let pass. It would be an impertinence to descend to them in this hour of our solemn mourning. It is enough to claim our everlasting gratitude that he has done this' work: and especially because this national spirit, so purified and deepened, has become more and more imbued with the ideas of justice and liberty. He, indeed, would be the last to claim that he *led the way* in this. He has the truer glory of having followed the popular will, and of having caused these ideas, already accepted by the people, to become a part of their fundamental law. And so it comes, that, wherever the word Freedom is spoken, there his name will be uttered with benedictions. Through him, the starry flag has come to shine undimmed by oppression. That hapless race, who sat in bondage so long, have learned to recognize him as their great deliverer, and to lift their hands in prayer for him toward heaven. They will feel that now they have lost their truest friend. If we carry from these funeral rites a quicker heart for the demands of justice, — a more living love of human freedom, and a steadfast purpose to do our part in the great work of re-organizing the society of the South on a truer basis, — we shall bear the best witness to the reality of our sorrow, and the sincerity of our affection.

But this work, wrought on the spirit of the people and in our fundamental law, could never have been accomplished save by such a man as he. A man of the people, through and through, he has had entire faith in the people. And this faith has been his tower of strength. Out of the hardships of his early training, he brought a heart thoroughly in sympathy with the common people. Add to this the qualities peculiarly developed by that wild, frontier life, and which were his to an eminent degree by natural endowment; that strong, plain, good sense; that practical shrewdness; the power of ready adaptation to unforeseen emergencies: add that capacity for continual growth in character, which he has clearly manifested, and those qualities which have been the very ground-work of his character; the absolute honesty, the brave simplicity, the manly tenacity of purpose, the power of true and single devotion to a great cause, — and where, in all the records of the past, has ever risen one who seemed more providentially prepared for his great place, than he? Yet, with all this, so far was he from being stern, as we are apt to think a leader must be, — so far from the rugged hardness of character which we attribute to the rude civilization where his boyhood and youth were spent, — that we have felt at times that he *erred* on the side of gentleness. The object of such contumely and violent hate as no other in our history has ever had to bear, it never cast even a shadow over his spirit. What nobleness of heart, what grand magnanimity, has it not required to keep him utterly free from words of unkindness or thoughts of hate, so that the words of kindly good-will toward his enemies, which he spoke on the last afternoon of his life, came out of the transparent depths of a soul into which no bitterness had ever entered! And so it came, that, more and more, the nation has felt that it could trust him to the uttermost, and love him to the fullest. Here in our need, was a genuine man, — when "a man was more precious than fine gold, even a man than the precious gold of Ophir." Gradually all hostile tongues have been stilled, and those who thought him too fast or too slow, learned to think his judgment safe and wise. So, too, with that criticism of his homely Western speech, — his unsophisticated ways, — as beneath the dignity of his great office. We have learned that *character* is a jewel beyond price, — and having *that*, we have more and more learned to be grateful.

Shall I speak of those other qualities which so strongly marked his character; of that fearlessness which could walk composedly in the streets of Richmond with a meagre body-guard of six sailors; and which, in a different manifestation, has enabled him to stand again and again, in the four years past, almost alone in unpopular solitude on that height of place where the cold wind of criticism blows sharp and keen; or of that sublime self-forgetfulness which labored on for the single end of his country's welfare, which never sought to lay hold on the laurels of others, which modestly disclaimed his own honors? Do not those generous words yet ring in our ears, in which he put away from him whatever credit of recent triumphs it was sought to give him, saying that he had only been a *spectator;* that all the praise was due to the generals and the army? Or shall I say how his conviction of the right of our cause sustained him in our darkest hours, so that that was true of him which John Maidstone said of Cromwell, "He was a strong man in the dark perils of war; in the high places of the field, hope shone in him like a pillar of fire when it had gone out in the others"? Shall I speak of that simple religious conviction which has manifestly been deepening in his heart, till it uttered itself in that Inaugural where even *English* eyes have read a sincere humility, and a true religious spirit? No! these things are too sacred to be touched with careless hand. In the silence of the heart let us meditate on them; and pardon me that I have even put into words the thoughts which are the reason of our deepest grief to-day.

I do not attempt to draw the portraiture of this great ruler whom we have lost. My heart would not let me do it. You do not need to hear it. He stands before us all, as he has stamped himself ineffaceably on the pure silver of the national heart, all fluent and melted in the fervid heats of this time of fiery war. Six days ago I listened to an earnest voice which claimed for him, that his name stood side by side with the highest on our history; that, as one is called the Father of his Country, so his successor should be known hereafter as the Saviour of his Country. To-day the sorrow of a whole people gives him the name, and the mysterious consecration of death sets him apart forever from all carping tongues or differing thoughts. He belongs to us all, — a part of our glory; and even in our grief we lift our hearts in thanksgiving that he has been ours so long. Nor should we let the deed of violence which took him from us cause us to forget still to be grateful that he lived long enough to see the dawn breaking into glorious day; to know that his fidelity, his patience, his bearing of weary burdens for us all, was to reap its great reward; that though, like the great leader of the chosen people, he has died on the very verge of the promised land, to his eyes, like those of Moses, it was permitted to see the future which the Lord would give to a nation chastened by suffering, and endeared to Him by adversity.

Nor let us fail to join in our thought of him, as he would have us, all that innumerable company of witnesses, whose blood has been given for our national life. Our heroic dead! from the general to the private, this day we remember them all in our solemn commemoration. In our warmest love, in our deepest prayers, they hold a place sacred and imperishable. That holy seal of martyrdom is now set on them, and on him whose word they obeyed. We bring hither our proud sorrow, our reverent affection, that it may be consecrated by the Spirit of God; and we do but repeat the voice of all the future when we say, "Honor, honor, honor, eternal honor to their names."

But in this hour, we turn, even from the purest earthly fame, to the consolations which we need. For the greatness of the honor tells us of the greatness of the loss; and we *must have* the faith that it is yet God's will. Blessed be the Father of our Lord Jesus Christ, that we do *know*, under mystery and terror, that still we can recognize in him a God of infinite wisdom and perfect love. The body may perish, but the soul lives forever and forever; and He has higher ways of service for his faithful servant, than any ways of earth. Nor will He, who suffers not "one of his little ones to perish," let the long agony of this nation be in vain. He may call his workman hence; but the work of God goes on, and is sure.

The long procession of a nation in sorrow bears him with reverent hands to his grave and our hearts yearn to bring him the offerings of our love and reverence.

That we may best remember him, we should carry a deeper purpose into our own lives. I hear that voice which spoke at Gettysburg, and the words seem addressed to our own hearts this hour. "The world," said he, "will very little note, nor long remember, what we say here; but it can never forget what they did here. It is for us, the living, rather, *to be dedicated* here to the unfinished work that they have thus far so nobly carried on. It is rather for us to be here dedicated to the great task remaining before us; that from these honored dead we take increased devotion to that cause for which they here gave the last full measure of devotion; that we here highly resolve that these dead shall not have died in vain; that the nation shall, under God, have a new birth of freedom; and that government of the people, by the people, for the people, shall not perish from the earth."

In a true devotion to our dear country, — the mother of us all, — let us, standing here, as it were, by the bier of our chief magistrate, consecrate ourselves anew to her love and service. Let us resolve to give a true support to him who is called to that lofty place by such an awful messenger. Let not the shock of our bereavement cause us to forget the Christian spirit which breathed six weeks ago in that Inaugural.

"With malice towards none, with charity for all, with firmness in the right, — as God gives us to see the right, — let us strive on to finish the work we are in; to bind up the nation's wounds; to care for those who shall have borne the battle, and for their widows and orphans. And with all this, let us strive after a just and lasting peace among ourselves, and with all nations."

With these words of peace yet, as it were, on his lips, he has gone into the higher kingdom of perfect peace, where the weary weight of cares, borne for our sakes, is laid aside forever. We would not sit by his grave desolate in our tears; we would be grateful that He whose cross is to us the sign of hope, has assured to us the promise of eternal life. And, as we look up after that departing presence, with the cry, " My father, my father ! the chariots of Israel and the horsemen thereof," it shall not be in despair, but in the spirit of perfect trust.

REV. F. D. HUNTINGTON.

EMMANUEL CHURCH.

It being the Easter Communion, after an extended service, in which the liturgical and musical portions were very rich and solemn, the rector, Dr. Huntington, addressed the congregation from the chancel, substantially as follows:

WE have finished a week of which it seems not too much to say, that, in the concurrence of public glory and public crimes, it is without precedent or parallel in the *human* history of the world. No doubt, as these strangely contrasted events have been announced to us, first filling the land with a joy that could scarcely find moderate expressions at the sudden prospect of an early, successful and righteous termination to four years of bitter alienation and bloody strife, and then overwhelming it with alarm, affliction, and indignation, equally sudden and even more unspeakable, at that appalling act of infamy that has struck the civil head of the nation from his seat and his life together,—many of us have inquired within ourselves whether there is any one thought, or truth, or doctrine, large enough, powerful enough, and reconciling enough to subdue this awful sense of discord, and to harmonize the terrible contradictions, under one benignant law of love. Is there any solid shelter, any holy pavilion, where we can take refuge, and find these distracting transactions falling into place as parts of one perfect plan of God? And probably many of you have already found a consoling answer to that question.

The solemn path through which the holy evangelists, in their narratives of our Saviour's last days, and before he suffered, have led us, to his sacrifice, to the sealing of his grave, and to its miraculous opening as on this morning, has brought us to just that comforting and immortal truth, — deep enough, high enough, and wide enough to take in and interpret every one of these conflicting emotions. For there is no possible joy of deliverance, or jubilee of victory, where the feeling of both public and personal sin, and the need of a Redeemer, does not pursue us. Nor is there any secret heaviness, nor any national mourning, where the cross of Christ will not support us, and his resurrection from the dead re-assure us. Here, then, is the reconciliation. Here is the complete and sufficient declaration of our peace. Here is solid rock, be the earth never so unquiet! There is nothing we have felt, as citizens or as men, that may not find its needed ministry in the scenes where we have walked and lingered, — Bethany, the Mount of Olives, Gethsemane, Calvary, and the broken sepulchre. In the most exultant emotion of triumph at a re-established government we have seen the Prince of Peace marching, with palms and hosannas, in front of the great procession of kings and commanders. The intensest and most loyal patriotism is sanctioned by Jesus weeping over Jerusalem. Every bereaved household is solaced by going to Bethany, where Lazarus was raised, and by hearing the Son of Mary commend his mother to the beloved St. John, amidst the agonies of the crucifixion.

When we lift up our hearty praises and thanksgivings, as we must day by day, that the God of Liberty has struck off the bonds from four millions of enslaved men, and set our whole country free from that wretched wrong, how can we help remembering that it is all the working out, at last, of his infinite mercy by Whom all the families of men are made of one blood, Who shed his own most precious blood in sacrifice for all alike,— the poorest and weakest and darkest as much as any, and whose Christian service, as our daily collect says, is alone " perfect freedom" ? Nay, more, we learn how to look on this appalling assassination, and every attendant enormity,—leaving retribution to divine and human courts,—when we hear the Crucified, who was anointed to be betrayed, praying for his murderers, " Father, forgive them, for they know not what they do!" When we turn our eyes forward into the future, with whatever misgivings or anxieties, who can deny or doubt an instant that all our best and sure hopes rest on the one inestimable and transcendent fact, which we are now commemorating, that the Blessed and Holy and Almighty Lord has so loved us as to give himself for us, the just for the unjust, bringing life and immortality to light? Our only safety from coming evil, as a people, is in *righteousness;* and that not of our own obtaining, but obtained for us by the wonderful grace of an infinite and everlasting Mediator. Therefore, dear friends, we do and we will, to-day, joy and rejoice in Christ Jesus, the resurrection and the life, by whom we have received the atonement; who hath broken down the middle wall of partition, reconciling man with his brother man, and with his Father, God. For God commendeth his love to us in that, while we were yet sinners, Christ died for us. And if we are reconciled by his death, much more, being reconciled, shall we be saved by his life.

REV. WARREN H. CUDWORTH.

.

DANIEL IV:35.

All the Inhabitants of the Earth are reputed as Nothing: and He doeth according to His Will in the Armies of Heaven and among the Inhabitants of the Earth; and none can stay His Hand or say unto Him, "What doest Thou?"

We would have celebrated the joyous festival of Easter to-day. Generous hands had provided the flowers that were to adorn our altar, and tuneful voices had made ready the anthem that was to hail the resurrection of our Lord from the dead. Next to Christmas, this is the great feast-day of the Church; and believers of all denominations are uniting to appreciate and observe it in a proper manner.

But, yesterday morning, like a clap of thunder from clear skies, came the appalling announcement, "The President has been assassinated." "Impossible; it cannot be!" we all exclaimed, because we felt it should not be, it must not be. But when it was re-affirmed, and the official statement, spread before our strained and eager eyes, forced the unwilling conviction upon us that it was, alas! too true, how startling and dreadful the blow! We all felt personally bereaved. About our streets the people walked with mournful faces, as though each one was bowed down by a personal sorrow. We all seemed to have lost a father, a brother, a dear bosom-friend. How much we loved, how much we trusted, how much we leaned upon him, we never knew before. How can we bear it? what shall we do without him? what could have provoked such an atrocious crime? what does it all mean? Such were some of the questionings which darted through all minds, and formed the burden of conversation passing from lip to lip.

We can now understand, somewhat, how the apostles felt when our Lord was arrested, and cruelly put to death. They had leaned wholly upon Him, supposing that it was He who should have redeemed Israel; and when He was taken from them, and ignominiously crucified as a common malefactor, no wonder they were scattered, each one to his own place, leaving Him alone.

The week through which we have just passed has not been unlike that Holy or Passion Week, which, in Judæa of old, was so eventful to the Saviour and his disciples.

It began in triumph and rejoicing, not only because Richmond had fallen, but because Lee and his army had been compelled to surrender, prisoners of war, and our country was saved at last. It seemed impossible to express the universal exultation. Churches were thronged; cannon boomed from the forts; assemblies, gathered from all classes of society, were extemporized in hall and mart; flags fluttered on every breeze; buildings were gayly decorated with the emblems of rejoicing; schools were dismissed; stores and workshops closed; bonfires, illuminations, and fireworks brightened the night, and every loyal heart was full of happiness. But, alas! it ended like the week of sorrows, in gloom and blood. And is it not strange that Good Friday was the day, of all days in the year, chosen by the murderer for his infamous deed? It is one of those remarkable historical coincidences, which, whether we will or not, challenge observation and cause remark; and, no doubt, could our President have spoken after he was shot, he would have forgiven the cowardly perpetrator of this inhuman act, and rounded the parallel with a final and complete imitation of our Lord's example.

Let us not imagine that the evil of this deplorable event is unmitigated and unrelieved; for, in the worst condition of human society, and amid the most disastrous circumstances connected with human affairs, "God is our refuge and strength, a very present help in trouble. Therefore will not we fear, though the earth be removed, and though the mountains be carried into the midst of the sea." God maketh even the wrath of man to praise Him, and the remainder He restraineth.

"All the inhabitants of the earth are reputed as nothing; and He doeth according to his will in the armies of heaven, and among the inhabitants of the earth; and none can stay his hand, or say unto Him, 'What doest Thou?'"

This awful occurrence has not taken God by surprise, for known unto Him are all his works from the beginning of the world.

Death is an experience of such magnitude, that, as we are assured, not even a sparrow falleth to the ground without God's notice; and surely an event of such transcendent moment as the brutal murder of the ruler of a great and free nation, in the zenith of his popularity and usefulness, cannot occur without the oversight of an all-controlling Providence.

"The very hairs of our heads are all numbered." "The steps of a good man are ordered by the Lord, and He delighteth in his way."

Let us never forget that God gave us President Lincoln in the first place. That He led his father to move across the Ohio River when he was as yet but a child, leaving that condition of semi-bondage in which all poor whites were then compelled to live in the slave States, and settling down where he could breathe the air of freedom. Let us remember the struggles, labors, and aspirations of his boyhood, youth, and early manhood; how he toiled, as a boatman, up and down the great rivers of that region; how, axe in hand, he hewed his own way through the world; how he studied, thought, observed, prepared himself for the bar, and finally entered upon his political career; how he distanced all competitors in the nomination for the presidency; how he was elected, after the most exciting canvass ever known in this country; how his life was preserved during the passage through Baltimore to his first inauguration; how signally he has been directed and sustained throughout his official career thus far, and how really he has not been taken from us until his work was done; his enemies scattered, the rebellion put down, the Union restored, and the country saved.

Though dead, he yet speaketh to us, in that earnest request of his, for the prayers of all Christians throughout the land, that he might be guided and controlled of God. And who knows, but the Most High, how much he owes to the prayers of righteous men and women, which have been going up day and night for him, accordingly, ever since he entered upon the discharge of his duties. As a nation, we have relied too little upon God. Ever since the war broke out, we have been seeking and trying General this and General that, — feeling sure, at each fresh selection, that at last we had hit upon the right man, and he would prove our national deliverer. But as one after another our Generals have been tried and found wanting, how plainly has God revealed to us, that " all the inhabitants of the earth are reputed as nothing; and He doeth according to his will in the armies of heaven, and among the inhabitants of the earth, and none can stay his hand, or say unto him, ' What doest thou ? ' " How clearly and irresistibly, after every fresh disaster, has He led us back to himself, and taught us that vain was the help of man ; that " the race was not to the swift, nor the battle to the strong," and that we were to prevail over our enemies, not by might, nor by power, but by his blessing and favor.

Never had nation stronger reason for reliance upon God than has ours. The location of our Puritan ancestors here, after a vain endeavor to settle in Holland ; the Declaration of Independence leading to the Revolutionary war, during the first years of which hardly glimmered the hope of our success ; the final achievement of national existence; the adoption of the Constitution; the federal Union of States, growing stronger and more numerous every generation, and the survival of political convulsions caused by the overthrow and destruction of powerful parties, — these prove that God had a purpose to accomplish in the preservation of the country, which not all the malice of its foes nor the folly of its mistaken friends could thwart.

Who may say that that purpose is yet attained? And if not, who can deny that God is ordering the course of events so as to secure its attainment? Let us rely upon Him, therefore; assured, that, having begun a good work among us, he will carry it on to a successful termination.

Was it not a signal manifestation of Divine favor, that the assassin was not allowed to triumph until the very work he would interrupt had been completed? No doubt this deed had been long premeditated by more than one of those domestic traitors who have been tolerated in our midst, and opportunities may have been sought, again and again, to take the lives of our honored Chief Magistrate, and all associated with him at the head of affairs. No doubt it was the hope of the miscreants, directly and indirectly engaged, had their nefarious schemes succeeded, to have thrown the administration into embarrassment and confusion: profiting by which they hoped to seize the reins of government, and have everything their own way. Man may propose, but God disposes. It was not to be. The cowardly assailant of the President could not even pretend to any such motive. He exclaims, "*I* am revenged!" His feelings were wholly personal. His act was the wilful, deliberate, execrable crime of a hireling cutthroat and ruffian, unattended by a single palliating circumstance.

He was too late to arrest the mighty current which this war has started in favor of universal liberty, and his act must tend to make that current wider, deeper and stronger than ever.

Thus will God overrule what was intended to be a fatal blow to all our hopes and prospects, for their speedier fulfilment and their brighter realization.

President Lincoln was the most prominent representative and illustration of the great national idea upon which all our free institutions are founded. He was emphatically a man of the people. He spoke the language of the people. He thought and acted after the manner of the people; and his assassination, at such a time, will lay broader and firmer the foundations of popular liberty in the heart of mankind, than could years of common life and labor.

God may have seen that a sterner hand than his was needed to hold the helm of state during the next four years of reckoning and reconstruction. We all have marked how gentle and kindly he has been; with what forbearance he has treated enemies; how he has warned, expostulated, and entreated rebels to return to their allegiance; how he has given them time for repentance, and foretold plainly the doom which sooner or later must overtake their cause. Hundreds of men whose lives were forfeit by the law, he has pardoned and released. Of all papers, the hardest for him to sign was a death-warrant; and, whenever he could, consistently with his duty as Chief Magistrate of a great nation, he has commuted the death-penalty to labor or imprisonment. I have seen him at many reviews of the national troops, and his face always wore a genial and friendly expression. He was approachable to all, and as courteous in his manner towards the private in the ranks as the officer on the line. The soldiers loved him. Thousands who voted against him at his first election voted for him at the second, not because their political preferences had changed, but because they had come to believe in the man; and upon no hearts has fallen the burden of a heavier grief than rests upon those who have fought for the country he has served so well.

His death, under God, will do as much for the cause he had at heart, as did his life : for all great causes need martyrs quite as much as they do men. If the blood of martyr believers is the seed of the Church, surely the blood of martyred patriots is the seed of the country. Not a few the noble souls who have risked and lost all during the fearful conflicts of the last four years. And now, as he led them in life, he leads them in death. They were allowed the privilege of meeting their foes in fair fight. He fell, the victim of unexpected butchery; and, as men can never get out of their hearts and souls the honest indignation such a deed excites, so they will never dismiss from their minds the noble principles for whose dissemination he labored, and in defence of which he died.

President Lincoln, as the victim of an assassin, will have vastly more influence in the future than would President Lincoln the successful ruler of a great people. His very wound will cry out against the spirit and belief of those who have connived at his destruction. The man might provoke animosity; the martyr will command respect. We know that, already, several of the leading supporters of his administration, hitherto, had taken issue with him on important points connected with reconstruction in the rebel States, the confiscation of property, the unconditional abolition of slavery, the extension of the right of suffrage, and the publication of an act of amnesty offering pardon to everybody willing to renew allegiance. Hundreds of perplexing questions would no doubt have arisen, splitting up his former sympathisers into conflicting parties intent on compassing their ends, and willing, for this purpose, to separate from him. This was evil to come. He has been removed from it; and, high above the storms it may cause to gather and break, his image will be treasured in every heart, his example be an inspiration to every life.

He has left, in sacred trust to every person in this country, a legacy of invaluable principles, far more likely to be carried out because adherence to them has cost him his life.

There is an element of reverence for the heroic dead in human nature, which wields constantly-increasing sway over human faith and action. We never know how great or good are the prominent men among whom we live; or, if we know, we do not seem to realize it so keenly while they are moving in our midst, as when they have left us forever. So we ride past one of the stately churches which adorn our streets. The symmetry and grandeur of its proportions do not catch our eye when near; but as we are borne farther and farther from it, its walls and towers loom up higher and higher, its harmonious outlines stand out more and more boldly, it separates itself faster and faster from the ranges of common buildings around it, and becomes in the distance the most prominent and commanding feature of the view.

Had President Lincoln lived on through the entire term of his office, being in our midst, and not always the representative of our ideas, no doubt he would often have failed of appreciation, had he not provoked opposition, and some of his measures or recommendations would have been sharply criticised, if not severely censured.

But now, as it were, he has bequeathed to us the principles of his administration as an inheritance bought and sealed with his blood, all the more sacred and binding upon us because he no longer lives to expound and enforce them himself. The more they are examined, applied, and tested, the more they must be valued; the more thoroughly and faithfully they are adhered to, the more highly will they be esteemed.

God would have such principles — though obnoxious to a large number of the American people — brought into bold relief before the eyes of men; and, in spite of every effort to the contrary, it has been done. Truly, "All the inhabitants of the earth are reputed as nothing: and He doeth according to his will in the armies of heaven, and among the inhabitants of the earth: and none can stay His hand, or say unto him, 'What doest thou?'"

Let me remark, in conclusion, that the assassin's act

shows the terrible depravity of human nature. There are many who call him fiend and demon, but to me he seems to be only a bad man. So low will human nature sink when left to the unrestrained control of hatred, selfishness, and passion; so vile and base and brutal will a man become, if he is wholly bent on evil. Let us not deceive ourselves with words. Call the act devilish and infernal if you will, for it deserves all the epithets that depravity has forced into our language; but let us not forget that once the actor was an innocent, harmless child, and that he has been sinking to the infamy of his present condition, step by step. His whole life seems to have been filled with flagrant violations of the moral law. A traitor from the beginning, without manliness enough to induce him to enlist in the rebel army, he has preferred, like thousands of others, to stay at home, and meanly appropriate the blessings, comforts, and protection of a country which all the time he was endeavoring to destroy.

No wonder the conspirators against the life of our beloved President found in such a man a willing tool all ready for their purposes. What he has done is only a practical re-affirmation of God's holy word, that "The heart is deceitful above all things, and desperately wicked," and should convince us that the germs of all possible iniquity, latent, undeveloped, it may be, are in all our hearts; and we need, without exception, the presence and the grace of God to prevent them from springing into a vigorous and powerful growth.

Finally, God has again providentially lifted the veil that apologists for slavery — Northern and Southern —

have drawn over its hideous features, and shown us just what spirit it is of. Thank God, the utterances from this desk, while I have been in it, have been uniform and incapable of misconstruction upon this point. A tree is known by its fruits. It was slavery, in the person of Preston S. Brooks, that made the brutal and cowardly attack upon Senator Sumner, but a few years ago, in the Senate chamber of the United States, supported by armed abettors, approaching him from behind, and beating him over the head until he fell from his desk, bleeding and insensible!

It was slavery that induced the mob of Alton, Illinois, to surround the printing-office of E. P. Lovejoy, on the 7th of November, 1837, destroying not only the press and building, but the life of their fearless and faithful defender.

It was slavery that chained the Boston court-house, some ten years ago, and led off its chattel in triumph through our streets, escorted by an irresistible military force. Slavery for years has controlled congressional action, and forced even Presidents into compliance with its wishes.

It was slavery that trained and fired the first gun at Sumter, and, without justifiable cause or provocation, precipitated upon this great country the horrors of a civil war. And can I trust myself to speak of the starving, shooting, and torturing of our captured troops in the prison pens of Andersonville, Salisbury, Dalton, Columbia, Wilmington, and Danville, when, without the least necessity, without the shadow of an excuse, their infernal captors slowly and pitilessly forced them into their graves by thousands? No, I cannot! They were all slaveholders, or the tools of slaveholders, and they but exhibited the temper slavery has developed and encouraged from the beginning of time.

What but the barbarism engendered by this "peculiar institution" has violated the sanctity of the grave, and, disinterring the remains of fallen soldiers, made of their bones trinkets and mementoes to amuse friends at home?

Shall I remind you of the invariable custom of rebel artillerists to shell our hospitals upon the field of battle, and that again and again their troops have bayoneted the wounded? Who has forgotten the massacre at Fort Pillow; the upsetting of a whole train of ambulances filled with wounded men in Tennessee; the hanging of loyal persons, in the presence of their agonized families, in all the Southern States; the slaughter at Lawrence, Kansas, of inoffensive citizens, and the burning of their habitations and effects by the infamous Quantrell; the attempted destruction of all our Northern cities, crowded with inhabitants, by incendiaries; and the robbery and murder at St. Albans? It would have seemed impossible to outdo the horror of such atrocities, but even that has been done. This last act crowns and completes the whole. Slavery has lost all disguises forever, and must now stand forth to the end of time in all its natural and revolting hideousness.

Because I have felt this to be its character for many years, I have been unable to endure the thought that members of this society, otherwise lovable and engaging, should be ranked among its defenders, and so have spoken strongly and repeatedly, though always in a spirit of charity and affection to them. Let me entreat of them again, if any there be here, or ask their friends to entreat of them if not, to reflect upon the stand they have taken, to view it in the light of this last deplorable event which has overwhelmed our whole nation with sorrow and gloom, and acknowledge that slavery has indeed proved itself to be the sum of all human villanies, and deserves the abhorrence and execration of mankind.

"Once to every man and nation comes the moment to decide,
In the strife of truth with falsehood, for the good or evil side:
Some great cause, God's new Messiah, offering each the bloom or blight,
Parts the goats upon the left hand, and the sheep upon the right,
And the choice goes by forever, 'twixt that darkness and that light."

Whether we will have it so or not, it is very evident that God has decreed the abolition of American Slavery. Whatever door He opens, man may not shut; whatever door He shuts, man may not open. God is now, and ever shall be, what He has been from the beginning. "All the inhabitants of the earth are reputed as nothing, and He doeth according to his will, in the armies of heaven, and among the inhabitants of the earth; and none can stay his hand, or say unto Him, 'What doest Thou?'" Amen.

REV. CHANDLER ROBBINS.

PSALMS LXXVII: 19.

Thy way is in the Sea, and thy Path in the great Waters, and thy Footsteps are not known.

How mysterious are the ways of Providence! We have passed through such a week of wonders and contrasts, through such quick alternations of fierce extremes of emotion, out of long anxiety into sudden hope and joy, and anon, from highest jubilee to lowest mourning, that — may God have mercy upon us — we come into the sanctuary to-day with our minds so agitated, jaded, amazed, that we are unfit to offer anything except a profound acknowledgment of God's inscrutable designs, and an humble prayer for his most needed succor.

How mysterious are the ways of Providence! We felt this, and we said it here — but under what opposite conditions! — only three days ago. We had assembled then, at the call of a human magistrate, to humiliate ourselves for our sins; but He who overruleth all had recently sent us such a joyful surprise as to turn our Fast into a Thanksgiving. And now, on this blessed Easter Sunday, which we were expecting to celebrate with double gladness, through the association of our joy for our country's triumph with our rejoicings for our Redeemer's victory, He has permitted our land to be shrouded with such a tragic gloom as even the radiance of the resurrection cannot wholly dispel. Alas! that the same loving hands which were preparing to grace this sacred altar with those simple but fragrant tokens of our Christian gratitude, should have been called, at the last moment, to entwine around them those drooping emblems of our patriotic woe.*

How mysterious are the ways of Providence! The life which He had protected for four eventful years amidst a thousand dangers; the life which was dear, and every day becoming dearer to all who love our country; the life which, in human view, was most important to the nation's welfare; the life upon whose continuance, more than upon any other mortal pillar, we hung our hopes of a brighter era of justice and of peace; the life which the myriads who are coming out of bondage have daily commended with prayers and thanksgivings to God; the life which foreign nations, both friendly and jealous, were beginning to respect and honor; the life which, in its peculiar way, was exerting an influence more powerful and extensive than that of any potentate of the old world; the life which legions of armed men stood ready to protect with their own, He has permitted a vile assassin's hand to destroy at one fell blow.

---

* Several ladies of the church had prepared a cross of "Mayflowers" for the front of the pulpit, and a large basket of rich flowers for the communion-table, in honor of Easter Sunday. On hearing of the President's death they draped the pulpit with flags of the United States, dressed with mourning.

We are told in his holy oracles, that, without Him, not a sparrow falleth to the ground, nor a hair of His servants' heads can be harmed. But He has not interposed secret hand to shield that honored head from such an ignoble fate. We are told that He counts the tears of His children, and hears every sigh of the solitary sufferer. But He has not thwarted that murderous purpose which has flooded a nation with grief, and extorted a simultaneous wail of anguish from millions of wounded hearts.

Yes, His ways are indeed mysterious! But who of us would question His wisdom or His mercy? "As high as the heavens are above the earth, so are His thoughts higher than our thoughts." Only because they are so exalted are they incomprehensible to us. The darkness which shrouds His plans is caused by their unfathomable depth. We fail to see His goodness, because His love is infinite.

What know we yet of the purposes of His providence in permitting this horrid crime? Who can tell us what consequences God may have foreseen would have resulted from the disappointment of that infernal design? What consequences to the distinguished victim himself, and what to the nation and to humanity? You must discover that secret before you begin to question His wisdom. Who can tell us that greater evil would not have accrued from the arrest, than from the execution of that satanic deed? — greater evil to him whom we lament, to the people to whom he was so unselfishly devoted, and to the cause of those principles which, as he himself once said, were dearer to him than life, — and which ought to be dearer to us also than the life of any mortal, however honored and beloved. You must solve that problem, before you can begin to arraign His goodness. You must pry into the future, and foresee the results which will actually follow from this tragedy, the influence it is to have upon the course and welfare of the country, upon the settlement of the momentous questions that are opening before us, upon the feeling and action of the North and of the South, upon our domestic and foreign relations and policy, upon the great interests of justice, freedom, and Christian civilization, — you must look forward and acquaint yourself with these things before you begin to murmur at what He has done, " who seeth the end from the beginning."

Yes, His ways *are* mysterious, — dark, very dark, and awful, as we contemplate them amid these first pangs of bereavement. But not wholly dark even now. Already gleams of light flash upon us through the gloom. Already some tokens of loving kindness find their way to our hearts.

He who so reluctantly inaugurated the war of defence and retribution which treason had forced upon us; he who till the last moment cherished the delusive hope, offspring of his own generous nature, that his rebellious countrymen would relent; he who, through all the stages of the fierce conflict, in spite of the bitterness which it has engendered and the spirit of retaliation it has provoked, has invariably leaned to the side of forgiveness and mercy; he who, whatever errors he may be judged by any to have committed, has under God conducted the nation safely and honorably through its long path of peril; he who, as the event has proved, was the providential man for the last four years, and whom we could not have spared during their progress without far worse disasters than any which have befallen us, — he has been graciously preserved to rejoice with us all over those last victories which have vindicated the violated authority of the nation; he has been spared to hear the shouts of our armies hailing the glorious issue which has crowned their valor, and repaid them for all their toils; he has been spared to see the flag of the Union floating over the strongholds of rebellion; to contemplate near at hand the blessed prospect of peace; to meditate a proclamation of amnesty; to consider with his Cabinet the terms of reconciliation, and to send abroad to foreign nations those significant messages which re-assert the suspended rights of the nation, and demand the unqualified recognition of its re-established dignity and power. In these providential favors, which come at once to remembrance, we should be ungrateful not to recognize the divine benignity, both to him and to us.

Moreover, we cannot but feel that he has died in a good time for himself; in a moment of joy, in an hour of hope and triumph, in the midst of peaceful and generous thoughts, while offering grateful aspirations to God, and devising acts of forgiveness and magnanimity towards man. Though the manner of his death is shocking to *us*, yet we should not forget that to *him* it was without a pang. Though *we* contemplate the vileness of the instrument with indignation and abhorrence, yet he himself had no suspicion of the malignity of which he was the victim, and no feeling of revenge towards the murderer who hurried him to his rest.

Whether he has died also in a good time for his country and for us, remains yet to be revealed. That Providence designs this event for the ultimate good of the nation we will not, we cannot doubt. But of what nature that good may be, and in what ways it may be accomplished, only the future will disclose.

Perhaps it may be His holy purpose to subject us to yet new tribulations. Perhaps He sees that we have not improved as we ought the discipline which has been hitherto laid upon us. Perhaps He perceives that it is necessary that we should pass through yet another furnace of affliction before we shall have become purified like gold tried in the fire. Perhaps He has seen that we have trusted too much to an arm of flesh. Perhaps He knows that the awful lessons of the war have not sunk deep enough into our hearts; that vanity and pride, frivolity and luxury, intemperance and dishonesty, reckless speculation and greed of gain, immorality and ungodliness, have not been rebuked and abashed and awed as they ought to have been by His judgments, by the vast bereavements and calamities which have been visited upon us for our public and private sins.

If such as these are among His purposes, — and that they may be, the consciences of many must bear witness that there is too much cause for believing, — then it rests in no small measure with ourselves whether this sudden chastisement shall eventuate in our good. O my countrymen, my countrymen! let us suffer ourselves to be implored and admonished, by all that is solemn and shocking in this bereavement; by this startling evidence of the brittleness of human life and the vanity of human hopes; by this awful warning of the fearful crimes to which wicked passions lead; by all that is instructive and exemplary in the life, and all that is impressive and touching in the death, of the honored head of our nation; by all that our country has suffered and is suffering; by all the precious blood which has been shed in its behalf; by all the claims it has upon its children; by all we owe to God, to our families, to our fellow-men, and to our own souls, — let us be admonished and implored to put away the evil of our doings; to cast out all low and selfish passions from our hearts; to watch and pray that we ourselves may not fall into temptation; to watch and pray and work, each one of us in his place, for the promotion of public virtue and the correction of the national sins; to dedicate the remainder of our lives to wisdom and righteousness. It is upon the *moral* results of these times of trial that the salvation both of our country and ourselves depends; and for these, let us remember, God will hold our citizens individually responsible.

But the oppressive sense of our great bereavement must not be permitted to draw our thoughts away from that sublime and joyous event which the whole Christian world commemorates to-day. Indeed, it is all the more salutary and needful, amidst this national distress and perplexity, while the winds and waves are roaring, while the earthly foundations of our confidence are shaking beneath us, and the pillars of human pride and hope are falling around us, that we should turn anew to the bright revelation of immortal life, and contemplate afresh the radiant pledge of the incorruptible and unfading inheritance.

Christ is risen! Thanks be to God, who has set this transcendent fact over against all the gloom and misery and mystery of man's earthly lot; thanks, that the interposing love of our Maker has inwrought it as a vital reality into human experience and history; thanks, that the heel of the woman's seed is actually planted on the serpent's head; that redeeming energy has manifested itself in human flesh; that the Eternal Word has spoken its life-giving truths through human lips; that that "Eternal Life which was with the Father" has been upon the earth, seen by mortal eyes and handled by mortal hands; that power and love divine have come down from heaven and dwelt among us, healing our diseases, comforting our sorrows, forgiving and taking away our sins; that the Son of God, the "Wonderful," the "Conqueror," the "Prince of Peace," of whose "kingdom there shall be no end," has taken upon himself our own nature, — dignifying it by his perfect life, redeeming it by his obedient death, renovating it by his quickening spirit, raising and glorifying it by his own glorious rising, — that he is bound to us and identified with us by the ties and sympathies of a common humanity, and has promised to love and guide and save and sanctify, and bring home, at length, spotless and joyous, to his Father's presence, every one who believes in him.

To-day, in the midst of our gloom, we will fix our thoughts and our hearts upon this "mystery of godliness," this miracle of the divine mercy, wrought in with the course of human events as palpably as the saddest reality of our experience, — more vivid and more impressive than the most tragic scene of history, — till all that is dark, disheartening and appalling fades into comparative obscurity, and the whole soul is irradiated with the glory of that majestic vision.

Come, then, all ye who believe that " Christ died for our sins, and rose again for our justification "; in this hour of general Christian jubilee, lift up your eyes, swollen with weeping, lift up your hearts, burdened with grief, and bear your part with the vast chorus of believers, who are raising, in ten thousand temples, their song of Christian triumph, — " Thanks be to God, who giveth us the victory through our Lord Jesus Christ!"

REV. W. S. STUDLEY.

LAMENTATIONS V: 15, 16, 17, 19.

THE JOY OF OUR HEART IS CEASED; OUR DANCE IS TURNED INTO MOURNING. THE CROWN IS FALLEN FROM OUR HEAD. WOE UNTO US, THAT WE HAVE SINNED. FOR THIS OUR HEART IS FAINT. FOR THESE THINGS OUR EYES ARE DIM. * * * THOU, O LORD! REMAINEST FOREVER! THY THRONE FROM GENERATION TO GENERATION.

This bright Easter morning is one of the saddest, and, at the same time, one of the most hopeful mornings that ever dawned upon the American people.

In the vigor of his days, in the ripeness of his experience as a ruler, in the midst of duties which no man knew or was better qualified to discharge than he, the foremost man of this nation has been struck down by the hand of an assassin.

Abraham Lincoln, our President, whose mental and moral vision was as clear and true as a sunbeam, and whose great heart was as tender and loving as a woman's, a man who possessed such a genial and generous nature that he had scarcely a personal enemy in the world, — having guided the republic safely through the darkest night of trial that ever gathered about any people since the foundation of the world, — just when the morning light begins to dawn upon us, giving promise of a long and glorious day, — this wise and just and merciful ruler lies murdered in the capital!

What language can express our horror of the blow which struck him down? And what shall we say of the hellish power which prompted and aimed the blow?

We thought we had already seen the utmost reach of barbarism and savagery of which the slave-power is capable. We had seen it trample on the rights of four millions of people, using them solely for its own infernal lusts. We had seen it make war on the most beneficent and kindly government that was ever devised among men. We had seen it take the *slain* victims of that war, and of their bones make toys and playthings and personal adornments for its wives and children. We had seen it take the *living* victims of that war, and transform sixty thousand of them into idiotic skeletons or ghastly corpses by the torturing process of starvation. Ay, in a land teeming with abundance, in the very heart of Georgia, tens of thousands of Federal soldiers, — under the direction of Jefferson Davis, and with the consent of Robert E. Lee, — were literally and deliberately and vindictively starved to death, or into hopeless idiocy; and the last breath of many a brave man was spent in offering a pitiful but unanswered cry for bread!

And now, to fill the measure of its wickedness, slavery has done — WHAT? How shall we characterize its latest deed? What lexicon contains the word by which to fitly call it? What shall we name the act of one who comes behind an unarmed, unsuspecting man, — surrounded by his family, enjoying an hour's respite from the weightiest burden of responsibility and care that ever rested upon a single mind, — and deliberately shoots him down? What shall we call the act of one who goes to the darkened chamber of an almost dying man, — a man whose bones have just been so shattered by accident as to make it doubtful if he ever moves again, — and, leaping upon the bed, with the fury of a fiend, plunges a dagger, again and again, into his helpless and almost lifeless form? And these nameless deeds slavery has just done to increase and perpetuate its previous record of infamy!

Marc Antony, standing above the body of the murdered Cæsar, is represented by the great dramatist as saying what we might say to-day above the scarred remains of the late wise and generous President of this republic:

> "Thou art the ruins of the noblest man
> That ever lived in the tide of times!
> Woe to the hand that shed this costly blood!"

Ay, woe to Slavery! — woe to its perjured, bloody-handed champion, Jefferson Davis! — woe to its adherents and defenders, its advocates and apologists, whether in Carolina or Massachusetts! Behold, the hour of its destruction is at hand! Nay, this very Easter Sunday is the day of its resurrection! — its resurrection to everlasting shame and contempt! — its resurrection to complete and eternal damnation! Its doom is sealed!

To-day, for one, I would rather be the murdered

President, or the wounded Secretary, than to be the man, who, in this hour of the nation's sorrow, has no prayer to offer for the final and utter extermination of that system which has lifted itself so long against our peace.

When Slavery did this last and most brutal of all its deeds, it doubtless thought to intimidate the future rulers of this land from meting out to traitors the punishment which their crimes deserve. But it made a fearful mistake. In dealing with traitors, Andrew Johnson's little finger will be thicker than Abraham Lincoln's loins. If the OLD president chastised them with whips, the NEW president will chastise them with scorpions. Here is what he said only last week in a public address on the occasion of the fall of Richmond:

"Treason is the highest crime known in the catalogue of crimes; and for him that is guilty of it,— for him that is willing to lift his impious hand against the authority of the nation,— I would say death is too easy a punishment. My notion is that treason must be made odious; that traitors must be punished and impoverished: their social power broken.

"You, my friends, have traitors in your very midst, and treason needs rebuke and punishment here as well as elsewhere. It is not the men in the field who are the greatest traitors. It is the men who have encouraged them to imperil their lives, while they themselves have remained at home, expending their means, and exerting all their power, to overthrow the government. Hence I say this: 'the halter to intelligent, influential traitors.' But to the honest boy, to the deluded man, who have been deceived into the rebel ranks, I would extend leniency. I would say return to your allegiance, renew your support to the government, and become good citizens; but the leaders I would hang."

Nor is this a new-born sentiment in the heart of Andrew Johnson; for as long ago as the second of March, 1861, in a thrilling speech, which created an unparalleled outbreak of enthusiasm in the galleries of the Senate Chamber, he said:

"Show me the man who makes war on the government, and fires on its vessels, and I will show you a traitor. *And, if I were President of the United States, I would have all such arrested, and when tried and convicted, by the eternal God, I would have them hung!*"

There is hope, therefore, in the bright beams of this Easter sun! Our new ruler knows how to deal with traitors!

. . . . .

Abraham Lincoln is dead: slain by the hand of slavery! He lived long enough, however, to see the promised land from Pisgah; long enough to witness the triumph of that army and navy of which he was the commander-in-chief; long enough to walk through the streets of Richmond, clad in magisterial authority; long enough to insure for the American people "liberty and union, now and forever, one and inseparable"; long enough to insure for himself a spotless record — a deathless name. That which the poet sung of the Greek hero is peculiarly applicable to our departed leader:

"Thou art FREEDOM's now, and FAME's!"

. . . . .

There is hope, I say, as well as sadness, in this hour;

the joy of our heart may have ceased; our dance may have been turned into mourning; the crown may have fallen from our head, but " THOU, O LORD, REMAINEST FOREVER; THY THRONE FROM GENERATION TO GENERATION. And, while God remains, truth cannot be shorn of its beauty or strength by any of the machinations of error.

On that dreadful Friday, when the enemies of Jesus nailed Him to the cross, they thought that they had silenced Him for ever; but there was never a greater mistake. They had only placed Him where His divine beauty could be more clearly seen, and where His divine power could be more widely exerted.

And so it will be always. Every purpose of evil is certain to be overruled for good. No outrage upon religion, or humanity, is permitted to go unavenged forever.

Four years ago the arch leader of the rebellion declared that the war should be waged on northern soil; that, within their own State lines, the people of the North should smell southern powder and feel southern steel. But God ordained it otherwise. His decree went forth that the power of injustice should be destroyed on the very spot where it had been exerted. And this latest crime of treachery and oppression, which has filled every loyal heart so suddenly with mourning, by God's overruling grace shall work out more perfectly the redemption of our land. Amen.

REV. RUFUS ELLIS.

LUKE XXIV: 5, 6.

AND AS THEY WERE AFRAID, AND BOWED DOWN THEIR FACES TO THE EARTH, THEY SAID UNTO THEM, WHY SEEK YE THE LIVING AMONG THE DEAD? HE IS NOT HERE, BUT IS RISEN.

THE voices still sound for the ear of faith; and he who hath that ear, let him hear what the spirit saith unto the churches to-day. It is our resurrection-morning, a time consecrated to gladness; and yet it finds a nation in tears. Our tower of strength is fallen. Bloody violence has invaded the high places of the land; and he who was in deed as well as in name the head of the people, more and more trusted, more and more loved, as he was better and better known, lies dead, — our country's martyr. Only on the last Thursday I tried to acknowledge, in a few earnest words, the eminent worth and high services of our noble President, and now he is no more with us on earth; and, saddest thought of all, the wrath of man hath wrought for us this woe. Let every believing soul exercise a high and serene and Christian trust, according to the great necessities of an hour which hath no precedent in our history, and be wise and calm and faithful in the persuasion, that, in the providence of God, the wrath of man shall accomplish all the more completely that divine purpose which nothing can defeat or so much as delay. Our Easter* flowers shall remain in the house of prayer, not because we are glad, — we cannot be glad to-day, — but because we are full of the great hope which is the Christian's anchor, and which holds in the stormiest sea. They are providentially here to grace the burial of our Chief Magistrate, honored and well beloved, the best defence of the nation, under God, only yesterday: they shall be eloquent symbols of immortality, shining witnesses of the light that burns behind the darkest clouds, and of the love which is unchanging; of the earth, earthy, and yet fragrant as with the airs of heaven, and telling us of things heavenly, that —

> "Sweet fields beyond the swelling flood
> Stand dressed in living green."

I am not sorry that it is Easter-morning; that the sad message has found us at the open tomb of Jesus, thankful, with a Christian thankfulness, that death is for ever abolished, and taught, by that look of triumph in the eyes of our risen Lord, how surely and how swiftly sometimes God brings the best things out of the worst, and clothes the heaviest spirits in the most radiant garments of praise. Let us confess his hand; and that known unto him are all the works of man from the foundation of the world; and that this blow also was needed, else it had not been given in the providence of One who never willingly afflicts.

* Easter Sunday, April 16.

"Why seek ye the living among the dead? He is not here, but is risen." It is a pious, faithful, and most tender office to go to the graves of our loved ones; and not to weep there were to be less than human. Know ye not, said the apostle, that ye are the temples of God; and that your very bodies are consecrated, fashioned into majesty and beauty by the life within? And we have all seen how the departing spirit sets upon the lifeless form its own lovely image; and, in proportion as we honor the soul, we deal very tenderly with the soul's wonderful tabernacle. Nevertheless there is need of the question, "Why seek ye the living among the dead?" — need that, even here in Christendom, we should again and again be told, "He is not here, but is risen." They are not the words which man's wisdom teacheth. Science does not announce them amongst her discoveries, old or new. The heart of nature hath no such burden as that to roll forth from its burning core, persistent as is its hope, deep as is its desire of immortality. The voices are the voices of angels; they come to us from that tomb in which Christ and his gospel seemed to be for ever buried; they are the echoes of those early testimonies which declared to all the world, beginning at Jerusalem, that he who "suffered under Pontius Pilate, was crucified, dead, and buried," rose from the dead on the third day, to be called, ever after, the Lord's Day, to be the Easter of each week,—

> "Till week-days, following in their train,
> The fulness of the blessing gain;
> Till all, both resting and employ,
> Be one Lord's Day of holy joy."

It is an unspeakable privilege to live in days when the angelic voices are to be heard; and we never hear them more distinctly, and are never more sure that they are from heaven, than when, in our human weakness, we are afraid, and our faces are bowed down to the earth. It would be agony sometimes to look upon the poor stricken body, over which the change may have passed almost in the twinkling of an eye, if the spirit which leads us into all blessed and consoling truths were not waiting for the opportunity to say, "He is not here, but is risen;" for that is what the spirit whispers in the heart of every true believer since the Lord abolished death. The bridegroom has been taken from them, and the children of the bridechamber may well mourn; but it is a holy and hopeful sorrow which moves their hearts, and they are lifted at once into heavenly places with the departed, and he is transfigured before them; and the eyes which were holden before that they could not see are anointed; and, because he lives, we live. Listen now, as you never yet have listened, for the angelic voices. It is a nation's opportunity to grow into a deeper faith in the everlasting life,—a faith that death only sets free, and reveals the bound and hidden soul. It is a faith which we owe to Christ. He changed the philosopher's opinion and the people's hope into a practical and abiding persuasion. The angels did not light up the tomb with their glowing faces and shining garments until he was laid in it. Then words of good cheer were heard, which were not passed by as the idle tales of the superstitious, but were taken up as most authentic gospels, and proclaimed wherever men, from fear of death, were subject to bondage. It is our blessed heritage from those who were glad because they had seen the Lord. It is a faith which we can have in its power and fulness only so far as we are thoroughly Christian, not merely in the reception of the outward facts, but in a conformity to the very heart and mind of Christianity. It is a faith which must be proportioned to our other faiths, and chiefly to our confidence in truth and goodness and immortal love. Not to all the people is Christ revealed, but to witnesses chosen before of God, who, though like Thomas they might hesitate for a moment, could not scoff like the Athenians when Jesus and the resurrection were named together, since nothing could be more credible than the rising of such a Lord.

Not of us is it to believe; and yet God's gift is also our act, and we must exercise ourselves in this grace; and a public grief so heavy and so unlooked for, and so suggestive of anxious questionings as this, which presses upon all hearts to-day, may challenge and exalt our faith in things unseen, and help us to taste the powers of the world to come, even more than a private sorrow. Let this be the measure of our Christianity. By this let us know whether we have been the companions and friends of Jesus, — whether we look at the things which are seen, or at the things which are not seen, according as we shall be able to look up from the grave, and to seek for the living in their appointed and exalted places. God is not the God of the dead. Truly to confess Him is to confess the life everlasting. No hand of violence can rob you of aught living, or consign you to hopeless sorrowing for the dead, if you yourself are truly alive. Find the soul in the body whilst the body lives, and you cannot be persuaded, — no, not though an angel from heaven should say it, — that, when the body dies, the soul too goes down with the dust into the grave. "Neither wilt thou suffer thine Holy One to see corruption." Oh, for that strong and ardent faith, which, in losing a visible person, gains an invisible life! — a life which is ours no more by virtue of corporal contact or contiguity, but flows in upon us through channels hidden and divine.

It is a blessed faith which enables us, when the man is gone, to rejoice as we never rejoiced before in his high and gracious manhood; and, when the countenance is changed, to walk more gladly and steadfastly than ever before in the pure light which illumined it, and made the hard lines of a plain and often sad face soft and flowing and almost comely. It is a blessed faith which so joins us to the wisdom and goodness, to the honor and gentleness, and all the fair and sweet humanities of our friend, that, when he is taken from us in a moment, we find that what made him justly dear is more ours than ever; not to be groped for among the dead, but already abroad in this world of the living; accomplishing still the will of God on earth, and amongst the children of men. It is a blessed faith which suffers us not to linger over our dead beyond the just time of a natural and healthy sorrow, but commits and commends us, as soon as may be, to the paths of our daily life in which he walked; to the works which he was not permitted to do, and to the greater works which he promised; which makes him more to us, in the way of inspiration and guidance, than he could have been whilst he was in the body. In mourning for the tabernacle which a mad and wicked hand hath invaded, do not forget to seize and appropriate the great life which hath been not so much unclothed as clothed upon. Disappoint any who may have secretly desired or planned this great crime, by showing forth, with the enthusiasm of a new discipleship, the very being, the very persistent purpose, which they would have put out of the world had it been possible. And what vengeance is to be compared with that divine vengeance which multiplies a thousand-fold the one voice that a cruel death has silenced, and makes of the truth which was buried in the ground a word of strength and joy for the whole world?

There is a crime unto death. It ought not to be lightly dealt with. Let no man ask that it may be forgiven; but, when the ministers of God who bear not the sword in vain have fulfilled their office, and the criminal has received the stern sentence, let us remember, were it only for the honor and the love which we bear to our dead, the generous and humane spirit that was so large a part of his noble manhood. I confess that I have not thought that they mourn for him wisely, who, renouncing his spirit before his poor outraged clay was cold, propose to be bitter and revengeful in fact, though not of course in name, as he was not. Friends,— *Christian* friends, — followers of him whose first disciples were as loving as they were just, let us not forget the many sad warnings of man's history, the cheats which his deceitful heart has put upon him; let us not forget that what is begun in righteousness and love is often ended, and not well, in unrighteousness and wrath. We shall have lost our noble leader indeed, if we lose his spirit, the wise and considerate mind, the excellent judgment, the tender, humane heart, that were in him; if, with all the wrongs, cruel wrongs, foul wrongs, that we have suffered as a nation, we forget that we are a Christian nation, and proceed to demand, and that, too, in the name of our gentle sufferer, measures of severity which he would never have sanctioned; so taking advantage of his dying, to thwart one of the high aims of his living. You know that I have spoken in but one voice from the beginning of this war, pleading for its rightfulness in the sight of the highest Christianity; and so you will not misunderstand my warning, lest, misled by passion, and not following, as we suppose, our man of peace, we inaugurate a reign of terror and blood. God grant that our martyr may be our deliverer; that he who was raised up in the most manifest providence of the Lord to be our counsellor and guide in our years of sore trial, may still rule and bless the people from the hiding-place of spiritual power; and, if we have had occasion to distrust him who is now called to the highest seat, may our fears be changed into hopes, and the desire of the nation be accomplished! *

---

* The preacher desires that the paragraphs above may not be interpreted as recommending lenity to the authors of privy conspiracy and rebellion; and he is glad to add that the circumstances, well known to the country, which led so many to distrust our present national Chief Magistrate, have been explained, by those who speak with authority, to his entire satisfaction.

REV. SAMUEL K. LOTHROP.

2 SAMUEL XIX: 2.

And the Victory that Day was turned into Mourning unto all the People.

Brethren, but one theme can command your attention this morning. Only the contemplation of one event, solemn and momentous, looked at in the light of that inscrutable providence which is ever wise and merciful, studied in its social and civil, its moral and religious aspects, is in harmony with the painful emotions that swell our hearts, the troubled thoughts that are pressing upon our minds.

Three days since, we gathered here for a service of humiliation, of human appointment, at the call of the civil authorities; God so ordered it, that it became of necessity a service of gratitude and thanksgiving. The black cloud of treason and rebellion, which for four years had lowered over the land, seemed distinctly broken and scattered, floating away in the distance. The dawn of approaching peace, of reunion, of prosperity, of a glorious and honorable future for the nation, gave clear indications that it must ere long burst upon us in splendid effulgence; so that, though conscious of our unworthiness, we could not think of our sins so much as of the divine goodness and mercy.

We expected to gather here this beautiful Easter Sunday with our thoughts far away from present scenes, undisturbed by civil cares or anxieties; travelling back to that holy morning hour when the gates of the sepulchre, sealed and guarded by all the power of the Cæsars, were riven, and "the Crucified" came forth, and the world awoke to find itself bathed with new light, clothed with an immortal hope, refreshed with a heavenly benediction, that would be felt anew in our hearts on this grand and solemn anniversary. But again God has otherwise ordered. We cannot forget that blessed and stupendous fact in his providence, — the resurrection of our Lord and Saviour Jesus Christ, — but the echo, coming down to us through the ages, of that glorious declaration, "He is not here, he is risen," which we expected would break upon our ears, filling our hearts with peace and gladness, is lost, as it were, overborne by the stunning announcement which burst upon us yesterday morning: "He is dead, — Abraham Lincoln, the President of the United States, is dead, — felled by the hand of a dastardly assassin, in the midst of a scene of quiet and peaceful relaxation from the oppressive cares of state." We cannot put from our thoughts that sudden and startling announcement, that sad and solemn event. It is not necessary that we should; nay, it is every way meet that we should not. The true place to which we should bring this great bereavement, this atrocious crime, this national calamity, this loss to the world, this event, the magnitude of whose influences, as they touch the relations and affect the policy of our own or other nations, cannot be computed, — the true place to which to bring it and all the thoughts and emotions it awakens, is the altar of God; that we may bow there with a submission as profound as our sorrow, with a trust as deep and strong as our necessities.

Brethren, I feel almost incompetent to direct your thoughts this morning, as I have scarcely been able for the last twenty-four hours to collect and guide my own. Language seems impotent to give utterance to all that I think and feel. But, doubtless, your experience has been similar to my own. Yesterday, after the first outburst of my sorrow, and, I am not ashamed to add, of righteous indignation against the fiendish author of this terrific tragedy, the instincts of faith and the habit of my heart prevailed, and I heard, as it were, the Holy Spirit breathing in my ear the solemn and sublime injunction, "Be still, and know that I am God;" and there was borne in upon my mind, also, that declaration of the patriarch Jacob, uttered for the comfort of his children as they were about to be deprived of the counsels of his wisdom and the joy of his presence, "Behold I die, but God shall be with you." Our first duty, my friends, in this sad hour, now, as in all great emergencies, public and private, the only help, comfort, and strength of our souls is to turn unto God, and lean upon Him. We must strive to be calm. This calamity which seems unspeakably great, this bereavement which makes a nation weep and covers a mighty land with mourning, this demon deed, instigated by the brutal passions, and perpetrated in the utter moral bewilderment, which, as many incidents in this war, and the war itself, so painfully and so conclusively testify, the barbarous institution of slavery begets in the human heart, was within the control of the Almighty Providence; and, in some way, which we cannot fathom, it will be made to contribute to our good, and the furtherance of the benignant purposes of that Providence. We believe this; we must strive to feel it, and be calm. Many have been accustomed, of late, to regard, and to speak of Abraham Lincoln, as a *providential* man. Political opponents, as well as friends, have been disposed to acquiesce in the epithet; the idea was fast getting to be the general feeling, the conviction of the nation. It was natural that this feeling should have arisen, have grown so strong, and been so cherished as to become a conviction. His history and character, his slender opportunities, and marked abilities, the wonderful way in which, under providence, he has presided over the nation, and by a singularly wise, calm, unimpassioned, but firm and persevering policy, carried the country, with honor before the world, through four years of a civil war which has no parallel in the record of the nations, seem to justify and demand that he should be regarded as the man for the crisis, "*a providential man.*"

"I called thee from the sheep-cote to be ruler over Israel," said the Lord to David, and the words have an application and significance here. The shepherd of Hebron, called to the throne of Israel, and the humble citizen of Illinois, raised from the lowly sphere of private life to the most august position, and the charge of the most momentous affairs, as President of the United States, have a providential similitude, which we may rightfully recognize. The care of sheep seemed no meet preparation for the cares of state: and the humble duties, the limited range of action, and small experience in public national affairs, embraced in Mr. Lincoln's previous life, seemed but a meagre preparation for the exalted post he was called to fill; the weighty and responsible trusts he was summoned to discharge. It will be the verdict of history however, it is the admission of to-day, it is the testimony of every honest and unprejudiced heart in the land, that he has discharged these duties amid circumstances of unparalleled embarrassment and difficulty, with vast and singular wisdom. Even his peculiarities of person, manners, and character, unchanged by his elevation to exalted station and large power, have contributed to his usefulness and increased his personal influence, because they have been rightfully interpreted as indications that the man was greater than his office, and therefore competent to its duties and worthy of its honors. Never before, I apprehend, has any man been invested with the august dignity of the Presidency of this great republic, and been so little changed by it; so little affected by the personal aggrandizement, so free from the intellectual and moral giddiness often consequent upon the position. He has grown, undoubtedly, since his entrance upon his high office; grown immensely and continually; enlarged intellectually, developed morally: but he has shown all along, and concentrated in himself thereby, more and more, the confidence of the nation, that his heart was as warm, his nature as simple, his purpose as honest, his judgment as strong and clear, his head as cool, amid all the grandeur and glory of the nation's palace, and the shaping of the nation's course and policy, as they were beneath the humble roof of his private dwelling, and the little routine and the petty cares of his attorney's office on the Western prairies. Such indifference or superiority to the influence of outward position is a clear indication of something great and strong in the character.

Forty hours ago, my friends, I presume we should all have acquiesced in speaking of Abraham Lincoln as "*a providential man*"; and the expression would have been an indication of a patriotic cheerfulness, trust, and faith in our hearts. If called upon to justify it, we should have spoken briefly of these four memorable years; of his unquestionable escape from assassination on his journey to Washington for his first inauguration; of the dark prospects, the extraordinary embarrassments under which he assumed the reins of government, and entered upon the administration of our affairs; of his sagacity, his mingled moderation and firmness at the outset; of his wonderful wisdom in following the leadings of Providence and the course of events, as evinced in his various proclamations and the successive steps of his policy; of the feeble life of the nation, — its existence hanging upon a thread, — and of the all but impotence of the government, as he received it from the hands of his predecessor; and of the healthy, deep-throbbing life of the nation at this hour; and of the government, strong, nay, mighty and irresistible, through the nation's confidence, — and we should have felt that in all this there was an ample justification of the faith which turned trustingly to him as a man of wonderful endowments, raised up by Providence to meet a momentous emergency in our national career.

We should have been right in thus feeling; but — and here is the point and purpose of what I have said — if his life was providential, is not his death providential also? If God raised him up for a grand purpose, for a great and noble work, would he permit his death, and that purpose unaccomplished, that work not done? He has not fulfilled all our wishes, answered all *our* expectations, discharged all the trusts we reposed in him; but has he not done God's work, — the work God gave him to do for us? Who shall dare to assume that he has not? Who shall refuse to hope and to believe, that events will reveal the Providence in his death to be as wise and benignant as the Providence in his life. Ah, how sad, how bereaved the Israelites felt when Moses went up into the mountain, and returned not, but died there alone! For forty years he had led them in the wilderness, and, after many misgivings on their part, become the object of their reverence and their trust. By counsel and encouragement, by instruction and example, he had sustained them in all the perils and privations of their wanderings, and brought them at length, under the divine guidance, to the banks of the Jordan, which they were about to pass, and to the sight of the promised land, which they were about to possess. He beheld that land, and saw that it was beautiful and good, but was not permitted to enter it. Israel wept at his fate and mourned his loss, but found in Joshua another leader adequate to their great necessities. So our Israel mourns this day its providential leader and head. A resemblance to David, in his elevation from a humble to an exalted station, there is a resemblance to Moses in the time, though not in the manner, of his departure. He has led us through four years of terrible civil war; amid the occasional misgivings of some of his friends, and beneath the conflict of parties, he has steadily gained upon the confidence, the respect and affection of the nation: till at length it may be safely said, that, on Friday last, there was no man living in whose political wisdom and sagacity, in whose moderation and magnanimity, in whose simple honesty of purpose, and broad, unselfish patriotism, the great mass of the people, of all sections and all parties, reposed such confidence, as in Abraham Lincoln's. It was the general, the all but universal feeling, that, in some just and right way, he would pilot the nation safely and honorably through to a glorious peace and a blessed reunion. Like Moses on the banks of the Jordan, he saw this peace in near prospect, and felt that the object of all his noble efforts, his days and nights of anxious thought and painful solicitude, was just within his grasp. But, like Moses, he was not permitted to enter into that peace, to attain personally that object. Suddenly, like a bolt from heaven, the dastard hand of an assassin did its work, and

> "He who cared not to be great,
> But as he served or saved the State,"

passed from the scene of his glory and his usefulness;

and the universal joy in our recent triumphs and cheering prospects, "*the victory of that day is turned into mourning unto all the people.*"

Brethren, our first and our last duty, the beginning and the end of our consolation, our only help, is to turn unto God, and trust; to feel that the Lord God omnipotent reigneth, and that all will be well. Even beneath this trust there is sorrow and anxiety in our hearts. The death of our President at this crisis is a tremendous loss, and I would not say one word to diminish your sense of it; for it can hardly be over-estimated. It is a great national calamity, and I feel it to be so. Every nerve and fibre of my being vibrates to it. I would not feel it less, or have you feel it less. It comes also in the form of an atrocious public outrage and murder, with a fearful shock to us and to the world. For the first time that monster crime, — to be abhorred by every citizen in every land, but most of all under a government like ours, — political assassination from the unhallowed promptings of political and party passions, stains our annals, startles us from our security, ay, and from our dreams of forbearance and tenderness. How far the rebel government or leaders, recently at Richmond, were privy to the fiendish purpose so fatally executed, remains to be ascertained and proved: it is not to be assumed. That they were vindictive, desperate, and cruel enough for such privity, the stories, too terribly authenticated to be doubted or denied, of the Libby, of Belle Isle, and of Andersonville, are conclusive evidence; and I confess that my strong disposition to forbear, forgive, and trust, grows weak; it melts away almost, before that indelible record of inhuman barbarities, deliberately, perseveringly practised, month after month, upon defenceless men, prisoners of war, within immediate reach, within sight almost of the headquarters of the most distinguished general of the Confederate armies, whose friends claim for him that he is a chivalrous, magnanimous, high-toned gentleman. Let him show that he had no knowledge of these barbarities, or having knowledge, had no power to prevent them; let him show that he ever uttered to his soldiers or his government a word of remonstrance against them; then, but not till then, may his claim to magnanimity, and the sympathies of his former fellow-citizens, and the compassionate regards of honorable and merciful men, be admitted. Judging from what we know of his position and his power, the record is, at present, a foul blot against his name. Let him wipe it out if he can. None will rejoice more than I, if he can do so. I wait, the country waits, the world waits for him to do it, ere the decision is made as to the estimation in which his treason, and his character as the great military chieftain of the rebellion, are to be held. As the record stands, the rebel government and leaders at Richmond have shown themselves base and cruel enough to be privy to this dastard deed of outrage and murder, but it is difficult to conceive that they were weak enough for that privity. All human experience, the history of all similar crimes, would teach them that this would recoil upon themselves with a terrible vengeance and fearful retribution,—would dishonor them before the world, make them and their cause infamous in the judgment of every civilized government. They must have known, also, all the leaders and people of the rebel states, if not utterly bereft of reason, and blinded by passion, must have perceived and felt that the death of Abraham Lincoln would deprive them of the best and strongest friend they had at the North; of the man whose disposition prompted, and whose office and influence would enable him to secure for them as large a forbearance, as generous and magnanimous a treatment as could possibly be granted to the authors of so much mischief,—the instigators and leaders in a political crime so gigantic in its proportions, its monstrous purpose defeated at such cost of blood and treasure to the nation. No! There must be clearer proof before I can believe that the leaders at Richmond were so weak and bewildered as to be privy to this conspiracy for assassination. There is no heart in the land, I apprehend, to which this terrible event will bring a sharper pang than to that of the President of the Confederate States: a pang not of sympathy, but of fear; because he will read in it the foreshadowing of his own doom, the closing of the gates of mercy against himself, should he ever be brought within the grasp of that government whose laws he has defied, whose liberties he has trampled upon when he could, and whose existence he has attempted to destroy.

But though there were no privity,— and for the honor of our common humanity, I hope it may be clearly shown that there was none,— a fearful responsibility rests upon the rebel leaders and government. This crime, "the deep damnation of this taking off" by assassination, runs back to them by the irresistible logic of cause and effect. It is the natural product of the spirit and principles they have constantly manifested. It is the full and perfect out-flowering of that ignorance and passion, that rancor and hate towards the North which they have studiously endeavored to cherish in the southern heart. It is the last, culminating, decisive testimony to the debasing, morally bewildering, and unhumanizing influence of that institution of slavery which they would have made the corner stone of the political edifice they proposed to rear. The judgment of the world, therefore, the verdict of history, I apprehend, will hold them largely responsible for a deed which secures to its perpetrator an unenviable immortality in the records of crime, gives his name a conspicuous place on the dark list of those around whose memories gather more and more, as the years roll on, the execrations of mankind.

But let us turn from these thoughts. They would come up in my heart; I could not prevent it. But I did not wish to keep them there; I preferred to let them out, and so have given them utterance. We have been stunned by a sudden calamity, and stand aghast at the awful mode of its coming. In the midst of our cheerfulness, under the smiles of a brighter day than we had known for four years, and whose to-morrow promised to be brighter still, we have been suddenly thrown into utter darkness, by the foul murder of the President of the republic. Without warning or preparation, we have been visited by what to our short-sighted wisdom seems an irreparable loss, and in a moment all our joy in "the victory of that day is turned into mourning unto all the people"; and again I urge that our first duty is to turn unto God and be calm, our only strength to have the thought of our hearts and the prayer of our lips, " the Lord's will be done." God is still with us, —here is the great consolation and help of the soul.

> " Human watch from harm can't ward us :
> God will keep, and God will guard us."

Human wisdom, the prophet, the counsellor, the mighty man, may depart; but the wisdom of God abides to illumine a new generation, and to guide his children in the way. From the beginning until now, and especially in the great struggle, which, notwithstanding this sore bereavement, we may still devoutly hope is approaching its conclusion, our land has received so many tokens of the divine favor, that to doubt the guardian care of God, and the merciful purposes of his providence towards this nation and the interests of liberty and humanity, so bound up with its preservation, would be a sin. We may still trust, it is our duty to trust, that behind this dark cloud there is wisely hid some great mercy, which shall one day be revealed amid the adoring acknowledgments of ourselves or our children.

After this trust in God, our next duty is to cherish in grateful reverence the memory of the man and the magistrate whose, to us untimely, fate we mourn, and gather up the lessons which his example teaches and his death enforces. I am not adequate, had I time, for the presentation of the prominent points in his life, or a sharp analysis and delineation of his character. I remember, in the only interview I ever had with him, in the autumn of 1861, at Washington, in company with twenty or thirty other persons, each of whom had his special purpose in the visit, and went up in his turn to present it, that I was at first amused, not to say offended, at what seemed an undignified levity, and a marvellous facility in conveying or enforcing his answers to the various requests presented, by telling some story, the logic of whose application to the case in point was unmistakably clear. During this part of the interview I was led to wonder where was the power? how had this man so impressed himself upon the people of the country, as to be elevated to the position he occupied? That wonder ceased, that inquiry was answered, before I left the presence. A lady made application for the release of her brother, who had been arrested for disloyalty by the major-general commanding in the vicinity of Frederick, Maryland. The President declined to interfere, on the ground that he knew nothing of the circumstances but what she had told him, and that the arrest and detention were, necessarily, within the discretionary power of the major-general commanding in the district. Considerable conversation ensued, and some tears were shed; and, at length, the President consented to indorse upon her petition, which was to be forwarded to the major-general, that he had no objection to the release, provided the general thought it compatible with the public safety. As he gave her back the petition, with this indorsement, he said, and I think I remember very nearly his exact words: "Madam, I desire to say that there is no man who feels a deeper or more tender sympathy than I do, with all cases of individual sorrow, anxiety, and grief like yours, which these unhappy troubles occasion; but I see not how I can prevent or relieve them. I am here to administer this Government, to uphold the Constitution, to maintain the Union of the United States. That is my oath; before God and man, I must, I mean to the best of my ability, to keep that oath; and, however much my personal feelings may sympathize with individual sorrows and anxieties, I must not yield to them. They must all give way before the great public exigencies of the country!" I shall never forget the simple majesty, the grandeur and force with which these few sentences were uttered, or their effect. In a moment the room was as still as death. The little audience that had, just before, been laughing at his stories, were awed and impressed, thrilled through and through by these few solemn and earnest words. They were a revelation of the man. They made me feel that there was a power in him that gave him a right to be where he was. That right he has vindicated more and more every hour since his first inauguration. That he has made no mistakes, that he was at all times superior to the weaknesses of our nature, or the faults of humanity, it would be neither wise nor truthful to maintain. I look for light and explanation to be thrown upon some acts and incidents of his administration; but I have confidence that that light will reveal reasons which will show them to have been wise and right, and establish a patriotic integrity of purpose that will do him honor. In general, the exhibition of himself, made these last four years, is proof to us, and to the world, that he was largely endowed with many large and noble qualities; and for his fidelity in his high office, for his wisdom, firmness, and moderation, for his genuine simplicity and homely ways, for his tenderness and compassion, his watchful guardianship of the great interests of liberty, and all his incalculable services to the country, which he has done as much as any man to save, I hold him in grateful reverence and honor; and now that he has fallen, a noble martyr to a noble cause, coming generations will rise up, and bless his name, which will grow grander and brighter through all coming time, and stand highest among the names of those whom the world cannot afford to forget. In some lines from Tennyson's Ode on the Duke of Wellington, I find the most fitting description of his character and our duty to his memory:

> "O, friends! our chief State oracle is mute;
> Mourn for the man of long-enduring blood,
> The statesman, moderate, wise, resolute,
> Whole in himself, a common good.
> Mourn for the man of amplest influence,
> Our greatest, yet with least pretence,
> Rich in saving common sense,
> And, as the greatest only are,
> In his simplicity, sublime.
> O voice, from which their omens all men drew,
> O iron nerve, to true occasion true,
> O fallen at length that tower of strength,
> Which stood four square to all the winds that blew.
> His life was work, his language rife
> With rugged maxims hewn from life,
> His voice is silent in your council hall
> Forever; and whatever tempests lower
> Forever silent; even if they broke
> In thunder, silent; yet remember all
> He spoke among you, and *the man who spoke*."

But there is other work for us than remembrance. We may not dwell always on the past. The exigencies of the country, the duties of patriotism, the calls to be faithful in the great struggle to which the nation has been summoned, and which is not yet ended, these abide; and the national calamity over which we mourn should be in all our hearts a quickening incentive to persevering effort. "God buries his workmen, but carries on his work." The individual dies, the generations pass; but the interests of humanity remain, and the nation continues. Abraham Lincoln is dead. Peace be to his memory, and immortal his fame. But the President of the United States still lives, the embodiment of the nation's life and power; and the first duty of patriotism now,— the duty to which this open grave around which the nation is standing gives a mighty emphasis,— is to gather around that President, and by the fresh, earnest, manly expression of our sympathy and confidence, give him strength and assurance for the high duties he is suddenly called to discharge. There is one dark hour, which he perhaps remembers with a keener sorrow than any of us. Is not a ray of light thrown upon that hour by recent events? What one conspirator accomplished by a fatal pistol-shot, may not another in another instance have attempted through the poisoner's drugs, so that an incident of the fourth of March last, especially when the subsequent illness and prostration are considered, ought in justice perhaps to be interpreted not as a personal fault, but the crime of others? This is clear: we are not to confound an accident with a habit, and our first duty— the first duty of the nation— is to let the new

President see that it remembers only, and recalls with grateful confidence, his undaunted loyalty, his noble efforts, his patriotic labors and sacrifices from the beginning of the war until now. As yet, he is to a certain extent an unknown quantity to us, as Abraham Lincoln was four years ago. It depends largely upon us, the people, to afford the elements that shall solve the problem, and determine what this unknown quantity is, its value and its power. Let the new President feel that he has the respect and confidence of the people, and it will help mightily to make him and keep him worthy of them. Let him feel that he has the respect and confidence of the people and it will be to him a great power, whereby to maintain the honor and glory, to secure the peace and prosperity of the nation.

In conclusion, my friends, let me urge you to a personal improvement of this solemn event. While it reveals to us the depths of wickedness and of moral madness into which the soul may be plunged, it gives an impressive emphasis to the injunction, "Be ye also ready, for in such an hour as ye think not the Son of Man cometh." Of what awaits us beyond the present moment, we know with certainty but this one thing — death. Exalted station, important services, noble usefulness, the charge of public trusts and interests of unspeakable magnitude, these nor aught else can avail to stay the hand or avert the blow of death. In his presence and before his power there is a stern and solemn equality of all men. All must die. But how, or when, or where? All inquiry is baffled, speculation is vain, reasoning at fault. In apparent peril, we escape;

seemingly secure, we fall. The President at Richmond, we feared. It was an exposure, but a beautiful and touching drama. Returned to Washington, we breathe freely. He is safe. Nothing can touch him in the capital. But there, unannounced, with no foreshadowing, the destroyer met him; and, in a moment, of all that he had, and of all that he was, nothing is of importance to him, nothing stands him in stead now but his goodness of heart, the simple honesty of faith, through which he sought to do God's will and promote man's good. Our death, the death of any one of us, can never attract the attention, or be the great public event his was, but to ourselves personally it will be more important and solemn; and, like his, may come suddenly, when we least expect it. By holiness of heart and life, by consecration of ourselves through faith in our Lord Jesus Christ to great purposes for which he suffered and died, by a daily walk in the light of his truth and the culture of his spirit, let us be ever ready, so that life, if prolonged, may be noble, useful, holy; and death, when it comes, may be gain, — the gain of heaven and immortality.

REV. EDWARD E. HALE.

23

1 *CORINTHIANS XV:* 57.

Who giveth us the Victory through our Lord Jesus Christ.

The contrasts of Passion Week are those of human triumph, of death in agony, and of Eternal Life.

The week begins with the Sunday of victory, — Palm Sunday, — when the Lord rides in triumph into the city. From day to day the triumph takes different forms, till on Friday the whole changes. His life ends at the hands of treachery and murder. Then comes the last of Jewish Sabbaths, — that Saturday sad beyond words. And then on this first day of the week, He rises: all the chains of earth are broken forever; and, from that moment, man knows he is immortal. Human triumph! Then, death in agony! Then, the unveiling of Eternal Life. These are our contrasts. Hidden in them are our lessons. Never since has the world needed them as we need them this day!

Of their Sunday of triumph we cannot paint the picture, without recalling their year, as it had gone by. These apostles, who could not understand, could feel and wonder. They had walked up and down through the cities of Israel. They had proclaimed the new kingdom. They had named the King. Nay, they had heard him sometimes make fit promise of his empire. He had spoken of it as the one thing certain. He had laid down its constitution and laws. At his word thousands had followed. To his word thousands had listened. At his word, again, the multitudes had melted away. The very voice of God had testified that here was God's beloved Son.

Yet there was, till now, no sign of empire! He would not give a sign. If he fed these thousands, it was that they might leave him. His prophet, John, had been beheaded by a tyrant. His own overtures to the rulers had been rejected with scorn. We can imagine then the darkness which brooded over even the faithful's faith, till the Sunday of victory came. Then, after such anxiety, all seems changed. They have endured to the end. Surely now they are safe. Hosanna! hosanna! Victory! victory! Even the capital has opened its gates to us. Here are coming out its very children, with their palms and their songs. "The Son of David! The Son of David! Hosanna! hosanna! Blessed is he that cometh in the name of the Lord! Hosanna in the highest!" Thus the week begins.

Easy to picture such exultant joy, when seen on a background of a year's defeat, anxiety, long-suffering, and gloom.

Nor, as the week goes by, does their mood change. True, the capital can open its gates but once. There can be but one triumphal entry. When the enemy sur-

renders Sunday, he cannot surrender again on Monday.
But the week seems victory! Speculators and brokers
are driven, crestfallen, from the temple. The lovers of
the nation's enemies follow them, — the Herodians. The
lovers of wealth; they are driven out also, set to scorn,
— the Sadducees. The hypocrites who exalt themselves and curse the people, all are rebuked in turn, —
the Pharisees. "Lord, what shall be the sign of thy
coming?" That question is key-note to the apostles'
feeling, when the eve of Friday comes.

And then, victory is changed in a moment into
treachery, blood, and death!

Of his feelings we can say nothing but what he tells
us. There is no likeness which we can compare to him.
But, his enemies: ah, wicked men and mean men are
so common, that we have seen them with these eyes.
Whether they deal with the son of God, or whether they
work in some mean cabal of their own lust, they are
always the same. What the soldiery of Herod could
not do; what the officers of Caiaphas could not compass;
what Pilate was not mean enough to descend to, —
could be wrought out, when that fatal Friday came, by
this coward Judas, with his midnight kiss. Of Judas,
the world has never known precisely what was his
fate, or what his character; whether he were finished
villain, or whether he were fanatic fool. Satan chooses
such accomplices. Such tool served the purpose
of crafty Caiaphas; and, by the work of such tool,
even the Lord of Life can be betrayed. They seize
him; they lead him out to Calvary; they kill him,
the world's best friend; nay, their best friend, if they

knew it; the only friend in the Universe of God, who, at that hour, was seeking to save them. So that never were words so terribly true as the words of his prayer, — "they know not what they do." From the terrible retribution which came upon them so soon; the retribution in which women drank the blood of their own infants; in which brothers fought brothers to the death, in the ruins of their own temple, — he whom that day they slew was the only being who could have saved them. And so, praying for them, he died.

And his mother and his well-beloved crept out from their hiding-places, and wept over him! And they laid him in a tomb, wherein never man lay. And his enemies sealed the stone with such cements as man can devise; and set over it such sentry police as Roman wit in arms had trained. And then came the Sabbath, — the Jewish Sabbath, the last day of the week; — saddest of days till then.

"Is this the end?" we can almost hear Nathaniel saying to Philip; "better I had staid brooding under my fig-tree; my poet-dreams, so vague and dim, were yet better than this horrid certainty!" "Is this the end?" might Andrew say to Simon Peter; "better we had swept the lake, — better traded fish in the market-place our lives long, than come to look on such horror!" "Is this the end?" might John, son of Thunder, say to his fierce, brother James. "Better had we cast in our lot with Theudas, rushed on the Roman spear and shield, and died in fight like men!" "Is this the end?" might Mary mother, whisper; "better had my child died in his infant innocence, when Herod slew the others in Bethlehem." But no, this is not the end.

"Lo, I am with you always, even unto the end of the world."

"The works that I do, shall he do also; and greater works than these shall he do."

Such is the promise. And when the sad Saturday has at last crept by; and when the light of this darker morning just begins to break; when, on that night, so cold, and black, there just creeps up the ray of promise, lo, it is a blush of hope! The grave cannot hold him. These keepers fall fainting on the ground. This man-sealed rock rolls, tottering, from its bed. And he is risen! as he said.

He was the well beloved Son of God. Yes; and we are all God's children. Children of God's nature,— and therefore immortal, as is he. We are his children. Children? Yes! and therefore he gives to us the victory.

God is with us, and we are with him. Therefore there is no death to us, nor to his purpose failure. It may please him to call away even our Saviour from our sight. But if he goes away, the Holy Spirit comes! It may please him to bring in his kingdom, as Israel has not dreamed. But, none the less certainly, does his kingdom come! It may please him to win that victory by the Saviour's death on Calvary; nay, to give to a dying thief at his Saviour's side the first laurels of triumph. The victory may be won when Stephen faints; when James is beheaded; when Paul and Barnabas are stoned. But none the less is it victory! It is not upon fields of battle only that he asks for his martyrs. At the hands of Herod, dying of lust, he will call away St. James. At the wish of a dancing harlot, will John Baptist give his head. But they are martyrs still! And when their Master dies, because he has given a Judas the access to his person; when, on the morning of this " day of days," he rises; to all such martyrs, nay to all God's martyrs in all time, — to all their brethren — nay, to all his brethren, in all time, — God promises, that, while they will and do of his good pleasure, He will give to them the victory!

[The choir then sang the anthem, by Rev. Henry Ware: "Lift your glad voices in triumph on high." After the anthem, Mr. Hale said:]

I cannot think that it is necessary for me to try to illustrate the lesson of scripture. The contrasts which we have been tracing in the history, as we might have traced them last year or any year since that history passed, teach us the lessons of to-day, so that we cannot fail to learn them. We often tell you from the pulpit that there is no experience of your lives, however glad or however painful, however great or however small, for which you do not find fit lesson in these experiences of your Saviour's life. I do not know whether you always believe this. But I am sure you feel it and believe it in the great trial of to-day,— in these terrible contrasts of the week that has gone by. Sunday, our day of triumph: and, Monday, again, we thronged the temple here with our praises. Each day, a new victory; each day a new congratulation; till, when Thursday came, — the fast day of our old Puritan calendar, — we did not know whether fasting belonged to us. Could the children of the bride-chamber fast indeed? Who were we that we should condescend to fasting and humiliation?

My friends! in the few words which I spoke to you on that day, — the last words which I spoke to you before this morning, — I said that Christian humiliation and Christian thanksgiving belonged together. We gave God the glory, which we dared not claim ourselves. "When I am weak, then I am strong." That is the Christian's ejaculation, and on that Thursday of victory and thanksgiving, it was very easy for us to repeat it!

It ought to be as easy to repeat it to-day! Would God it were! Fasting and rejoicing are strangely mingled indeed to-day. The day of a nation's grief is the day of the church's rejoicing. Fittest day of all, indeed, for the day of such grief; for, but for this resurrection, this immortality of which to-day is token and symbol, such grief were intolerable! But for to-day's promise of victory, what should we have worth living for? It is not simply that this day assures us of the immortal life of the good, great man, who, in an instant, puts off this mortal body that he may put on his spiritual body. It is not simply that to-day tells us all is well with him. It is to the country, which he loved and served, that to-day, in its promises, gives a like assurance. That death has no power over the immortal spirit; that is the lesson of to-day. That Jesus Christ gives victory to his flock, in giving them the help, comfort, and blessing of the Most High; that promise is sealed to-day. That the eternal laws of God reign in men's affairs, and that men may trust him if they strive to follow those laws; that is the promise of his victory. That the republic is eternal if it makes itself a part of his kingdom. If its laws conform to his laws, no cerements can bind it, and no tombs can hold it. If it serve God, God gives to it immortality.

I dare not trust myself to speak a word regarding this simple, godly, good, great man, who, in a moment, has been called from the rule over a few cities to be master over many things, in that higher service where he enters into the joy of his Lord. To speak of him I must seek some other hour. Our lesson for to-day is, that the kingdom of God comes, and is eternal. The republic, if in simple faith it strive to make itself a part of that kingdom, lives forever. When we built this church, four years ago, we painted here upon the wall before you the beginning of the angels' song, in the words:

"Glory to God in the highest."

It was in the very outset of war; our own boys were coming home to us bleeding from the field, or were lying dead after the battle. And we stayed our hands at those words. We did not add the other words of the promise. But when last Sunday came, with its glad tidings, when it seemed as if we had endured to the very end, we ventured, in the fulfilment of the glad prophecy, to complete our imperfect inscription, and to add here the rest of the blessed legend:

"And on earth peace, good will toward men."

The martyrdom of Good Friday does not make us veil the motto, though we read it through our tears. Of such martyrs, it is as true as ever, that their blood is the seed of the church. Because they die, the kingdom comes! We do not forego our hope in the promise, "On earth peace, and good will among men." The President may be killed to-morrow, and his successor may be killed to-morrow, and his successor, and his; but the republic lives! While it seeks to do God's will, to will and to do of his good pleasure, He works with it, and gives it immortality. "Fear not little flock, it is your Father's good pleasure to give you the kingdom."

REV. A. A. MINER.

24

PSALMS LXXXIX: 18.

The Lord is our Defence, and the Holy One of Israel is our King.

Most welcome truth when the current of events seems sweeping us away. Scarce two short weeks ago, powerful armies were watching each other at the gates of the rebel capital, as a beast of prey watches his victim. The invincible army of Northern Virginia had been assailed in the terrible battles of the Wilderness, had been forced to retreat, day by day, until they were driven within their intrenchments at Richmond, and, for nearly a year, had been held in the mortal grasp of the Federal power. By a constant tension of forces, and a steady pressure of military vigor, our Lieutenant-General had extended his left, threatening the rebel communications, until Petersburg and Richmond became untenable, and the news of their hasty evacuation, leaving behind five hundred guns and vast military stores, filled the whole North with joy and exultation.

Hotly pursued by the cavalry of the eagle-eyed Sheridan, the retreating hosts were harassed on their flank and rear, depleted in numbers, despoiled of their weapons and supplies, broken in spirit, and compelled to surrender, as prisoners, an instalment of a half dozen major-generals and thirteen thousand men. It was a prophecy of what a few days more of unflinching purpose would accomplish upon the foe.

Scarcely had the echoes of this triumph died away, when the stillness of our Sabbath evening was broken by the news of final and triumphant victory in the capitulation of the rebel commander, and of all that remained of his traitorous hordes. From within the city of Richmond, our noble President sent despatches to Washington, assuring the country that the rebel stronghold had surrendered, that the boastful army of treason had become a humbled fugitive, and, at length, a subdued and prostrate captive. Joy was unbounded. Gratitude surged in our hearts, like the heavy swell of the sea. Spontaneous assemblies burst forth in praise, rent the air with their acclamations, and pledged anew, everlasting fidelity to country and to God.

But, while the glorious hope of coming peace and of universal freedom was gladdening our dreams, we were aroused by another voice. Our noble President is dead, — died suddenly, — died by the hand of the foul assassin, — died surrounded by his friends, and in a public place. Terrible is the revulsion of feeling occasioned by this event. The public heart is paralyzed. We are cast down from the very summit of joy into the deep abyss of grief. Oh, how changed the aspect of the country! Yesterday we were strong in the confidence we reposed in the best of earthly rulers. To-day man seems as nothing; less than a feather borne on by the breeze. We involuntarily feel after the Unseen. We listen for the echo of Jehovah's footsteps along the hillsides of our country. An audible voice from the heavens seems to say, "Be still, and know that I am God."

It were vain, in this hour of excitement, to attempt a delineation of the good man's life. Born in a State which could by no means claim to be in the van of our civilization, of parentage in the narrowest circumstances, with only the rudest and most meagre instrumentalities for culture at command, he acquired but a very inadequate education whether general or professional, and entered upon the practice of the law. In the great school of life he soon rose to eminence in his calling; and the people of Illinois, in an hour of sharp political conflict, called him to bear up the standards of liberty. It was by his famous senatorial contest with the late Hon. Stephen A. Douglas for the championship of the State, that he became most favorably known to the country at large. They were accustomed to meet assembled multitudes, and, face to face, on the same day, canvass the principles to which they were respectively consecrated. I well recollect how deeply at the time I was impressed on reading those debates in a western paper, by the tone of candor exhibited by Mr. Lincoln, by his great tact in the conduct of his argument, as well as by his shrewdness of retort and quaintness of reply. The *argumentum ad hominem* was a favorite instrument with him, and was rarely employed in vain. His fulness of anecdote, so effective in quickening the pulse and cheer-

24*

ing the heart, served a most valuable ulterior end, in compassing all the elements of a forcible argument, and carrying deep conviction to his auditory.

It was from the conspicuous position he had thus gained, that he was called, in the providence of God, to the first place in the gift of the nation. You remember the great enthusiasm of the people as they skirted his pathway from Illinois to Washington. You remember his hair-breadth escape from the hand of the assassin as he passed through the notorious city of Baltimore. You remember the surprise of the dignitaries at the capital of the nation when they awoke of a morning, and found the "coming man" already there. You remember the meekness with which he has borne himself through these four long years of fratricidal strife. You have observed his condescension to all classes of persons, official and private, high and low, rich and poor, learned and ignorant, white and black.

Nor is our admiration of this great man excited alone by his private walk and bearing. To the virtues of temperance, integrity, and honor, he has added the example of magnanimous and lawful rule. True, great needs have compelled great sacrifices, and we have reared our hecatombs of slain, and have poured our treasures without stint into the seething caldron of this rebellion. Great dangers have called for unusual measures,—unusual in a country where peace is indigenous, and the citizens are strangers to the arts of war. But these have all been lawful and just. Whatever have been our judgments in the past, the voice of calumny, at home and abroad, is now hushed forever; and craven monarchs, strangers to his virtues, will henceforth sing

> "He
> Hath borne his faculties so meek, hath been
> So clear in his great office, that his virtues
> Will plead like angels, trumpet-tongued, against
> The deep damnation of his taking off."

But this crime is not solitary. The bayoneting of our colored prisoners of war, the tortures of death by slow starvation, the stripping of prisoners and exposing them to death by cold, the converting of the bones of the dead into amulets, the hanging of inoffensive citizens for opinion's sake, and a thousand other untold enormities, bear it dreadful company. The foul institution of slavery is the accursed mother of them all.

Not only is this crime not solitary, but it is not the crime of a single man. Whether the recognized conspirators are few or many, the animus of the assassin's blow flows from a million hearts. It is found in that wide-spread disloyalty that has brought upon the nation all the woes of a protracted civil war. The crime itself is but a single drop of the spray from the topmost wave of the rebellion.

Hence it is a crime of startling magnitude. Loved as was our revered Chief Magistrate, an assault upon him is an assault upon the nation's heart. The constitutional head of the government, the executive power centred in his hands. The vast responsibility of our military and naval operations; the condition of our internal relations, not undisturbed by the Indian tribes upon our borders;

our judicial, postal, financial, and industrial affairs; and especially the delicate and difficult duties growing out of our foreign relations, — all demanded, and received, his most careful and candid thought. The protection we enjoy in our homes, the continuous workings of our institutions, and the security we feel for the future, are all promoted by the fidelity of our now-lamented President. To twenty millions of people he has been a leader in the darkest hour of civil war; to four millions more he has been a deliverer from the infuriated oppressor; to yet eight millions more he has been an unrecognized saviour from utter extermination by their own suicidal passions. When the assassin deals a blow at such a man, and breaks into the citadel of life, he deals, at the same time a blow at the life of the nation itself, and, consequently, at the liberty and justice and equality which the nation represents. Such an act is most damningly infamous in the eyes of men, and inexpressibly blasphemous in the eyes of God. Unhappy city that gave the assassin birth! The home of disorder, the nursery of rioters, the shelterer of those murderers that shed the first Massachusetts blood in this great struggle, and now the mother of the nation's parricide! Pity, oh, pity unhappy Baltimore!

Such a crime naturally begets sad apprehensions. It breaks down our confidence and stuns the public heart. It distracts and confuses the public mind. It produces a chaotic state of feeling incompatible with the duties of the hour, and unfavorable to unity of effort. The executive chair being vacant, some may fear that the affections of the nation will not so warmly welcome another occupant, especially as he will be a Southern man. The blindness of the South may give new sustenance to the rebellion, and the leaders may be inspired (the Satanic influence seems sufficiently potent) to renewed and more vigorous efforts, taxing the energies and still further trying the patience of the loyal men of the land. The news of such a crime may unfavorably influence foreign governments. They little appreciate the unguarded freedom with which our magistrates mingle with the people. They may not at once comprehend that this enormous crime is as foreign to the genius of our government and to the spirit of the loyal North, as is the accursed institution that inspired it. England may forget her gunpowder-plot of two hundred and fifty years ago, aimed at the destruction of the king and the whole parliament, and defeated alone by one of the conspirators desiring to save a Romish lord. She may forget the unsuccessful attempts made upon the life of her noble Queen. France may forget that her military Emperor has been a target for the assassin's pistol. And, forgetting those and the like transactions, they may find it convenient to consider this great crime as a peculiar symptom of Democratic turbulence, and thus construct it into a barrier against Democratic tendencies in their own lands. There *may* be new danger of foreign complications on another ground. Murder knows no rank. Murderers at St. Albans, fleeing to Canada, have been treated simply as raiders and belligerents. Should the assassins at Washington make a similar escape, and find a similar welcome, what can save us from a new and terrible conflict? These and like considerations will have different degrees of weight in different minds.

For myself, I turn to the future full of hope. Dark as were the heavens yesterday, already the clouds begin to lift. The people will rally from this stunning blow; not simply to the level of their former purpose, but to a more discerning and a more determined purpose. The probable comprehensiveness of the conspiracy is baffled. However it may have aimed at the heads of several of the departments, it counts but a single victim; others escaping by a seeming interposition of providence, impressing us with the truth that "the Lord is our defence; and the Holy One of Israel our king."

Perhaps we were in danger of forgetting this. The rebellion was manifestly waning: apparently breaking up. We had out-numbered the rebels, out-generalled them, out-flanked them, out-witted them, and whipped them. Were we not too confidently feeling that we owed it all to a few *men?* Was not our trust too much in man, too little in God? Did we sufficiently remember that the "Holy One of Israel is our King?"

Perhaps, also, we were too little disposed to be thorough in our work. The well-defined labor of war appears to be chiefly past. The difficult, the untried, the unprecedented task of re-construction is before us. Perhaps we had not the nerve for it; were not equal to the stern work of dealing with arch-traitors, of meting out punishment to leading rebels, and hanging wholesale murderers, as we would those of less criminality. Who can say that we have not had a lesson on this point? Who can deny that the magnanimity we were cherishing has received a severe shock, and that we have been made to feel that we should deal with great villains as certainly as with small offenders, and far more severely? Some of our cotemporaries may, indeed, invoke endless perdition on the heads of these assassins of a nation's life; and they as richly deserve it as mortals can. But between endless ruin and absolute exemption from punishment, there is a very broad margin within which the line of duty *may* fall; and when we remember the very general inclination of the people, the various sects of religionists included, to mitigate the punishment provided by *human* laws, thus showing, on a broad scale, the popular notion of justice unwarped by religious theories, such inclination may be regarded, within certain limits, as the voice of God, who always mingles mercy with judgment. Let us, then, with one voice, grant forgiveness to the ignorant and deluded, but now repentant masses, and demand expatriation or death for the ambitious, crafty, and fiendish leaders. Thus may we teach all future traitors the hazards of their enterprise, and their probable doom.

However such matters may be adjusted, let us not doubt that the people of this widely extended country will prove even more determined than ever. The institutions of the land have lost none of their preciousness. They are not weakened by this sad event. The assassination of our honored President shocks all our hearts; but it gives no shock to the machinery of government. All the heads of departments, and every member of Congress might be cut off, and we should spring to our feet, extemporize another government, and demonstrate to the world that we live in institutions rather than in men.

Why, indeed, should we be apprehensive? The army remains intact. Our military successes, under God, will continue. Our Lieutenant-General has been thoroughly proved, and bears with him the entire confidence of the nation. His forces are now within supporting distance of each other, while the army of treason is shorn of half its numbers, besides being dispirited and broken. Having accomplished so much, with the blessing of God, how can we fail to finish the work? If there has ever been an hour when we have faltered in our purpose, that hour has now gone by. Henceforth we are a unit, whose energies are consecrated to the most patriotic service.

And shall we not find a satisfactory leader in our new, let me say, God-given President. It is true he is as yet untried. But four years ago Abraham Lincoln was untried; and the trial has endeared him to all hearts — has called forth a nation's gratitude in his re-election to the highest office in our gift, and made his death the occasion of a deeper and more general sorrow than we had ever before known. Who can say that his mantle has not fallen on one altogether worthy of it? President Johnson, though untried in that office, is not unknown to the country. Through a long public career, his fidelity has been unquestioned. Born and reared in the midst of slavery, he knows its baneful influence and its crushing power. Cherishing in purest affection the Union and Liberty, he has felt the iron of secession enter his soul. Acquainted minutely and in detail with the spirit and purpose of the rebel leaders, he may be better prepared than Mr. Lincoln himself to estimate their deep demerit, and mete to them the meed of justice as traitors before the law.

It is narrated of Mr. Johnson that, in October last, on an occasion of addressing some thousands of colored people in the city of Nashville, if I remember correctly, he exhorted them to patience, and assured them that God would raise up for them a Moses to lead them out of the wilderness. His auditors shouted, "You shall be our Moses!" Mr. Johnson modestly replied that he was not equal to so important a labor. But they repeated their claim, "You shall be our Moses; we want no other than you." "Well, then," said Mr. Johnson, "I will be your Moses." Was this incident prophetic?

I have rejoiced that our merchants and men of business, both in Boston and New York, have made haste to give him assurances of confidence and support. He will be surrounded, I trust, by the same experienced advisers who have stayed up the hands of his predecessor, and can command the same resources, and the support of the same constituency, as have borne us through the storm of the last four years. Shall we not all welcome him, then, to our hearts, and pray the blessing of God to be with him?

These are grave experiences through which our nation is passing. The discipline of a life-time is condensed into the lessons of an hour. The significance of all history from the beginning of the world is in the events of the last few days. Can these events fail to bring us profit? Can we fail to discern the dangers whence we are escaping; the deep wickedness whence they sprang? Can they fail to snatch us out of the ruts of custom and of customary prejudices, and to teach us, mid the sharp chastisements of the Divine hand, the dignity and the glory of right, and the fearfulness of injustice and wrong? Can they fail to purify the nation's heart, and enlarge the promise of its coming glories? Will they not tone down the rebellion itself, and make the leaders turn back from their purpose as from a fathomless abyss?

Who shall assign limits to the providential blessings which late events, victorious and tragic, may be made to yield? A transcendently good man has been taken from us; but other good men remain. Since " God is our defence," since " the Holy One of Israel is our King," we may affirm his continuous watchcare. The very existence of our nation seems providential. The great eras in our history reveal the divine purpose. But no period is equally instructive with that of the last four years. No work is more important or glorious than the emancipation of the slaves. No agent has been more conspicuously providential than Abraham Lincoln himself. Startling, then, as is the manner of his death, who will exclude the event from the overrulings of the divine hand?

> " God moves in a mysterious way,
> His wonders to perform."

Providence does not skip events, or omit opportunities. If the crucifixion of our Lord, through the malignities of the Jewish hierarchy, is made a means of the salvation of the world, is it too much to hope that the death of Abraham Lincoln, through agencies not less malignant, may be overruled to the good of our deeply afflicted country? Called from us at the culmination of his fame, he may be more to us in the coming years, than he could have been had he still tarried in the flesh. He died as a martyr dies.

> "The voice at midnight came;
> He started up to hear:
> A mortal arrow pierced his frame;
> He fell, but felt no fear.
> * * * * *
> "His spirit, with a bound,
> Burst its encumbering clay;
> His tent, at sunrise, on the ground,
> A darkened ruin lay."

Bowing here, at the altar of God, shall we not renew our zeal in the great cause of liberty and righteousness? Standing upon those principles, which are the foundation of our national edifice, shall we not hold ourselves ready for every needed sacrifice, of time, of ease, of resources, of sweet life itself, if we may perpetuate the blessings which have been transmitted to us? Especially should you, young men, and particularly those of you, who, through liberal culture, are seeking fields of widest usefulness, enter in at the open door of opportunity, which the new order of things proffers you. A nation waits your service. Our country calls for help. "The Holy One of Israel" sanctions the call. In patriotic devotion, then, consecrate yourselves anew to the good of man and the glory of God.

REV. JAMES REED.

ADDRESS.*

The event which calls us together is unprecedented in the history of our country. It seems almost incredible that in this nineteenth century of the Christian era, and in this land of free self-government, so horrible a deed could have been perpetrated, as that which has taken from us, almost in an instant, our beloved and honored President. War is bad enough. It is tolerated by well-disposed men, only as a painful necessity. The nature and condition of mankind at present are such, that, so far as we can judge, certain evils cannot be removed without it; and, as we have lately had abundant opportunity to prove, individuals may be actively engaged in it without any revengeful or unkindly feelings. Yet, war, at best, is bad enough, and every good man must rejoice when its ends have been successfully accomplished, and a genuine peace is the result of it. But there are no terms too scathing to designate the bloody work of the assassin. It seems to be the very sum and substance of human wickedness. The blood

* Delivered Wednesday, April 19, 1865.

in our veins runs cold, as we read the harrowing details, — how the villain, armed to the teeth, pursues his innocent and unsuspecting victim; watches his opportunity from day to day, and from hour to hour; then approaches him stealthily from behind, and, all unseen, inflicts the fatal wound. When at last, rejoicing in his infamy, he shrieks out his exultant motto, it does, indeed, appear as if hell itself had broken loose, and were enjoying a momentary triumph.

The unparalleled atrocity of the crime is heightened in the present instance by its striking contrast with the character of its victim. However much many may have differed from him on questions of political expediency, all men bear witness to his singular purity and tenderness of heart. If he had been capable of intrigue and violence, — if he had shown signs of a vindictive and unforgiving temper, — this deed, terribly dark at best, would not have shown in such appalling blackness. But it is probable that he who was thus remorselessly shot down had not a single unkind feeling towards any one, The saying is in everybody's mouth, that those, on whose behalf this villany was done, have lost thereby their best friend.

At this very moment the funeral obsequies are progressing at the capital of the nation; and, by official invitation, all churches and denominations are contributing their part towards them. It is for this purpose that we have now assembled here.

There is no reason why we may not perform all the essential part of a funeral service. To be sure, the remains of the illustrious deceased are not with us.

But that matters not. He who considers the subject will see, that the religious exercises in connection with a burial are never for the sake of him who has gone, but solely for those who remain. The departed spirit stands in need of nothing which men can do for him. He is entering upon a new and active life in the spiritual world. He has left his material body behind him. It is a matter of concern to him no longer. Nor are the realities of his spiritual existence in any way affected by the eulogies or prayers which may be uttered in this world. But if by means of them those who listen are lifted up to a higher and better state, so that they can more clearly

> "Assert eternal Providence,
> And justify the ways of God to men,"

then surely the services have fulfilled their legitimate purpose. Hence it makes no difference whether the corpse is present or not. The religious exercises can be just as real and useful without it as with it.

It is a doctrine of the New Church that the Lord is Love itself, and Wisdom itself; and has created all things from Divine Love by Divine Wisdom. Because He is Love itself, therefore has He created human beings to the end that they may become angels of heaven, and be conjoined with him in eternal blessedness. The infinite love yearned for that on which it could be bestowed, and by which it could be reciprocated; and man was created. But, inasmuch as freedom is the indispensable condition of all genuine reciprocal love and all true happiness, therefore the

Lord made man a free agent; and His constant effort with regard to him is to lead him to shun evil and do good in freedom. Yet he may abuse his freedom, and act in opposition to the Lord's wishes; and so obtain eternal misery instead of blessedness.

If we bear in mind this great principle, that the Divine Providence has for its object a heaven of angels from the human race, we can understand, in a general way, all the Lord's dealings with men. By means of the various events which befall them from sources beyond their control, He designs to bring them into the highest degree of happiness which they are capable of. "The Divine Providence looks to eternal things; and no otherwise to things temporal, than as far as they agree with things eternal." The Lord's view of events is not limited and contracted like ours. Not only does He look infinitely beyond the present moment, but, in all that He provides or permits, He has regard to the effect which is to be produced on every human being. We may truly say, therefore, that no event can come to pass except in the precise way which is best calculated to benefit all who are in any degree affected by it, either directly or indirectly, now or hereafter. The only condition imposed upon us is, that we should freely make use of the providential opportunities which, in His infinite wisdom, our heavenly Father offers. Unless we do so, we throw away the benefit which forms the chief part of His merciful designs.

Accordingly, even this barbarous and inhuman work of the assassin has been divinely permitted for the good of our beloved country and of the whole human race, to the end of time.* By means of it, each and all of us may be strengthened. if we will, for the heavenly journey. As for him who has been struck down, we cannot doubt that he, in his new abode, is inspired with the same trust in Providence which was so conspicuous a trait of his character while he was in the flesh. Nor can we doubt that he is able to see more plainly, by far, than he could here, the reasons why Providence leads mankind through such strange and devious paths.

The Lord, I say, has permitted this shocking deed. But let us remember that He has not caused it. He is the cause of no evil whatsoever. But all evil has its origin in man himself, and is occasioned by the abuse or perversion of his divinely given freedom. No belief could be more false, than that the Lord put it into the heart of the murderer to do this thing. On the contrary, His infinite love was extended over him, as it is over all of us, to lead him to put away the fiendish lust and thought which impelled him to the fiendish act. But he would not yield to any divine or heavenly influence, working within and upon him. He listened to the voice of hell in preference to that of heaven. And the Lord, knowing what was best for all concerned, interposed with none of those events, which we call accidents, but permitted him to carry out his bloody purpose. The successful villany is no more wicked in itself than if it had been unsuccessful. As far as the spiritual condition of the criminal is affected, it is no worse than if his plot had failed. The murderer of the President is no more worthy of condemnation than the would-be murderer of the Secretary of State. But as for the results, reaching far beyond the deed itself and the doer of it, what a wondrous difference! Who can measure them? Who can conceive of them? Who can adequately estimate them even during the past week, if we take into account nothing more than what we have seen in our own immediate community? And who can doubt that the Lord of love and mercy is directing, and will direct, them to His own infinite purposes?

That our heavenly Father provides good, and good only, for all of His children, must be clear to those who regard Him as infinitely good and wise. That at the same time He permits the existence of certain evils, is evident from the simple fact that they exist; for how could this be without His permission?

It is a somewhat striking fact that the day on which this terrible deed was perpetrated, is celebrated by the greater part of the Christian world as the anniversary of the Lord's crucifixion. The Sabbath following is, in like manner, supposed to be the anniversary of His resurrection. It matters little whether these suppositions are correct or not. The great truth remains the same, that the Lord was crucified, and that he rose again. So too, there is no event, however dark and sorrowful, which has not, if we but use it rightly, its day of resurrection, in which it re-appears, not in the same form, indeed, but transfigured; its aspect changed from deformity into beauty, from grief into gladness. So are the Lord's doings made acceptable, as well as marvellous, in our eyes.

We may not, and doubtless do not, see clearly why the horrid events of the past week should have taken place. But surely we cannot question the goodness and wisdom of the Lord. We cannot doubt the tender mercy of that Divine Providence which has so wondrously preserved us hitherto, and has apparently brought us to the end of this unnatural and distracting war. Our Heavenly Father is not changeable as we are. If he has been kind in raising up for us a great and good ruler, He has surely been no less kind in suffering him to be removed from us.

Certain it is that our President would never have been taken away, if he had not finished his appointed work. As for that work, the memory of it will live forever. A greater work is seldom performed by a single man. Generations yet unborn will rise up, and call him blessed.

But, as for what remains, the true spiritual welfare of the country and of mankind, requires that it should be done by others. It may be that we need still further discipline and trial before the full measure of national prosperity can be allowed to us. Or it may be that he who was the best leader in time of war is not best fitted for the new exigencies which are arising. We cannot tell now, but we shall know hereafter. Our present duty is to trust. He who has guarded us hitherto will not fail us in the time to come. In the hollow of His hand let us rest, doubting not that if we strive to do our part, He will do His; and though we now are sorrowful, our sorrow shall be turned into joy.

The primary object in such services as these ought unquestionably to be, the effort to see and acknowledge as far as possible the guiding hand of our heavenly

Father. But in the case of a public man, whose obsequies are performed by an entire nation, there is also the further object of paying respect to him and his office. In the present instance, the office has been foully desecrated by the impious hand of violence. For this reason, if for no other, the whole people would rise up as one man in the fury of their indignation. But now we have lost a magistrate, who, to the faithful discharge of his official duties, has added the most endearing of personal characteristics. His uniform gentleness of heart, his almost womanly tenderness, his unaffected frankness of manner, and straight-forward simplicity of speech, have brought him wonderfully near to the hearts of his countrymen. We all feel to-day as if a father had been taken away from us.

I shall not attempt any minute analysis of his character. You all have a clear perception of the man; for it was his nature to make no concealment of himself. Indeed, he was so transparent, that it seems almost as if we had had a personal acquaintance with him, even though we had never seen him. His acts and words show what he was, more plainly than any labored eulogy can do; and I have thought that I could not show forth in any better way his purity of purpose, his disinterested patriotism, his genuine reverence for the Lord and the Word, than by reading to you the inaugural address, which stands, and will forever stand, as his last words to the American people:—

"Fellow-Countrymen:—

"At this second appearing to take the oath of the Presidential office, there is less occasion for an extended address than there was at the first. Then a statement, somewhat in detail, of a course to be pursued, seemed very fitting and proper. Now, at the expiration of four years, during which public declarations have constantly been called forth, on every point and phase of the great contest, which still absorbs the attention and engrosses the energies of the nation, little that is new could be presented.

"The progress of our arms, upon which all else chiefly depends, is as well known to the public as to myself; and it is, I trust, reasonably satisfactory and encouraging to all. With high hope for the future, no prediction in regard to it is ventured. On the occasion corresponding to this, four years ago, all thoughts were anxiously directed to an impending civil war. All dreaded it, all sought to avoid it. While the inaugural address was being delivered from this place, devoted altogether to saving the Union without war, insurgent agents were in the city seeking to destroy it without war; seeking to dissolve the Union and divide the effects by negotiation.

"Both parties deprecated war; but one of them would make war rather than let the nation survive; and the other would accept war rather than let it perish, — and the war came.

"One-eighth of the whole population were colored slaves, not distributed generally over the Union, but located in the southern part of it. These slaves constituted a peculiar and powerful interest. All knew that this interest was, somehow, the cause of the war. To strengthen, perpetuate, and extend this interest was the object, for which the insurgents would rend the Union by war, while government claimed no right to do more than to restrict the territorial enlargement of it. Neither party expected the magnitude or the duration which it has already attained. Neither anticipated that the cause of the conflict might cease, even before the conflict itself should cease. Each looked for an easier triumph and a result less fundamental and astounding. Both read the same Bible, and pray to the same God, and each invokes His aid against the other. It may seem strange that any man should dare to ask a just God's assistance in wringing his bread from the sweat of other men's faces. But let us judge not, that we be not judged. The prayer of both should not be answered. That of neither has been answered fully. The Almighty has his own purposes. " Woe unto the world because of offences; for it must needs be that offences come, but woe to that man by whom the offence cometh." If we shall suppose that American Slavery is one of these offences, which, in the providence of God, must needs come, but which, having continued through His appointed time, He now wills to remove, and that he gives to both North and South this terrible war as the woe due to those by whom the offence came, shall we discern therein any departure from those divine attributes which the believers in a living God always ascribe to Him?

" Fondly do we hope, fervently do we pray, that this mighty scourge of war may speedily pass away. Yet, if God wills that it continue until all the wealth piled by the bondsman's two hundred and fifty years of unrequited toil shall be sunk, and until every drop of blood drawn with the lash shall be paid by another drawn with the sword, as was said three thousand years ago, so still it must be said, that the judgments of the Lord are true and righteous altogether.

"With malice towards none, with charity for all, with firmness in the right, as God gives us to see the right, let us strive on to finish the work we are in, to bind up the nation's wound, to care for him who shall have borne the battle, and for his widow and his orphans, to do all which may achieve and cherish a just and a lasting peace among ourselves and with all nations."

26*

REV. GEO. PUTNAM.

ADDRESS.

What was mortal of Abraham Lincoln, President of the United States, is at this hour being borne to the grave. How are the mighty fallen! He who but yesterday was the top and crown of this vast political fabric, the peer of the world's foremost men and mightiest potentates, stricken by the assassin's hand, has fallen from that great height. His word of power is hushed; his great heart, embracing a nation in its love, has ceased to beat. His body is given back to the dust as it was, and his spirit returneth unto God who gave it; and the man who has filled so large a space in the eye of the world has ceased to be an earthly presence.

The civil and military heads of the nation are burying their chief, at the capital, with such poor earthly pomp as befits his station; and we, who are so far away, yet as near as they in love and grief, do join in the obsequies; we, and twenty millions more, bowing down our heads, as one man, in deepest sorrow and awe; the whole land in mourning; the drapery of woe festooning the breadth of the continent; bell answering to bell, and gun to gun, from tower and town and hill top, from sea to sea; a more than sabbath stillness fallen over all the cities and the plains and the mountain-sides of our vast empire.

Verily, this funeral hour, so observed, is an hour filled with a solemnity, a sublimity, and a pathos, unequalled in all the hours that we have lived, or that our fathers have told us of; and such an one as might scarcely come to us again though we should live for centuries.

It is an hour to be much observed unto the Lord; and it was meet that we should come before his presence, and bow down, and seek his face in submission, in supplication, and in trust, if so be the hour might not pass away without leaving its blessing.

Friends, we will not give these flying moments to the indulgence of our sorrow, nor to vain attempts to express that sorrow. Deep grief does not readily betake itself to words: it rather craves the privilege of silence; and, if forced to speak, it does but stammer in half-thoughts and broken utterance. It is the better way for us, the more manly part, and the more patriotic and more religious, and a worthier tribute to the illustrious dead, to hush down the sobs of grief, and rise up into the realm of more tranquil meditation; to remember the virtues and the services of the departed; to study the lessons that Providence sets for us in his death; and gird ourselves up devoutly, bravely, for the work that is before us.

I will not cumber this day's brief solemnities with any biographical detail or careful analysis. All is said in two words: Abraham Lincoln was a GOOD and a GREAT man. He must have had faults, and he must have committed mistakes, for he was a man. But his worst enemy, — if, indeed, he had any enemy, except his murderer, and those whose system of war, conceived in treason, blazing in rebellion, and graced with thousands of slow murders in the prison-house, has at last inspired the heart and nerved the arm of the assassin, — excepting these, his enemy, if he had one, would not wish to have his faults recounted, here, as it were, beside his opening grave. Therefore, it is no matter that the speaking of these funeral words has fallen to the lot of one who has loved him with such a filial, grateful, and reverent love, as never to have been able to see any faults in him, and who confided in him with such perfect confidence as never to discover his mistakes.

A GOOD man. I catch no voices of dissent on that point, and never did, even in those dark days of national adversity, when the heart of the people seemed to be falling away from him. A conscientious and upright man. Just and true in every known act and word of his life. God-fearing, God-serving; just and faithful; anxious unto prayer to see his duty and to do it. And a warm-hearted man, disinterested, devoted; tender-hearted as a woman, gentle as a child; loving his country with his whole heart, and yet room enough in that heart for kindness to the humblest fellow-creature, and compassion for every sufferer; but with no room for one malignant or vindictive feeling towards his own or even his country's foes. If he could have had a moment's consciousness, after the accursed blow was struck, who will doubt that the sublime words of the

Son of God would have been on his lips and in his heart, "Father, forgive them, for they know not what they do."

This conjunction, of so childish a simplicity, so gentle and unselfish and tender a spirit, with imperial powers and functions, is so new a thing in the history of nations, such a strange spectacle to the world, that the world has not known what to make of it, and has yet to grow up to an appreciation of the unequalled beauty and majesty of it.

A good man, and as great as he was good. I know not that I could tell, if the occasion required it to be told, just wherein his greatness lay, or where was the hiding of his power.

The eye of the nation was first turned to him in that great debate which he conducted in Illinois, some six years ago, against an adversary who was regarded, perhaps, as the ablest and most skilful debater then known in the public councils of the country,—Judge Douglas. In that debate the great issues of the time were entered on fully, and to their utmost depths. Mr. Lincoln bore his part in it with such noble candor and self-possession, such breadth of views, such clearness and power of statement, and such masterly logic, that he became henceforth a marked and representative man, and could never again become anything less.

Since that time, whoso has been left to speak of Mr. Lincoln in slighting terms, as an ordinary man accidentally raised to power, shows himself forgetful, or but poorly read in the forensic history of the few years preceding the war.

Many persons make great account of the manners and personal bearing of eminent men, and not without some reason, for manners are an index of the mind.

In private circles, in hours of social converse and relaxation, there was undoubtedly in the President a freedom and a homeliness of manner, that showed other breeding than that of courts and fashionable assemblies. For he was a genial, humble, kindly man, all undazed by power and place, utterly devoid of egotism, and almost of personal consciousness, and unaffectedly regarding every man he met as his full equal before God. Yet, where or when, in any public place or function has he been found wanting in the stateliness and gravity that befitted his rank?

Our own consummate Everett, himself the embodiment of grace and dignity, has declared, that on the occasion of the funeral solemnities of Gettysburg, where were met together on the platform, and at the table, our own most eminent men, and the ambassadors of foreign courts, there was no man there who bore himself, or was capable of bearing himself, with more propriety and true dignity, than the President. And Goldwin Smith, the candid Englishman, said that not a sovereign in Europe, however trained from the cradle for state pomps, and however prompted by statesmen and courtiers, could have uttered himself more regally than did the plain, republican magistrate, on that solemn occasion.

Passing from mere manners, to official words, I think there is no potentate nor minister of state living, or who has lived in this century, who has spoken so many words so terse, so strong, so genuine, that history will make imperishable, as has Abraham Lincoln. I quote with pleasure the saying, not of an American partisan, but of a cold, critical, unsympathizing Briton, respecting the last inaugural address of the President, that it is "a state paper which for political weight, moral dignity, and unaffected solemnity, has had no equal in our time."

Of those intellectual faculties, which have constituted Mr. Lincoln's greatness in the administration of the Government, I can speak now only in the most general terms. It was not genius, inspiration, brilliancy: no man ever used those words in connection with his name. There was in him, the shrewdest common sense, a deep sagacity intuitive and almost infallible, though not rapid nor flashing. He had a strong grasp of principles, great patience of investigation, and a sound, sure judgment. These are not the shining powers of the human mind; and yet, wherever they are largely possessed, and happily combined and balanced, they go to constitute greatness, and produce the effect of greatness in any sphere of human action. They border close upon the moral qualities, and it has never yet been metaphysically shown to what extent high moral qualities combine with the intellectual ones to strengthen, enlighten, and direct them, so as to produce greatness of thought, action, and result. We cannot define how far a living, sleepless conscience, a sacred, singlehearted regard for truth and right, a fixed devotion to a noble end and purpose, a fervent love of country and of humanity, an unswerving fidelity to trusts, and a devout fear of God;—we cannot tell in what proportions these qualities have contributed to set the stamp of greatness on the name and life of the President. Neither can we so far penetrate the mystery of spiritual laws as to tell how far, or in what way, the spirit of the mighty God, who holds the hearts of all men in his hand, and by whom princes rule, comes to those who piously seek it, and humbly welcome and trust in it, and enters in by its secret course, to inspire, assist, and lead the Lord's anointed in the discharge of their great and solemn function. We only know that the men who have achieved the greatest things in any age, have been those who have been ready to say in such dialect of faith as they had attained to, Not unto us, O, Lord, not unto us, but unto thy name be the glory.

But what need of these inquiries? Look at what this man has done. He is great in the greatness of that. A stupendous work was given him to do, and he has accomplished it. Called, in God's providence, to a lofty destiny, he has gloriously fulfilled it. Placed on a pinnacle high as any earthly height, in the world's full view, he has won the world's respect and honor. He came to the capital, four years ago, and found it reeking with treason in all its departments, threatened on every side by gathering hordes of rebels, and the very roads leading to it lined with banded assassins; he leaves it to his successor, purified, fortified, impregnable as any seat of empire on earth; and not an enemy near it, unless it be another murderer lurking in its dark places.

Inheriting from his predecessors the seeds and necessities of a civil war of such vast dimensions and such intense malignity, he has conducted that war and fought it out through weary years, through seasons of darkness and discouragement; threatened with reaction among the loyal, threatened with bankruptcy and every form of national exhaustion, with foreign intervention, — he has fought it out to a complete and final victory. The rulers of Europe told him he was trying to do the impossible: well, then, he has done the impossible. When he took his seat of power, he found the nation drifting towards disintegration and anarchy, division and subdivision, the abyss out of which only could proceed ruin and eternal strife; and he leaves it compacted in unity, and power, and more imperial than ever before. The ship of state was strained in every joint, and crashing in the breakers, and the great seas going over her, and the skies were black with tempest, and the crew was in mutiny, and the wisest knew not what to do, and the bravest blanched with fear. Then this unknown and untried man comes forth at the call of the all-wise Providence, which guides and overrules the choice of men, and, with his eyes raised to heaven, lays his firm hand on the helm. And behold, now, the goodly ship rides at her anchors, and rests beautifully on her shadow; and he, the helmsman, stands confessed before the world as the pilot that weathered the storm. Firm and unwavering throughout, whoever might falter or play false, he has crushed the gigantic rebellion. Its power of resistance is broken, and on the verge of annihilation, and the day-star of peace is rising in the eastern heavens; and behold, now, it is accompanied, as it never has been before, with two glorious attendants, — so new, so beautiful, — namely, absolute and impregnable NATIONALITY, and universal FREEDOM.

If to have done this is not greatness, what is greatness among men? If he who has done this is not great, who is great among the living or dead of all ages? Shall we apply the title great to the man who composes a treatise or a poem, who invents a machine, who argues a cause, who wins a battle, or takes a city? Truly we may sometimes. But so applying the title, do we withhold it from the man who saves a nation? who, by the guidance of his mind and the strength of his arm, raises it up from the verge of destruction, leads it through its night of gloom, its wilderness wanderings, its seas of blood, and places it at last erect on the supreme heights of power and peace and glory? Truly, I think when the history of this era is written, and our posterity shall read it, and burn, as they will, with the admiration and the inspiration it kindles, they will marvel to learn, that, in the time of these great events, there was in any mind a blindness and narrowness that could so much as raise a question of the surpassing greatness of Abraham Lincoln.

From his work so accomplished, this man, so great and good, has gone to his rest, and his great presence has faded from our sight. He, the saviour of his country; he, who has so watched and toiled for us; our head, our guardian, our best earthly stay and staff, is fallen powerless and dumb! Oh, the bitterness of the grief! Oh, the immeasurable loss! Would God he had lived, our yearning hearts cry out,—lived, if it were only to come forth among his people, that we might throng his presence, and tell him of our love and reverence, and weave for him our garlands of honor and thankfulness, and call down heaven's blessings on his head, and see if we could not do something to make him as happy as he was good and great. But our prayer is denied, and we must submit; and we will, meekly, devoutly, God helping us.

And, indeed, apart from the yearnings of love and sorrow, rising to the height of calmer thoughts, can we not almost see already that God's time is the right time, and that this death was not untimely? He lived to see the work assigned to him substantially accomplished, and to witness his country's triumph. The measure of his fame was full. There awaited him, had he lived, duties less arduous, indeed, but harder for his tender heart to perform. It needs not a better or a greater man, but a sterner nature and a more iron hand than his, to do what yet remains to be done. God in his mercy has spared him the severe necessities that will soon press upon his office. He has gone amid the satisfactions of success and the rejoicings of victory, and the loud plaudits and affectionate appreciation of his countrymen; gone in a moment, and without a pang, from an earthly joy and glory to an heavenly; ascended into the bosom of his God, to whom he had lived so near in firm obedience and pious trust on earth. Peace be with him, the peace of God, which passeth all understanding.

Though dead, he yet speaketh. Though gone, he is still here. His memory and influence abide in his country's heart forever.

The visitation, so solemn and sad, while it dissolves us in tears, must also arouse us to our responsibilities, and brace us to our duties.

First, not his gentle and forgiving heart, but the sacred instinct of eternal justice, implanted in us by our Maker, demands, in his name and in God's name, that the whole earth be searched, in every nook and corner, if need be, for the fiendish murderers, that they may make to an afflicted nation and an outraged humanity the poor atonement of their accursed lives. Hell is agape for them; or, though God have mercy on them (which we will pray for), man cannot.

And not they only, but the spirit that has bred so many enormities, that has so long and in so many ways struck at the nation's life, and has only shown its full development in striking down the nation's head, must perish. The new President—God bless, preserve, and guide him—is right. That spirit, together with the foul slave-system that engenders, embodies, and perpetuates it,—that spirit, which is a murderer from the beginning, and forever will be while it survives, must be crushed into the earth. Justice is as divine a principle in God and in man as mercy. An unfit clemency to guilty individuals is cruelty to innocent millions and to unborn generations.

Not from the kindly lips and tender heart of Lincoln do we derive these stern counsels of duty; but from his gaping wound and flowing blood do we take them, and must heed them.

The awful duties of retribution rest, where they best may, with the law and the magistrate; and there we leave them in strong and faithful hands, I do believe.

And yet there are duties for the humblest citizens. We must raise higher, and hold firmly up, the standard of loyalty. The country that has been saved to us, given back, as it were, from the jaws of destruction, must now be devotedly loved, and jealously watched for, and guarded by all its people. No more careless paltering with treason and half-loyalty, North or South. Our grand and happy nationality, restored and rehabilitated, is henceforth our most sacred trust from God; and the arm that is lifted against it, be it palsied rather; and the false tongue that would profane its majesty by a word of treason, or of sympathy with treason, be it struck dumb ere it speak. Whoso does not love his country is unworthy to live in it. Let the people this day, bending in tears over the bier of their beloved chief, let them register in their hearts the solemn decree, that they will hold their country so dear a possession and so holy a trust, that they will not permit a drop of the deadly virus of disloyalty to circulate in its veins; and that traitors, and the apologists and supporters of traitors, must not share its blessings, nor enjoy its protection, nor so much as breathe its air. Tens of thousands of our dearest and our noblest have died to save it, and our great chief has died, because he had saved it; and shall not we, who are spared to enjoy it, — shall we not swear by that sacred blood, his and theirs, that henceforth we will love it with all our hearts, and live for it, and watch for it, and devote ourselves and all that we are and have to it, hold its enemies as our enemies, and have no friends that are not its friends, and love none that do not love it?

Perhaps at this moment, while we speak, they are lifting up the remains of our noble patriot, deliverer, martyr, to bear them from his palace-home to the dark and narrow house. In such a moment, of so great solemnity and tenderness, let the sacred fires of patriotism blaze up bright and aloft in millions of hearts; let hand clasp with hand in a solemn league and covenant of loyalty, and all true souls renew their vows of devotion to the country which he loved, and lived for and died for; and make that country, in its unity, its grandeur, and its peace, a fitting monument to his memory, worthy to record his earthly fame, and acceptable to the contemplation of his glorified spirit.

REV. GEO. L. CHANEY.

JOHN XIV: 19.

BECAUSE I LIVE, YE SHALL LIVE ALSO.

GREAT lives are never finished; least finished when the grave relieves them of their mortal part. Their biographer only drops his pen at the open sepulchre, because eye hath not seen, nor ear heard, nor the heart of man conceived the glories that succeed; or because his search is baffled as he seeks to trace the growing influence of these ransomed lives upon the thoughts, the habits, the principles and actions of an attentive posterity. Modern scholars have sought to discover a philosophy of history which should introduce into the reading of the history of man the precision of natural science, and enable them to predict the future as they review the past. Race, climate, physical environment, all external conditions of the human lot, and each new discovery of human wit, have been ascertained to affect the history of man; but no sufficient philosophy of human history has been reached, where the most potent factor in the problem refuses to be classified. The great man is the controlling power, and he cannot be anticipated. Guizot calls the appearance of a special great man, at a special time, "the secret of Providence." — "The great person, the great man," says another, "is the miracle of history."

The only prophetic history which deserves the name, that of the Hebrew prophets, turns with inspired truth to the great person. "His name shall be called 'wonderful, counsellor,'" and "the government shall be upon his shoulder."

The only good and sufficient biography, also, is to be found in the same sacred volume. For in the successive books of the New Testament, the life of Jesus Christ is given with a fulness that recognizes the truth we maintain. The biographers of Christ do not leave him in the grave, as if death were the end of life. To them was revealed, by the will of God, something of the glory that succeeds death; and in the re-appearance, further teaching, and final ascent into the heavens, of their Master, they describe his victory over death and the grave, and immediate entrance into the life eternal in the heavens.

Nor does the record end here; but, running over into the Acts of the Apostles, it shows how the life of Christ on earth was taken up and carried forward by His immediate followers. And, preserving the missionary epistles of apostles, it further shows how foreign nations felt its power and followed in its footsteps.

Taking the New Testament as a unit, it is the only good and sufficient biography; because it not only preserves the separate details of the thirty years of the life of Christ on earth, but follows him beyond the grave, adding that most glorious leaf from the Lamb's Book of Life, and then traces in the lives of his near posterity the quickening influence of his Master's spirit and life.

"Because I live, ye shall live also." If Jesus had designed to state the universal condition of life, he could not have chosen fitter words to express his meaning. Till we reach the spring of life,—the self-existent God,—every living thing implies a living author. And when we reach that life of the spirit, that higher life, which has no better definition than "energy of love, divine or human," they have it not, who will not confess that it was inspired in their hearts by some kindred life in another. Often, most often indeed, the awakened soul can gratefully remember the name, the word, the act of its awakener, and can recall the occasion of its waking.

Always some vitalizing word or deed of a living man or woman has kindled them into life. "Thou art Peter," says Christ, "and on this rock I will build my church." Signifying that men and women animated by the Christian spirit, speaking and acting out of their original conception and interpretation of the gospel, were to constitute the lively stones of his church edifice.

Only life is life-giving; and the more it gives, the more it has to give. Therefore I said, "Great lives are never finished." Therefore it is, that the life of Christ can never be written in briefer form than in the life of Christendom. For apostolic zeal and constancy, word of preacher, prayer of saint, fidelity of martyr, patience in suffering, comfort in sorrow, strength in temptation, confidence in death, all the grand and beautiful virtues that have graced Christian biography, acknowledge in Jesus, the Christ of God, their inspiration and support. Because he lived, they have lived also; and the followers of Christ will never lose the holy emulation excited by that one perfect life, till they all "come to the measure of the stature of the fulness of Christ." If the life of Christ could be studied in its effects, even if we could search no farther than to the direct influence of the New Testament record, doubtless it might be said with literal truthfulness, of these things which Jesus did, if they should be written every one, even the world itself could not contain the books that should be written: with such fulness has history verified that word of Christ,— "Because I live, ye shall live also." We find in these words a profound statement of the law of spiritual vitalization; and, although their brightest illustration is given in the life and influence of Jesus Christ, the special application of their first statement by him cannot conceal their large and universal significance. Life is life-giving! with only this, the most natural and self-evident interpretation of the text, we may venture to take up the burden of this day.

How shall I speak of him, the mention of whose name a few days ago, made our hearts glad and hopeful? This is no time for eulogy. All speech is so feeble in the presence of the national grief and indignation, that I would choose to be a silent worshipper with you, while each should listen to the solemn preaching of the event, as his own heart might inly interpret it. But since the occasion, and your general expectation, not unfairly demand speech, I will try so to speak as not to disturb your hearts' conference with its own bitter grief. Prayers, spiritual song, and hallowed word of Holy Writ, must take, for the hour, the ministry of consolation. In the words that I shall say, I am as one just bereaved, who can only repeat the virtues of the dead, and mourn.

He was a faithful husband and a kind father. All his virtues were homebred, and a domestic sweetness flavored his public acts. He was too much a father to conduct the pitiless discipline of an army. If a tired boy fell asleep on guard, he had not the heart to have him shot. Perhaps he was thinking of his own son, his Isaac, whom God has since rescued from the sacrifice of war, and restored to him, and in whose bright description of the recent glorious victory, Robert's father and our country's father took such honest pride, only the day before he died. Or, perhaps, he thought of his youngest, the little Benjamin of his home, the boy ever at his side. I have read nothing more sad, among the scenes of that saddest chamber death ever entered, than this. "Little Thaddeus will not look upon his father." Oh, with what poison did treason's malice inflame the dull temper of the fatal lead, that it could unman such a father, and estrange such a child!

He was kind and forgiving, forgiving to a fault (some have thought and said). But, my friends, if forgiveness be a fault, methinks saints, not sinners, should make the discovery. Our good President never knew, never could know, the wickedness and spite of the enemies of his country. We never knew them till they placed him beyond the fatal knowledge which this day we know. I say the "fatal knowledge;" for unless heaven forefend, the act which has opened the eyes of this people, till they stand out with horror, may wake such rage, hot indignation, and vindictive fury, in the breast of an excitable army and populace, that crime shall fall on crime, and the triumphant nation shall smear its garments with the bloody fingers of revenge. Abraham Lincoln never knew, while he lived with us, the hatred that was in the rebellious heart. I thank God that his tender heart has not been wrung and torn as ours has been, by the human contemplation of enmity's last curse. I thank God that if such depravity can be known by ransomed souls, the knowledge has come to him where love has no limitation, and where forgiveness is no fault.

In life, as every act shows, he was as little conscious of the spirit that fired the Southern heart, as at the last he was of the murderer's presence. When he left his Western home, four years ago, he sowed peaceful promises, of which his sincere soul was full, all along the route Eastward; and his first word in the Capitol was an anguished appeal in the form of a most tender remonstrance: "We are not enemies, but friends. We must not be enemies", he said. He was scarcely better schooled in enmity when he died. He could not learn it. He who so easily forgave injuries could not comprehend a hatred which had no injuries to forgive; a hatred which, with Jewish malignity, hated him because he was a Christian, and clamored for its bond.

He had a working religion, which believed that God helped those who helped themselves to right ends. He said, and said devoutly, "God is over all"; but he added, "We must diligently apply the means." He had not profited so little by his pioneer life, as to wait for the lightning to plough his land or the whirlwind to fell his trees; but he took the instruments that were at hand, the plough and the axe, and having well used these, he trusted to God for the increase. We must do our best, if we desire the best gift of God. In the practical application of this religious principle, he was never remiss and never discouraged.

He saw clearly that there were moral results from every act, but over these he disclaimed having any power. Men could not restrain, or much increase them, he said.

But he was sagacious enough to see that these moral results would, in process of time, work a change of policy in the administration of a people's government, and he doubtless kept equal pace, at least, with the advancing moral sentiment of the people.

The acknowledgment of a controlling Divine Power, was a frequent and sincere expression with him. He never forgot it, from the day when he parted from his Springfield home, and said to his friends there, " Pray for me," to the closing days of his life, when he ascribed all glory unto the wonderful providence which had guided the events of his administration. God was his Counsellor, but man was his instrument. He could counsel with God; he must work with man: and he showed a practical good sense in the use of his instruments.

Some have blamed him because he seemed to be so distrustful of committing his government to the policy which most engaged his moral approbation; the policy of emancipation: but events have showed that he only bided his time. He thought, if God could wait a hundred years for the destruction of American slavery, man might wait a hundred days.

The real cause of this delay, however, was his respect for the Constitution. He was scrupulously true to his oath to support that. He spoke of himself, in homely phrase, as of one who had engaged to do a job, and who felt morally obliged to do it well, according to the terms of the agreement, viz , the Constitution; and history will declare that there never was a President who took more conscientious pains to be faithful to constitutional government.

All his public documents, and all his published letters and speeches, bear witness to his fidelity to the Constitution as he understood it; and surely any construction less liberal than he put upon it, and any milder exercise of its war powers, would have exposed that instrument to the ridicule of the world, and flung us into the ancient chaos of disunited States. He suffered for long the moral disapprobation of men whom he profoundly revered, because of his delay in assuming the power conferred by war, to abolish human slavery; and when the proclamation of emancipation came, his impressive benediction commends it not simply as an act of justice, but of wise policy and constitutional validity :

"Upon this, sincerely believed to be an act of justice, warranted by the Constitution upon military necessity, I invoke the considerate judgment of mankind, and the gracious favor of Almighty God."

He was honest from the first, and lived so, four years, in Washington. His fairness in dealing showed itself in repeated offers of compensated emancipation to the Slave

States; in temperate delays and profitable warnings; in a hundred days of grace, before the consummate word was spoken that made us free.

A winning frankness made it impossible to double-deal with him. He made short work with all super refinements, curious subtleties, and specious insincerities. His kindly nature made him value the approbation of his people. To-day, when we cannot suffer a word to his discredit, we almost resent his own words, when we read, in a letter he once wrote to Mr Conkling, "But many people find fault with me." We feel ashamed that we ever doubted him, when we read further and hear him saying: "I certainly wish that all men should be free, while you, I suppose, do not." And then he proceeds to state, with that judicial clearness so characteristic of his mind, the emancipation policy.

The same regard for fair-dealing which led him to offer, again and again, compensated emancipation to the slave-master, made him determined to protect the men whom he had freed. "To abandon them now," he says, "would not only be to relinquish a lever of power, but would also be a cruel and astounding breach of faith."

He was a constant and self-sacrificing friend, and never allowed personal ambition to pervert justice. Early in the war, he showed a generous readiness to take upon himself the responsibility of unpopular acts. He laid aside the traditional dignities of his office, and mounted the rostrum, that he might defend the character and disposition of influential servants of the government. It is the singular truth that in the death of him we mourn, his enemies are even more bereaved than his friends. His cool assassin was a lunatic suicide.

But why prolong the mention of virtues that do but prolong our grief? These memories only deepen our sense of a loss already, at times, beyond our trustful submission.

Let me leave with you these words of sober prophecy and faithful advice. I need not tell you the name of their author:

"Peace does not appear so distant as it did. I hope it will come soon, and come to stay, and so come as to be worth keeping in all future time. It will then have been proved, that, among freemen, there can be no successful appeal from the ballot to the bullet, and that they who take such appeal are sure to lose their case, and pay the cost. Still, let us not be over-sanguine of a speedy, final triumph. Let us be quite sober; let us diligently apply the means, never doubting that a just God, in his own good time, will give us the rightful result."

REV. A. L. STONE.

LAMENTATIONS V: 15, 16.

The Joy of our heart is ceased; our Dance is turned into Mourning.
The Crown is fallen from our Head.

When, three days ago, the morning of the day appointed for fasting, humiliation, and prayer, rose upon a people jubilant with the joy of victory, many felt that both the designation of the day and the accustomed manner of its observance should be changed; that, instead of fasting, there should be feasting, instead of humiliation and supplication, thanksgiving and praise.

But some of us remembered, and we called it to mind, that the chief intent of the day, as our fathers kept it, was prospective. It did not look backward with penitential review, so much as it looked forward with forecasting deprecation to possible evils. The day was appointed in the spring season, when the great venture of the harvest was at hazard, and all the uncertainties of elemental blight and blessing hung poised in the scales of Providence. If there were confession, forsaking of sin, — as was always true, — it was as a preparation of heart for availing prayer, that "the early and the latter rain" might fall, each in its time; the hand of the reaper bind and gather its sheaves with joy, and the autumn granaries be full. Then should follow the commemorative festival, looking to the past, and celebrating the throned goodness that had provided abundance for the wants of man and beast. It was this ideal of the day recently observed, that held so many Christian pulpits and Christian people so closely to its first design.

We ought to have felt, more deeply than we did, that the future might bring up, into that bright morning sky, dark clouds big with storm and tempest, and have stretched our hands up with a mightier reach of supplication toward the sovereign hand holding the balances weighted with coming events.

The thought was on our hearts and on our lips that there might be perils brooding for our country, shadows gathering over the path of its future. But who could have looked forward to so dark a shadow as this which has fallen! who could have painted this sable cloud on that smiling sky!

There was talk, with some, of reversing our associations with this month of the Spring, and our religious observances wedded to its annual return, and making it henceforth our month of most tuneful rejoicing, — the coronal of the year. But not now! We cannot change thee, oh, weeping April! oh, month of tears! Pour down all thy warm showers: from our eyes the rain falls faster yet! Evermore, from henceforth, at thy return, thou and the sorrowing nation shall weep together.

How sudden the changes of the April sky, — sunshine! shower! And beneath, on our faces and in our hearts, how faithfully copied! What glad days they were that followed those two memorable sabbaths, freighted with such a gospel of victory and peace! What a deep and tender joy rested upon all our homes and temples! Richmond was taken. The sword of Lee was broken. Loyal and honest hands were on their way to run up the old flag above the battered and ruined walls of Sumter. Every eye was sunny with gratulant greetings to every other. How sudden the darkness! Night comes in nature with twilight herald running before. Our night came without precursor, — "in a moment, in the twinkling of an eye," as though noon and midnight had met.

There were beds the night before last, I suppose, restless with dreams; but with all the sleepers there was no dream so black as that awful fact that went pulsing and tolling through the night, and lies now like an incubus which memory cannot chase away, upon the shuddering national heart.

We have lost great and good men before. They have been taken from the high places of honor and of trust with their robes of office on. They have been taken from the scenes of retirement whither a nation's homage followed them, bearing in its offerings before their feet. Washington died leaving that one peerless title behind him, — "The Father of his Country." Harrison and Taylor died, sinking wearily down from that chair toward whose great vacancy our dim eyes look to-day. Our two great Massachusetts statesmen and orators passed away leaving us to feel that the world was less rich and grand since they were gone. But these were all led gently from our presence, by a messenger hand, whose power and whose right none of us could question. The Divine Will, by itself, and alone, made up and executed the summons.

But our dear President was snatched from us by the hand of violence. This was the bitter element in the cup. He might have lived. He was not sick. He was not old. "His eye was not dim, nor his natural force abated." All wantonly and wickedly his precious blood was shed; unchilled by age, untainted with disease. He had reached no natural bound of life. It was not a treasure expended, but stolen by forceful robbery. It is not simply bereavement, — but bereavement by such awful fraud, that tries us most sorely.

And yet none the less — but how it strains upon our submission — none the less is it the solemn, sovereign providence of the reigning God. Truly "clouds and darkness are round about him." In this visit to us "He maketh darkness his pavilion," and our hand cannot draw back the heavy folds. He is trying, by a hard test, our faith, our confidence, our resignation. Oh that our struggling lips could say clearly, if not calmly, "It is the Lord, let Him do what seemeth Him good." We must say that, before we can have any comfort, before our prayers can find acceptance, and before the divine hand will take from our suppliant hand the loose-lying reins of state. God help us to say out of the depths of this great grief, without a doubt, without any reserve, with our yearning affections still clinging around that pale, dead form, lying in the chamber of the White House, "Thy will be done!"

How dear he was to the people! That thought comes first after the loss. He was *of* them. He was not lifted above them, either in pride of place, or pride of intellect, or the kingly style of his greatness. He walked on our levels still. All his simple, plain, homely talk, kept him near us. He spoke our vernacular, the language of the fireside and common life, and not the dialect of courts. He did not leave us, and wrap himself in official stateliness, when he went up the hill of the capitol. His kindly face and voice, his cheerful, humorous, fireside English, his form and attitudes, and all his personal habits, made him seem of kin to each of us. A familiar, friendly, neighborly air hung about him everywhere. He *put on* nothing. He was always his own, true, hearty, republican self. The people loved him. That thin, swarthy face, that tall, angular form, drew after them, more than all beauty and grandeur in the land, the blessings of their hearts. And he loved them. He was thoughtful for the comfort of the aged, the poor, the hearts which war had made desolate. The humblest could go to him, finding an open door and an open heart. It seems to me that we have never held any other President so tenderly in our affections. And one reason is, we have never found any other so accessible to our thoughts and sympathies, and never one so much of our own mould and substance.

How we confided in him! He was a man to build trust upon. His honesty was a pillared rock. The pleasant air, with which, against whatever importunity, he kept his purposes, covered and mantled the sternest conscientiousness. The careless step with which he walked toward his objects in the country's welfare, neither wealth nor favor could make to swerve. All was simple, easy, and natural, but firm-fibred as oak, true as steel. The most faithful discharge of his great duty, — the highest good of the nation, — to this fixed, unrevolving star his soul was steady as the needle to the pole. He had a sharp insight that cut through all the rind of sophistries to the core of difficult questions, leaving such light on the stroke that other minds could follow. He was a man of parables, and translated the dark and vexed problems of political science into pleasant similitudes, transparent to the dullest eye. Where a diplomatic answer would have been dignified obscurity, he told a story through which flashed the honest light of clear intelligence. He was in this way a wonderful teacher of the nation. His brief, pithy, humorous narratives have made crooked things straight, through a thousand tortuous walks of State policy. This quaint, ever-ready humor was the soft cushion upon which the great burdens of his public cares impinged, covering and shielding his nerves from laceration. It saved him half the wear and tear of his official work. It kept his friends, and conciliated those who differed from him. He could convince with a smile, refute with a jest, turn the flank of heavy reasoning with this agile lightness of wit and conquer kind feeling, if not persuasion, — generally both.

His goodness was his greatness. His honest heart helped his straight-forward mind. He saw truth and duty more clearly by this inward illumination. His reach of genuine desire carried out his reach of intellect, and became genius. He was more sagacious than his advisers, partly because he was more single-hearted. He sought so earnestly the best means to the noblest end, that he was sure of an intellectual triumph in their discovery. He kept the moral sky clear, and it reflected light upon the mental. A pure patriot, who walked with honor, faith, and truth, though walking amid the defilements and corruptions of political life, and so kept his garments unstained. But this is no time, in the freshness of our affliction, for his eulogy. It is too soon to write that. We must wait till the clouds have risen from all the paths he trod, — till the smoke of conflict and the haze of prejudice are swept away by the sun-bright air of our newly-risen day. By and by the future will lead us up to calm heights that will give us perfect vision over all these fluctuating levels. We are too near Abraham Lincoln yet, fully to survey and respect his great nature and his great work. Not till the wave on whose crest he rode has receded with him a little, shall we be able to discover on the back-ground of these eventful times the true proportions of his greatness. Every coming day will add to his fame; and coming generations will testify that no purer, no nobler, no more fruitful life has been given to our nation and American history.

"We trusted it had been he," whom God had appointed to lead us through both the Red Sea and the desert beyond, to the Canaan of our future. But the dastard hand of treason struck, — struck as cowards always strike, from behind, — struck, with the confession of weakness and desperate inferiority which the assassin and his cause always make in the very act that gluts their hate, and the good, the great, the gentle, the kind, the large-hearted, the beloved President is no more! Whatever else may be dark about this mystery of crime, we cannot mistake the spirit that steeped itself in that sacred blood. It is the same spirit that has been deaf for generations to the groans and sighs of the bondman; the same that struck with parricidal hand at the breast of the country's life; the same that opened the murderous thunders of war in Charleston harbor, and has kept them resonant over the land through four wasteful, tragic years; the same that sent hired incendiaries to fire the mansions in our Northern cities, where women and babes as well as men slept in unsuspecting security; the same that laid in wait for the President elect, with murderous intent, when he first left his Western home for the Capitol; the same that advertised for bids upon his head, through the consenting press of the South; the same that administered keepers' discipline in Libby Prison and Castle Thunder, for a step or gesture amiss, with bullet and bayonet; that made grim Famine jailer at Belle Isle and Andersonville, over tens of thousands, to whom death only brought release. This black, consummate crime is only the ripe fruit of that system of barbarism which has struck its roots so deep, and had such stalwart growth in this continent. That barbarism has cheapened human life in hearts where it has had its hour; made shedding of blood like the pouring out of water; the cries of famishing men as whisperings of the idle wind; the striking down of senatorial dignity in its own place of privilege and unsuspecting safety, a deed of chivalrous gallantry; and now the cold-blooded murder of one who has led in the great marches of liberty to a whole race, and is hailed as deliverer and saviour by four millions of souls whose fetters have fallen at his word, and has disappointed thus the scheme to build a kingdom of darkness and of iron upon the necks of those millions, an act of fruitless though sweet revenge. It has delivered many a blow before, that has wrung and pierced the individual heart; but it has found here at last its opportunity, Nero-like, to gather in one the hearts and hopes of all loyal people, and pierce them through with a single thrust. Will any one say that I go too far in attributing this stroke of a single hand to the whole system which it so fitly represents? The evidence found in the papers of the assassin, the time at first arranged for the execution of the plot, the hesitation of an accomplice *at that time*, until WORD SHOULD COME FROM RICHMOND, and the mysterious threats and prophecies of Richmond papers of *that date*, of some great shock to the Union, and the world even, then just impending, which would be the deliverance of the confederacy, all go to show that the secret of this conspiracy, and its dark purpose, were in the hearts of the rebel chiefs in the rebel capital.

But what has it gained for itself by such triumphant guilt? Any reversal of its own infamy; a more clement judgment in history; the blossoming of fresh hope for its own dark designs; a change of sentiment and will with the loyal people; the blotting out of the great victories of the fortnight past; aught but a crimson hand whose stain strikes all through the soul, and the curse of earth and heaven? It has bought its revenge dear.

And what, we may ask, is the extent of this revenge? or, rather, in what aspects may we view it, that shall help us bear our loss, and show us the divine hand mingling in it?

That deadly aim took the life of Abraham Lincoln. But it could not touch his past. That is forever safe. It could not blot out one of those pregnant years through which his hand was on the helm of the ship of state, as she drove reeling over the great waves of the storm. It could not make good the threat, that he should never live to take his seat in the Presidential chair. It could not bereave the country of one counsel of wisdom, one firm resolve upon which she has leaned so steadily in her darkest hours. It could not put out the light of that shining example of truthfulness and dutifulness which has been to us all, in this night of gloom, a star of cheer and of guidance. It could not undo the policy which has gathered and marshalled invincible armies, and conquered peace by the sword, without one compromise of rightful, unfettered authority. It could not silence that voice that spoke out on the most illustrious New Year's morning of all our history, and said to Four Millions of slaves, "BE FREE!" — and the winds of heaven bore it out, "Be Free!" — and the sea repeated it, on all our shores, "Be Free!" — and the eagle of liberty, looking down on his own broad continent, screamed it, "Be Free!" — and the bending heavens with saluting angels sent it back to all our dusky homes, "Be Free!" — and the echo rose in unnumbered voices of lonely lips, toned with wondrous gratitude, "Free, Free, Free!" That word has been spoken. In that word the murdered

President "though dead still speaketh." That voice can never be silenced, though those pale lips shall never part again. The work that has been done, and so well done, by this faithful worker, cannot be undone. No power beneath the sun can roll back this nation to where she stood four years ago. Those grand acts of the drama that have moved across the stage will never retrace their steps. This final act of victory and certainty cannot be exchanged for that first act of surprise, confusion and fear. Our risen morning cannot sink down behind the orient, and hide again in the darkness of the past. The night of doubt and defeat, the night of slavery, the night of defiant rebellion, those deep shadows of the past, have fled; and the new day no man can sweep from the brightening firmament. All this has been gained, for us and humanity, under that leadership whose stricken hand has dropped the sceptre now. The sceptre has fallen, but this work remains. The past is secure. No murderer's hand has power to blot it.

In our hearts, too, our slain leader *still lives*. He lives more vitally than ever. Many hearts that were cool to him will have opened now, and taken him in. All prejudice will forgive him and accept him. He is no more an object of criticism; he is beyond the reach of hate. Hate itself will die out, and in its place will come a concession of his many virtues and peerless excellences. He is dead. All pens that write of him will write forbearingly, if not tenderly and admiringly. And those of us who loved and honored him before will take his name and image into some more interior chamber of our hearts, within some more sacred shrine, and guard them there. It was not Abraham Lincoln, it was our cause, the cause of liberty, the cause of humanity, the cause of government, the cause of the Union, that was doomed to the death by that felon hand. The victim stood on that perilous height, as the representative of this whole great scheme of human progress. He is its martyr. He died for that. He was slain because of his faithfulness to that scheme. Our hands led him up, once and again, to that eminence, and set him there as a target for the deadly malice of the conspirators. He fell because we laid upon him such trust, and because he discharged it all too well. We can but love him the more for this. Our noble, murdered witness, with his good confession, his home and his throne, are henceforth in our heart of hearts. The assassin's steel, the deadly aim, cannot reach him here. We will teach our posterity to honor him. Our children, and our children's children shall hear us speak his name as our fathers spoke to us the name of Washington, and shall grow up revering and guarding the hallowed memory of this second *Father of his country;* whom History will write, also, *the Father of a race.*

His future, too, is *safe*. There is no question now, in any mind, whether any eclipse can come upon his fame. Would he have guided the vessel as wisely, through the intricate channels of reconstruction, as over the tempestuous sea of civil strife? Could he have gained such wide assent and cheerful support to his measures, in the new exigencies of ruling, as in those through which he has safely brought us? Might not some, who have been his friends, have turned against him possibly, as the new questions of the hour, and of coming hours, came into sharp debate? Already there were fears that he would not prove stern enough for the stern work of retributive justice, and that his great, kind heart, rather than his bond to law, and to the destinies of the future, would have guided him in his treatment of the chiefs of the rebellion. But all fears, all questions, all doubts looking toward any qualification of his well-earned renown, are vanished now. He can show no weakness in the future, to reflect upon his strength in the past, commit no folly to reproach his old sagacity, make no blunder that shall leave him shorn of influence, and mingle large qualification with the praise of history. He is safe from all these possibilities of errors, frailties, and failures. History must take his portrait as he is, standing at the very highest eminence of a just and stainless life. Not one laurel which he has won, and which he wears, is ever, by any reversal of coming days, to be stolen from his wealth of power.

He was permitted, too, to see the great triumph toward which his hopes looked and his counsels helped. Thank God for that. He *knew* the rebellion doomed, the war ended, and the nation saved. That one supreme moment when his feet trod the streets of the conquered rebel capital paid him for all. He did not die like the old prophets "without the sight." He gazed with mortal eyes upon the glorious consummation, for which, with such grandeur of constancy and diligence. through four years whose weight would have crushed a weaker man, and would have crushed him but that he leaned on

Heaven, he had been toiling. If the assassin had struck before the rebel banner fell at Richmond, and the sword of Lee was yielded to the hand of Grant, if the sun of the President had gone down before the sun of our rescued nationality had fairly risen, that would have been a darker and more trying providence. But that sun was up. Those patriot eyes saw its morning radiance, and reflected it back. He might almost have said, like aged Simeon, perhaps he did so say in the silence of some secret and thankful prayer, "Lord, now lettest thou thy servant depart in peace, for mine eyes have seen thy salvation!"

It will not be too bold to say, that his work was done when it paused; for God, who gives each man his task, so judged and so appointed. His mission was accomplished. That for which God raised him up he had performed. All that was committed to him to do he finished, and finished well. That which comes after is assigned to other heads. God is not limited in the number or in the variety of his agents. Nothing is put in peril now by this falling of a trusted leader which God cannot as well provide for, and make even more victoriously secure.

Least of all are we to fear, that the great cause of progress in this land must needs be turned back, or even halt. That cause may be served and forwarded by men; but it is not dependent upon their living or dying. It is not invested in any vulnerable, human life. It is not something material which bludgeon or steel may strike to the earth. Its citadel is not within frail human flesh, or within the truest and noblest human heart. It is a kingdom of truth, — a life of ideas, invisible, invulnerable, — on all the air, — in the faith and testimony of millions of confessors, — in God's imperishable word, — linked with his invincible providence, — in living seed of thoughts and principles which righteous blood shed by the hand of violence only quickens to a more instant germination, and ripens to an earlier and broader harvest. That cause is God's cause. It is hid in his heart. It is carried on his eternal purpose. It is too high and safe for human desperation to strike.

Let none of us in his great grief despair or despond over his country. Recall to-day that word which has become in these stern times our national motto, " In God we trust!" He did not lead Israel through the Red Sea to forsake them in the wilderness. He will not forsake us on the shore from which we have looked down on our foes overwhelmed and broken. He has led us hitherto. He can lead us on. His counsels have not changed. His power is not baffled. He can appoint us a leader. Moses was not permitted to go over Jordan; but there arose a new captain of the Lord's host, and the sword of Joshua instead of the rod of Moses waved in the van of advance. David was not permitted to build a temple for the Lord his God, because he had been a man of war, and had shed much blood; but he prepared the way, accumulated the means, conquered the peace, and Solomon reared the magnificent, sacred pile. Through our tears let us look up and confide in that Supreme Leader.

He has mingled mercy even with this great tragedy. Part of the bloody conspiracy was foiled. The Secretary of State, and those smitten in his defence, we may hope will survive. The arm that conquered in the field, doomed in the foul plot with those who were stricken,— the arm of our hero, Grant, is nerved still with life and strength. God keep it so nerved. God shield the head of Grant. How wide the murderous scheme, and how many names were written on the assassins' roll, none of us can tell, but every great and precious life we can commend to his vigilant keeping who has numbered the hairs of our head, and without whom not a sparrow falls to the ground.

What if the new unexpected responsibility settling upon the legal successor of the slain President should fill him with another heart, call him up to the height of a great consecration, gird him with noble and faithful purposes, so that the memory of one hour of shame shall be remembered no more against him, in the splendor of a long and just renown? That issue is more than possible. This, too, may be given as the answer of Christian intercession.

And oh, we have that stricken household to bathe with a nation's sympathy; to beseech God's tenderest consolations for them; to lift them, and lay them for strength and comfort on the heart of Jesus.

Of what infinite worth to them now, and to us also, those words of tender confession which came a few months ago from the President's lips: "Yes, now I can say that I do from my heart love the Lord Jesus Christ."

We feel, many of us, that we could have wished, for him whom we mourn, a different scene for the last hour of his health and consciousness on earth, that he could have met the fatal missive on some stage of official duty, or in the retirement of home, or in the circle of religious worship, rather than within those festal walls. Yes, it would have been better.

But they were scarcely festal walls to him. They were a sort of refuge often, for one who had no retirement of home, from the incessant calls and wearying importunities of aspirants for place and office.

And it has seemed to be rather one of the penalties than pleasures of political rank and illustrious position, that they must yield themselves to the popular welcomes and fellowship in such festive gatherings. And the plea that prevailed with the President to visit the theatre on this particular night was that of his own kind heart, unwilling, in the necessary absence of their idolized general, that the waiting enthusiasm of the people should be altogether denied an object for its expression; his last thought not for himself, but for the gratification of those whom he loved and served.

And so he has passed from the midst of us. Our joy-bells have changed their merry peals for solemn tolling. Our festive banners droop at half-mast. Our purposed jubilant processions must become funeral marches to this new grave. "The joy of our hearts is ceased. Our dance is turned into mourning. The crown is fallen from our head."

We touch, in this event, one of the great pivotal points in our history and destiny. on which turn issues more momentous than we can now discern. But our future is with God, and not at the mercy of human scheming and human crime.

We shall not have much time for tears even over so great a sorrow. Our work is stern and pressing. One thing is beyond contradiction. Yielding rebellion has lost its most lenient judge,—returning rebels their best friend. His successor has always entertained towards these parricides a sharper and more incisive purpose. They will meet in him a face set like a flint, a hand of iron. They have not gained much by the exchange.

We shall none of us be any the more inclined to spare the last remaining weakness of the old system, from this new exhibition of its fell spirit, or to apologize for that temper in the midst of us that can make this day of broken-hearted mourning a day of glad tidings to itself. It is not wise just now for such minds to speak out their brutal gladness. Our hearts are too sore to bear it. They had better hide it, if they feel it, so deep that neither by look nor lip shall it get expression. We shall not be very patient with it. The law officers have found out that there is such a crime as being accessories to murder after the fact, and the spirit of Andrew Johnson is the downright kindred spirit of the Andrew Jackson of other days, and treason, North and South, will have a short shrift and a sharp doom. Perhaps we needed, all of us, to see more clearly the wickedness against which we have had to contend, and to be girded anew for its utter extermination. Let us crush it quickly, and forever.

And so, bereft of this one helper in whom we have felt strong, let us turn to God with a new spirit of dependence on his Almighty arm. and make our tears of mourning the waters of a new baptismal consecration to the service of our country and humanity, the supremacy of law, and the safety, honor, and perpetuity of this Union, for which we have paid so great a price.

REV. J. D. FULTON.

DEUTERONOMY XXXIV: 7.

"HIS EYE WAS NOT DIM, NOR HIS NATURAL FORCE ABATED."

An inscrutable providence crowds this and other sanctuaries to-day. A nation, redeemed by the blood and toil of her bravest and best, mourns the loss of a Chief Magistrate, who was the embodiment of a people's hope, and the object round which the affections gathered of every lover of liberty in the world. Abraham Lincoln was sincerely loved. That "peasant proprietor," and "village lawyer," whom, by some divine inspiration or providence, the republican party of 1860 selected to be their standard bearer; whose election was regarded as a calamity by many of his supporters; and as a justifiable cause for the most monstrous rebellion upon which the sun ever shone, grew to be the peer of Washington, and climbed to the highest peak of earthly distinction.

It was a great shock when half the nation attempted to make the dream of secession a real fact, and when the guns of Sumter sounded the call to arms; but it was trivial when contrasted with the emotions experienced as the tidings reached us that Abraham Lincoln had been assassinated. We were glad when the armies of the rebellion were beaten; when Richmond fell; when Lee capitulated; but we would rather have had Washington environed with the enemy and have had Lincoln alive, than to have had the armies defeated and Lincoln dead. This is a new crime. We are not used to the bloody hand in that shape. We have felt that "slavery was the sum of all villanies," and that men who could starve our brothers amidst abundance; who could suffer them to freeze, and go unsheltered amid primeval forests, were capable of any act of cruelty and injustice; but we had forgotten that sin is blinding, and that God often permits the wrath of man to work out his own destruction; and so we had somehow fancied that rebels had hearts and brains as other men; and that they would discover, what we have felt all the way, that our chief magistrate was a wall between the wrath of an outraged people and the veriest criminals of history.

They did not perceive the truth, and so they conspired against the life of their best, if not of their only powerful friend. There is no other like him. Death has frozen and hardened that loving face, and embalms it in the memories of mankind as a legacy of the past. That heart which felt its need of divine support when the nation's sky was o'erclouded, and the air was full of rumors and revolt; which nearly broke as the eye gazed upon the lifeless form of his idolized child; and which surrendered itself to Jesus as the boom of the cannon at Gettysburg assured us that the nation was in its Gethsemane struggle; which wrought, by the throes of an indescribable anguish, Emancipation for this nation; which was so full of gentleness and love, and so longed for peace, that already it was nearing the verge of injustice, in its search for its ways of being merciful, is stilled in death.

> "Yet a few days and thee
> The all-beholding sun shall see no more.
> Thou shalt lie down
> With patriarchs of the infant world, with kings,
> The powerful of the earth, the wise, the good,
> All in one mighty sepulchre."

Like Moses, he has died, not because of disease, nor of advanced age; his eye was not dim, nor was his natural force abated. He died because his work was done. He had passed through battle, sorrow, and war; had climbed the heights of Pisgah, and had gained a view of the Canaan of peace lying in the distance; and when the Lord had showed him all the land, and had assured him of the promise that the sons of freedom should possess it, by his providence he declared, "Thou shalt not go over thither."

The purpose which God had to accomplish through his instrumentality had been fulfilled; and, as there are dividing lines in time, drawn by God, over which men never pass, it becomes us to bow in meek submission, here as elsewhere, and to hear the words, "Be still, and know that I am God."

Four years ago we remembered him as he abode in hope. Then he found himself the object of Southern abuse so fierce and so foul, that, in any man less passionless, it would long ago have stirred up an implacable hostility. Mocked at for his official awkwardness, and denounced for his steadfast policy; beset by fanatics of principle on one side, who disregarded constitutional obligations, and by fanatics of caste on the other, who were not only deaf to the claims of justice, but would hear of no policy large enough for a revolutionary emergency; now tried by a long series of disasters which distressed and depressed the nation, and now by a series of successes that would have puffed up a smaller mind, he has preserved his balance, and walked on in the path of duty; never in advance of public opinion, and never far behind it; going more as a passenger on the ship of state, believing that the hand of God was on the helm, than as a pilot and commander, capable of mapping out new and untried paths; never trying to control events, but frankly confessing *"that events have controlled me;"* never attempting to compliment his own sagacity, but gladly admitting that to God belongs all the praise: like our Capitol, which has been pushed on towards completion amidst troublous times, though it lacks here a cornice and there a column, yet the statue of Liberty crowns its summit, and looks with glorious pride toward the east; so we remember that though his character was incomplete, yet like the Capitol, its main portions stood out in grand and type-like outline, crowned with the laurel wreath of victory, and bearing on its ample frontlet, the emblazoned word of *Liberty*. We remember that a little more than a month before he died, he stood forth on the day of his second inauguration, with a message so statesman-like, so imbued with Christian hope and charity, that even English critics declare that they can detect no longer the rude and illiterate mould of the village lawyer's thought, but find it replaced by a grasp of principle, and dignity of manner, and a solemnity of purpose, which would have been unworthy of none of the remarkable statesmen of the past: while his gentleness and generosity deserve to remain forever the wonder and admiration of mankind.

Death has done its work! That soul no longer lights up that tall, frail body. The window is darkened. The vital force is withdrawn. The heart ceases its beating. The tabernacle is emptied of its inhabitant and goes to decay. Rejoice that, though the assassin's bullet has wrought this, it could not accomplish its fell purpose. For though the earthly house of this tabernacle was destroyed, he had a building of God, a house not made with hands, eternal in the heavens. He obeyed his Master's injunction and literally knew no fear of men, who could destroy the body, but after that have no more that they can do; but having feared Him who can cast both soul and body into hell, he had learned to put away trouble; having believed in God, and having believed, also, in Christ. It is ours to rejoice. We had elected him to the highest of earthly positions, and made him an inhabitant of that house which is the goal of millions. Christ has lifted him higher, and made him a tenant of a mansion prepared for him in the heavens. Hence the loved wife, and those children, one of whom was just standing upon the verge of manhood, and the other "Tad," whom he loved so well, — a boy of hope and promise, — can exclaim, now that the soul has winged its way upward, " Our loved one is with God." With the Christian the separation of the soul from the body is but the throwing aside the curtains of time, and crossing the threshold of a blissful eternity. His eternal Sabbath has begun. Sin, which fettered his soul here, cannot touch him there. He has escaped, like the eagle to the mountains; the snare of the fowler is broken. He has kept Christ's commandments, and abides in Christ's love. He has fought the good fight, and finished the course, and kept the faith; and henceforth there remains for him a crown of righteousness. Let us rejoice that over his remains the light of a Christian's hope sheds its radiance. In spiritual death there is something frightful to contemplate. We all understand the meaning of the word "death" as applied to the body; none of us can comprehend the meaning of the term "death" as applied to the soul. We have seen the footprints of the destroyer, now in the wasted form, and sunken cheek and eye of those we have loved. We have seen the child of tender years lying, like a withered flower, in the lap of maternal tenderness; we have gazed upon the robust frame, plump cheek, and closed eye, over which the sporting ringlet played, and have cried, " He is not dead, but sleepeth;" we have seen death in horrid shapes on the battle-field, where giant men have fallen in the strife; we have walked beneath the shadows of the pestilence, and have seen manly forms pierced by the arrows which God's messenger has drawn from his quiver, and shot with unerring aim from his death-dealing bow; in fancy we have seen that bent head, that blood-crimsoned chair, that room crowded with senators and statesmen, and, ever and anon, vocal with the cries of a wife, who exclaims: "Live!" "*You must live.*" "*Bring Tad — he will speak to Tad — he loves him so!*" and yet there are scenes worse than this, — scenes which cannot be compared with those witnessed daily by the eye of faith; seen by us as through a glass darkly, but seen by Spirit eyes in all their hideous proportions, whenever they gaze upon a world lying under bondage of death. The sight beheld in the White House is full of touching sadness, but the sight beheld by angel eyes within these walls is still more gloomy. The dead in trespasses and sins, without God, and without hope in the world, — what sight can be more pitiable than this? "For the wrath of God is revealed from heaven against all ungodliness and unrighteousness of men, who hold the truth in unrighteousness."

It was this which brought Christ to earth. He came to bridge the bridgeless river, and to lead captivity captive. He was and is the way, the truth, and the life. His hand lifts heaven's window, and permits the eye to behold the streets paved with gold, and trodden by the feet of the redeemed. His revelation carries the torch through the vail, and permits us to see the fountain from whence the crystal stream flows forth, beside which the trees of life forever stand, and beneath which flowers bloom that delight the eye, and fruits abound which satisfy the soul. You feel that you have heard of that land as from a friend. In that land there are no gray hairs, no wrinkled cheeks, eyes do not grow dim with tears, forms are not bent with age. The step is always light, and the ruddy glow of health is ever on the cheek. In that land there are no creeping shadows, no wintry blasts, chilling the blood, and driving men to seek shelter. It is a place of rest, and a place of safety. Assassins cannot lurk there. The vile cannot dwell there. "And there shall in no wise enter into it anything that defileth, neither whatsoever worketh abomination or maketh a lie; but they which are written in the Lamb's book of life."

Spiritual life and spiritual death are determined here. As the tree falls so it lies. This hope animates our souls to day. When a man's feelings are benumbed; when his inclinations tend downwards; when his affections are bound around the decaying things of time, and you find it impossible to lift them up, and cause them to twine about the living realities of eternity, and he dies, you feel that the beyond is full of gloom. But when he is good, reverent, loving; when mellowness and greatheartedness, when faith in God, in Christ, and in the guidance of the Holy Spirit characterized him; when love for God begets a love for man, and the tie that binds him to the infinite links him to the finite; when kindness broods over the actions; when the blessings of those that were ready to perish rest upon him, and the peace that passeth knowledge flows like a river through the area of his life, it is impossible not to think that death is but the introduction to a more blessed companionship with Jesus:

> "Where rivers of pleasure flow bright o'er the plains,
> And the noontide of glory eternally reigns."

You feel that, in the description of this good and reverent soul, I have described the character of Abraham Lincoln. Never have we seen a nature more broad, a love of justice more strong, an incorruptibility of character more manifest, a loyalty to principle more binding, than distinguished the man whom we so profoundly mourn. As a denomination, we are indebted to him; for it was his innate sense of justice, and love of right, that gave protection to some who are dear to our brotherhood and to our hearts. Prison-doors have been unlocked by his hand. Soldiers condemned to be shot, rescued by him, have leaped into the embrace of heroic death with his name upon their lips. The fatherless, the stranger, the poor, and the desolate, rise up from this stricken land, and praise God for the benefaction and the benefactor.

We remember, with sorrow, the place of his death. He did not die on Mount Nebo, with his eye full of heaven. He was shot in a theatre. We are sorry for that. It was a poor place to die in. It would not be selected by any of you as the spot from which you would desire to proceed to the bar of God. If ever any man had an excuse to attend a theatre, he had. The cares of office were heavy upon him. His brain reeled. His frame grew weak. He longed for a change. He desired to get away from the crowd, from the cares and responsibilities of office. Washington's closet would have been preferable. In conversing with a friend, he said, " Some think I do wrong to go to the opera and the theatre ; but it rests me. I love to be alone, and yet to be with the people. I want to get this burden off; to change the current of my thoughts. A hearty laugh relieves me; and I seem better able after it to bear my cross." This was his excuse. Upon it we will not pronounce a judgment. This we will say: we are all sorry our best loved died there. But take the truth with its shadow. Moses was forbidden to enter the promised land because, at the waters of Meribah, he disbelieved God, was impatient, and took to himself the glory that belonged to God. Does not the rock in the desert stand as a finger pointing forward to our danger? does not Moses' life assure us that none of us can hope for heaven through or because of any merits of our own?

We have not tried to disguise his fault, if you choose to give it that name. Is it not strange that there is no other which suggests itself? But I know of none. Admit this, and answer me. If you were to send a man to heaven, to represent the American people there, would you not cast your vote for him? Who was his match in virtues? Who has used opportunities so well, and so wisely?

Some tell us that he would not have done for the hour. God knows best; and God took him: but do you believe that was the reason? Has he not always met the emergency, and did not his last act show us that he was ready to meet this? If he erred in leniency, did not he prove himself ready to be just, in condemning men who evidenced that they were ready to trifle with the imperilled interests of the country?

Is it not more just to say, God looked in pity upon a nation that had floated off the crime of slavery upon the outflowing currents of its own crimson life; and that, in one blow, God intended to prepare us to understand his purposes, and make us ready for his judgments? As another has said, "The cowardly crack of that pistol was the fitting knell of the infamous romance which ever belongs to feudal fierceness, and we shall probably hear no more of it. On Good Friday, long ago, the God of Martyrs was sequestrated from all apparent hope; but on the tomb of the Sacrificed arose the banner of freedom everywhere and forevermore. Coming ages will hold our beloved President in perpetually augmenting esteem, until the vestiges of his beneficent rule are found, not along the strand of an inland sea, but upon the highest range of central mountains, equidistant between world-washing oceans, with the old flag above and the youngest race beneath, free under every tint, and fearing only God!

In the future it shall be discoverable, as it is not at this time, that his work was finished. Our country resembled a magnificent war-steamer, lodged midway in the Mississippi, but destined to sail the ocean. When Abraham Lincoln stepped upon her deck, four years ago, he found her prow in the muddy bank, her wheels were clogged with flood-wood, and her stern was swept by the resistless current. When he began his work he did not do any remarkable thing. He loosened first one wheel and then the other. He turned on the steam, got her prow into the current, and began to sail down the mighty river. It was a perilous passage. Now she was swept along by rapids, now she moved amid frowning shores, alive with guerillas, and bristling with batteries. Now she was stopped by sand-bars, and now driven through perilous channels, and the nation's hope died out, at times, as night settled down upon the ship and its brave commander. At last the gray dawn appeared, and the morning broke. The ship was moving, and he was on the prow, and the brave old crew stood by his side. At last Vicksburg fell; the ship moved on. You remember his words: "The signs look better. The Father of Waters again goes unvexed to the sea. Thanks to the great Northwest for it. Nor yet wholly to them. Three hundred miles up they met New England, Empire, Keystone, and Jersey, hewing their way, right and left. Nor must Uncle Sam's web feet be forgotten. At all the water's margins they have been present, not only on the deep sea, the broad bay, and the rapid river, but also up the narrow, muddy bayou, and wherever the ground was a little damp, they have been, and made their tracks. Thanks to all for the great republic, for the principles by which it lives and keeps alive for man's future; thanks to all. Peace does not appear so far distant as it did. I hope it will come soon, and come to stay; and so come as to be worth the keeping for all future time." Sustained by this hope, how he worked, how he waited! Peace was coming; the current of a national purpose grew stronger and stronger; our ship passed straight into the Gulf, and our commander got a little taste of the salt sea, and a slight touch of the billow when he confronted the long swell of the Atlantic. At this point a strange Providence startles us. The assassin's bullet causes him to step aside, just as the nation begins to think of closing up the rebellion; and so, in a moment, as if summoned by God to new and fresh work, she lays aside her glove of kid, and puts on her glove of iron, — gets ready to answer the difficult questions and solve the knotted problems, and settle her running account with the traitors at home, and with the sympathizers with traitors abroad. A man falls, but a nation lives. A fact which would have thrown France into a revolution but steadies the American character, and solidifies our government. Yesterday, we considered the effects of this death upon the settlement of national questions and the jurisprudence of the land. To-day, let us confine our attention to the delineation of his character, and follow him as he enters upon his reward on high.

Consider now here God's goodness to our Chief Magistrate. Come with me to the eternal city, ye that know what it is to see a look of love come to you from the hungry whom ye have fed, and the naked whom ye have clothed, and behold Abraham Lincoln walking humbly the golden streets bearing in his arms the manacles of four million redeemed bondmen, and of thirty million emancipated freemen, and saying in his quaint way, Dear Master, these are the results of the washing of thy blood, and of the proclamation of thy glorious gospel. Behold the husbands and sons whose spirits have preceded him from battle-fields and prisons, from the slave-pen and from the dungeon, and hear them in their ascriptions of praise to Him to whom belongeth the glory forevermore.

It is hard to part with him, but it is cruelty to wish him back. His life was round, full, and complete. Can you not see Jesus opening the record of him whose footprints of love are found in every path where it was possible for him to be useful? Can you not see his face light up as Jesus leads him into the mansions hung with the pictures of his faithful acts? There is one where he saved the widow's son, whose father had been his benefactor in his youth. There is another descriptive of his thoughtful tenderness to his aged stepmother, who has been supported by his munificent care. Another reveals him writing sometimes five hundred notes per day for the poor and the destitute in Washington, asking a job for this laborer, a pass for this wife, granting a pardon for this innocent, and bending his tired frame over documents in which he can have no personal interest, in his search for justice. There are a few acts which will immortalize him in history. The Emancipation Proclamation is the crowning act. This secures him immortality. This lifts him to a niche in the temple of fame an arrow's shot higher than any ever held by any living American. But in heaven, methinks, I see Christ's eye reading records our eyes never will see, and hear him saying, "Inasmuch as ye did it unto these, ye did it unto me." The form of his beneficent face will be perpetuated in marble, and cities will vie with each other in piling up monuments, to attest their appreciation of his worth.

A Christian's monument is not built of any material as decaying in its nature as marble. It cannot be confined to any given locality. Would you see the monument of Moses you need not make a pilgrimage to Mount Nebo, or search with your eye the plains of

Moab for a mosque or a marble shaft. His monument is not there; still, he has one visible to every eye. Look over the records of the past and see how that name has ploughed its way into the history of the world. The monument of Abraham Lincoln rests in the heart-love of the American people. It is composed of acts which will glow with immortal beauty; with acts, rising higher than any mere monument of stone, round which loving recollections will eternally entwine themselves, and in which the hopes of millions are enshrined. Such characters are creations of God. They exist. They had a beginning, but their growth was almost unnoticed. All we know about them is, they were ready to bear any burden, to endure any hardship. Press them with cares you but hold them steady, as the beams strung along on the top of columns keep them from falling. There is nothing superfluous about them. Equal to every emergency, ready for every task, faithful in every crisis, they naturally become objects of almost idolatrous trust, and of malignant hate. Their lives are full of toil and hardship. As a workman often uses his best instrument to overcome the greatest difficulty, and to surmount the most perplexing obstacle, as the strongest men are sent to perform the hardest tasks, so God gives his chosen ones heavy burdens, and sends them forward on perilous enterprises, knowing that they have the nerve to attempt, the courage to endure, and the faith requisite to the accomplishment of the gigantic undertaking.

Abraham Lincoln's traits of character are easily described. His power of trust was marvellous. He believed in the structural power of our free institutions, which, without any statesman's coöperation, is slowly building a free nation on this great continent. He felt that the dogmas of the great past were inadequate to the glorious present. "The occasion," said he, "is piled high with difficulty, and we must rise with the occasion. We must disenthrall ourselves, and then we shall save our country." He believed in the logic of events, because in them he thought he saw the purposes of God.

He believed in the people, and longed to hear from them. He asked for discussion as for light, and awaited opportunity. At the outset he pledged himself simply "to hold, occupy, and possess the property of the United States;" and when he accomplished the task, he passed away. He was a conscientious and deeply honest man. He was afraid of gratifying self at the expense of duty, and of sacrificing duty for the sake of self. This explains many mysteries. The hand that wrote, "If I could save the Union without freeing any slave, I would do it," wrote, also, "I am, naturally, anti-slavery. If slavery is not wrong, nothing is wrong. I cannot remember when I did not so think and feel. And yet I have never understood that the Presidency conferred upon me an unrestricted right to act, officially, upon this judgment and feeling."

His integrity was thorough, all pervading and all controlling. He hesitated to put down his foot. There is little doubt but thousands of lives were sacrificed because of his slowness; but when he put down his foot it was as immovable as the rock itself, and his waiting may have saved the nation. We all remember his message in which he disclosed his purpose of giving freedom to the slave. It assumed the form of a duty. "In giving freedom to the slave we assure freedom to the free, honorable alike in what we give and what we preserve. We shall nobly save, or meanly lose, the last, best hope of earth. Other means may succeed: this could not fail. The way is plain, peaceful, generous, just; a way which, if followed, the world will forever approve, and God must forever bless."

The people confided in him, not so much because they believed in his genius, or in the quickness of his perceptions, as because of a sense of safety and security, which was begotten by the methods chosen to reach important conclusions.

He believed in God and recognized the value of prayer. Hence, when he left Springfield for Washington, fifty-three months before, he said to his old and tried friends, "I leave you with this request: pray for me." They did pray for him. Millions beside them prayed for him. To a company of clergymen he said, " Gentlemen, my hope of success in this great and terrible struggle rests on that immutable foundation, the justice and goodness of God. And when events are very threatening, and prospects are very dark, I still hope that in some way which man cannot see, all will be well in the end, because our cause is just, and God is on our side."

He was one of the people. Well do some of us remember standing upon the steps of the White House, as he came forth from the Presidential mansion. He bowed to us in passing. Our hearts were touched by his careworn, anxious face. Passing into the grounds, on his way to the War Office, he stopped to give a greeting to a couple of pet goats that waited for his recognition. While thus engaged, one of the party stepped up and said, "Mr. Lincoln, will you allow me to introduce to you two Massachusetts women." He drew himself up to his full height, swept his hand over his face, and said, "Yes, bring them along." We came, and were introduced. He chatted pleasantly until we grew frightened, and begged him not to allow us to intrude upon his time. We felt, it was said, that it would be a great pleasure to shake hands with our honored Chief Magistrate, here, beneath God's open heaven, and on this green grass. "Ah!" said he, waiting a moment, "such a privilege is worth contending for," and then, assuring us of his pleasure to greet the people, he passed on to his laborious tasks. Well has it been said, "No one who approached him, whether as minister or messenger, felt impelled either to stoop or strut in his presence." Edward Everett, after observing his bearing, at Gettysburg, among the Cabinet and foreign ministers, the Governor, and other notables, pronounced him the peer, in deportment, of any one present.

He was an affectionate man. He never forgot a favor or a friend. The men he loved before he was President, he loved even more tenderly after he learned the value of their disinterested affection.

He was a temperance man, and never used intoxicating liquors, or tobacco. After his return from Richmond, we are told, a cask of old whiskey, taken from the cellar of one of the southern grandees, was brought to the

War Office, and opened. He was urged to take it in honor of the occasion. He declined, and thus refused to lend the influence of his name and position to the support of a practice which has wrought such immense mischief in the Army and in the State.

In the poem which he was so fond of repeating, and which he learned when a young man, you discover a key which unlocks many of the mysteries of that marvellous life. There is a charm in them which will repay perusal not only because of their intrinsic beauty, but because when we read them we seem to get near his great and loving heart:—

Oh why should the spirit of mortal be proud?
Like a swift-fleeting meteor, a fast-flying cloud,
A flash of the lightning, a break of the wave,
He passeth from life to his rest in the grave.

The leaves of the oak and the willow shall fade,
Be scattered around, and together be laid,
And the young and the old, and the low and the high,
Shall moulder to dust, and together shall lie.

The infant a mother attended and loved;
The mother that infant's affection who proved;
The husband that mother and infant who blessed;
Each, all, are away to their dwellings of Rest.

The hand of the king that the sceptre hath borne;
The brow of the priest that the mitre hath worn;
The eye of the sage, and the heart of the brave,
Are hidden and lost in the depths of the grave.

The peasant, whose lot was to sow and to reap ;
The herdsman, who climbed with his goats up the steep ;
The beggar, who wandered in search of his bread ;
Have faded away, like the grass that we tread.

So the multitude goes, like the flower or the weed
That withers away, to let others succeed ;
So the multitude comes, even those we behold,
To repeat every tale that has often been told.

For we are the same our fathers have been ;
We see the same sights our fathers have seen ;
We drink the same stream, and view the same sun,
And run the same course our fathers have run.

The thoughts we are thinking our fathers would think ;
From the death we are shrinking our fathers would shrink ;
To the life we are clinging they also would cling :
But it speeds for us all, like a bird on the wing.

They loved, but the story we cannot unfold ;
They scorned, but the heart of the haughty is cold ;
They grieved, but no wail from their slumber will come ;
They joyed, but the tongue of their gladness is dumb.

They died, ay ! they died ; we, things that are now,
That walk on the turf that lies over their brow,
And make in their dwellings a transient abode,
Meet the things that they met on their pilgrimage road.

Yea ! hope and despondency, pleasure and pain,
We mingle together in sunshine and rain ;
And the smile and the tear, the song and the dirge,
Still follow each other, like surge upon surge.

'Tis the wink of an eye, 'tis the draught of a breath,
From the blossom of health to the paleness of death;
From the gilded saloon to the bier and the shroud,—
Oh why should the spirit of mortal be proud?

A man that revolved such thoughts in his mind was not likely to be elated by his position or place. There is one more fact which deserves to be mentioned, because it places the last stone upon the monumental pile of his greatness. He took time daily to peruse his Bible, and was often found up at four o'clock in the early morning holding communion with the Father of Lights in his word. Such is the character which America at this time places in her gilded bark of hope, and sends down the current of time to the distant future. Whoever in Europe or Asia or Africa shall behold its heaven-enkindling look, will find the face of him whose

"Patient toil
Had robed our cause in victory's light,—

"A martyr to the cause of man,
His blood is freedom's eucharist,
And in the World's great hero-list
His name shall lead the van.

"Yea! raised on faith's white wings, unfurled
In heaven's pure light, of him we say:
He fell upon the self-same day
A Greater died to save the world."

A PROCLAMATION.

Whereas, it appears from evidence in the Bureau of Military Justice, that the atrocious murder of the late President, ABRAHAM LINCOLN, and the attempted assassination of the Hon. William H. Seward, Secretary of State, were incited, concerted, and procured by and between Jefferson Davis, late of Richmond, Va., and Jacob Thompson, Clement C. Clay, Beverly Tucker, George N, Sanders, W. C. Cleary, and other rebels and traitors against the Government of the United States, harbored in Canada;

Now, therefore, to the end that justice may be done, I, Andrew Johnson, President of the United States, do offer and promise for the arrest of said persons, or either of them, within the limits of the United States, so that they can be brought to trial, the following rewards:

One Hundred Thousand Dollars for the arrest of Jefferson Davis.

Twenty-Five Thousand Dollars for the arrest of Clement C. Clay.

Twenty-Five Thousand Dollars for the arrest of Jacob Thompson, late of Mississippi.

Twenty-Five Thousand Dollars for the arrest of George N. Sanders.

Twenty-Five Thousand Dollars for the arrest of Beverly Tucker, and

Ten Thousand Dollars for the arrest of William C. Cleary, late Clerk of Clement C. Clay.

The Provost Marshal General of the United States is directed to cause a description of the said persons, with the notice of the above rewards, to be published.

In testimony whereof, I have hereunto set my hand and caused the seal of the United States to be affixed. Done at the city of Washington, on this 2d day of May, in the year of our Lord one thousand eight hundred and sixty-five, and of the [L. S.] Independence of the United States of America the eighty-ninth.

ANDREW JOHNSON.

By the President.

WM. HUNTER, *Acting Secretary of State.*

www.ingramcontent.com/pod-product-compliance
Lightning Source LLC
Chambersburg PA
CBHW030357230426
43664CB00007BB/639